Two week

Utica 1964

INFORMING
THE
PEOPLE

INFORMING THE PEOPLE

A Basic Text in Reporting and Writing the News

By CHARLES H. BROWN
The Pennsylvania State University

Holt, Rinehart and Winston
New York · Chicago · San Francisco
Toronto · London

Copyright ©, 1957, by Holt, Rinehart and Winston, Inc.

Library of Congress Catalog Card Number 57-5824

April, 1964

21102-0117

PRINTED IN THE UNITED STATES OF AMERICA

PREFACE

THE AMERICAN PEOPLE today have at their disposal more current information—more news—about the world than perhaps any other people anywhere at anytime. All the media of mass communication—newspapers, magazines, radio, television, motion pictures—place before them daily huge quantities of easily accessible information. Traditions of freedom, accuracy, and impartiality assure them that they can trust most of this information.

The situation, therefore, would seem to be ideal. Yet if public opinion polls are a reliable guide, there is basis for doubt as to how well the mass communication media keep the people informed. Surveys reveal that on the whole people devote little time to following the news and that many are appallingly ignorant about persons, places, and events which have figured prominently in newspaper headlines and in radio and television newscasts.

Aware of this gap between the amount of information people are offered and the amount they seem to absorb, journalists in the past few years have sought to trace the cause, making extensive use of research conducted by the social scientists. Despite magical developments in the methods of disseminating information, especially in electronics, they have found the core of the problem in something very old—the handling of words. The writing, as one newspaper editor put it, isn't good enough. His conclusion about newspaper writing applies also to radio and television, since news scripts must be written before being broadcast.

This book seeks to apply to the practice of news communication some of the findings of the social scientists about readability and listenability and about the interests of people. It is not the author's belief that this knowledge should, or can, revolutionize current performance. Rather, he has attempted to show how it can be used to modify and improve practices that have been tested by time.

The book gives more attention to newspaper work than to radio and television, because newspapers still employ more people specifically assigned to gathering and writing news than do the other

v

two media. Moreover, most schools begin journalism instruction with an introductory course in which newspaper training is regarded as basic. Much of the material, however, applies to all three media. Because students on the sophomore and junior level do not have sufficient facility in writing to switch back and forth readily from one form to another, instruction in the particulars of radio and television writing has been deferred to the final section. By the time students have practiced writing newspaper stories for most of a semester they should with comparative ease be able to make the change to writing for the ear.

The section on major news assignments deals with the fields which provide the bulk of general news in newspapers and broadcasts. The discussions supply background information that students are not likely to pick up in pursuit of their own particular interests or in other courses taken in school. Chapters 19 and 20, containing much detailed information on the court and trial systems, were included in the belief that this material would be of special value to the student of journalism.

Because of the great complexity of events today, there is increasing need for news interpretation. At appropriate places in the early part of the book, especially in the chapter on explanatory writing, interpretive writing is discussed. But since interpretation involves special problems much more difficult than those faced in routine news writing and reporting, it was felt that it should also be treated in a separate chapter after the student has become acquainted with the more elementary problems of journalism.

The assignments at the end of each chapter should be considered an integral part of the text. They are designed to amplify the discussion by suggesting additional lines for the student to follow and by presenting practical exercises in news writing.

Journalistic and public opinion research in the past few years has produced a great body of information which has been of immense help in the preparation of this book. Acknowledgment of this assistance is made throughout the text. For special advice the author is indebted to Frederick B. Marbut and James W. Markham of the Pennsylvania State University, and Robert O. Shipman of Principia College, Illinois.

C. H. B.

The Pennsylvania State University
January, 1957

CONTENTS

PART III. THE MAJOR NEWS ASSIGNMENTS

PART IV. SPECIAL WRITING PROBLEMS

PART I

News and News Gathering

CHAPTER 1

THE READER AND THE NEWS

The Nature of News

By NEWSPAPER, by radio, by television we are informed of the news of the day: the Big Four foreign ministers confer in London; a motion picture star elopes to Las Vegas; congress debates an increase in defense expenditures; a man is killed in a car crash; a strike of steelworkers closes mills throughout the country; the Kiwanis Club will meet at noon today for a report on its membership drive; the government of France falls over the issue of colonial policy in Africa; a woman finds in the crop of a chicken a diamond she lost last year.

Such information—from an event that will affect the course of history to one that will affect the lives of a few persons—is news. And it is brought to us by a huge expenditure of money, by the work of thousands of people, by a vast and far-flung system of communications utilizing sound and light waves.

Because of the range of news, we can be excused if we do not try to write a definition of it. No one has been able to write a satisfactory one. But though we cannot define news, we can learn a great deal about its nature. Obviously, news deals with what people do, feel, and think. Therefore, almost anything can be news. The journalist's first task is to select, from the multitude of actions of people and the manifestations of their feeling and thought, what he considers news. His second task is to convey this news to others.

Essentially, and in its most obvious aspect, news is an account or report of a happening. More than a quarter-century ago, Walter Lippmann, discussing the nature of news, explained that the recognition of news depended upon an overt manifestation. "The course of events," he wrote, "must assume a certain definable shape, and until it is in a phase where some aspect is an accomplished fact, news does not separate itself from the ocean of possible truth." He continued:

> Usually it is the stereotyped shape assumed by an event at an obvious place that uncovers the run of the news. The most obvious place is where people's affairs touch public authority. De minimis non curat lex. It is at these places that marriages, births, deaths, contracts, failures, arrivals, departures, lawsuits, disorders, epidemics and calamities are made known.[1]

This conception of the nature of news dominated American journalism for many years. It resulted in treating many events as news simply because they were recorded in the conventional places of surveillance—police stations, courthouses, city halls—not because they might have any interest or significance for readers. It is a conception that, in recent years, has been frequently attacked. For example, Lee Hills of the Detroit *Free Press*, discussing a content study made by the Associated Press Managing Editors Association, condemned the preoccupation with such surface news, describing it in a phrase as a "police blotter complex."

What we are increasingly recognizing is that merely reporting the facts about an overt manifestation is not enough: facts do not always add up to truth. Hence, there has been a demand for interpretation—explaining why an event took place and what it means. What went on before the event occurred, and what its effects will be, are considered as much a legitimate concern of the reporter as the collection of information about the current manifestation. While two of the requirements as set forth by the Commission on Freedom of the Press for adequate news presentation may be impossible to achieve, they must be considered in analyzing the nature of news. The commission asked for "a truthful, comprehensive, and intelligent account of the day's events in a context which gives them meaning" and "for the presentation and clarification of the goals and values of the society."[2]

---

[1] Walter Lippmann, *Public Opinion*. New York: The Macmillan Company, 1922, pp. 340-41.

[2] The Commission on Freedom of the Press, *A Free and Responsible Press.* Chicago: University of Chicago Press, 1947, pp. 20-28.

Even limiting our news to the reporting of overt manifestations is not so simple as it might at first appear. News is an extraordinarily complex psychological concept for those who gather and write it, and those who read and hear it. This aspect is stressed by Wilbur Schramm in an acute analysis of the nature of news. He wrote:

> News exists in the minds of men. It is not an event; it is something perceived *after* the event. It is not identical with the event; it is an attempt to reconstruct the essential framework of the event—*essential* being defined against a frame of reference which is calculated to make the event meaningful to the reader. It is an aspect of communication, and has the familiar characteristics of that process.[3]

The process includes the following steps: (1) the gathering of facts about an event by the reporter from eyewitnesses and participants; (2) the encoding of this information for transmission by the reporter in writing his story, and by editors in processing the story for publication; (3) the entrusting of the news to ink or sound waves or light waves for transmission to a potential audience; and (4) the reception of the news by members of the public. "No aspect of communications," Schramm wrote, "is so impressive as the enormous number of choices and discards which have to be made between the formation of the symbol in the mind of the communicator and the appearance of a related symbol in the mind of the receiver."

Since news gathering and news writing involve making a multitude of decisions, it is obvious that the journalist must develop his faculties for judging news. He must know enough about his public to be able to select the news that will interest and be useful to it. He will not be able to employ absolute rules or formulas in his judgment, but he can obtain useful guides in the voluminous research of recent years on how people read, what they read, and why they read.

How People Read

We do not require elaborate research to know that to speak of newspaper "readers" is something of an inaccuracy. It might be more accurate to call people newspaper "scanners." All we need to do is observe a person with his newspaper. Very likely, he begins

[3] Wilbur Schramm, "The Nature of News," *Journalism Quarterly*, 26:3, September 1949, p. 259.

with the front page, his eyes attracted first by the headlines in big type at the top. He may read the first paragraph of stories beneath, if his interest is aroused, or several paragraphs, if his interest is held. But he quickly passes on to other headlines and stories. Only occasionally does he hit upon a story that he reads all the way through.

Our reader follows his hit-and-skip method when he turns to the inside pages, though he may spend a little more time on some departments or pages than on others. If a sports fan, he may devote several minutes to the sports page; if an investor, to stock market quotations; if a politician, to comment on the editorial page.

To any casual observer of a newspaper reader in action, it should come as no surprise to learn that research shows people spend an average of perhaps 30 to 45 minutes a day informing themselves of the news through this printed medium. Similarly, it should be no surprise that research shows a low percentage of item readership.

The reading habits of people are thoroughly documented in hundreds of readership studies conducted in recent years. The most extensive project was the Continuing Study of Newspaper Reading conducted of 138 newspapers from 1939 to 1950 by the Advertising Research Foundation.

The Foundation's 138-Study Summary showed that men read about 18, or 14 percent, of the items in a paper, while women read 14 items, or about 11 percent. A more informative picture of readership is given in an analysis of 130 studies by Charles E. Swanson. Grouping the items in quartiles, he found that one in four was read by 4 percent or fewer readers; one in four by 5 to 11 percent; one in four by 12 to 29 percent; and one in four by 30 percent or more.[4]

A study by Schramm, based on 600 interviews, indicated a difference in the amount of readership of weeklies, small dailies, and large dailies. He found the average news readership for weeklies to be 27.8 percent; for small dailies, 21.5 percent; and for large dailies, 12.1 percent.[5]

Schramm's study also documents the fact that, though a person may be attracted to a story by a headline or lead paragraph, he usually does not read all of the story. It showed that a story loses

4 Charles E. Swanson, "What They Read in 130 Daily Newspapers," *Journalism Quarterly*, 32:4, Fall 1955, pp. 411-21.
5 Wilbur Schramm, "Measuring Another Dimension of Newspaper Readership," *Journalism Quarterly*, 24:4, December 1947, pp. 293-306.

readers rapidly in the first few paragraphs. On the average, a story lost 5 percent of its readers after the first paragraph, another 5 percent at the end of the second, and still another 5 percent at the end of the third. Thereafter, the decline continued, but the curve of loss flattened out.

While Schramm's study indicates that longer stories lose readers more quickly than shorter ones, the Swanson study suggests that brevity is not necessarily an inducement to read. Swanson found a progressive increase in readership according to the length of items. The average readership for items up to 3.9 inches was 13.1 percent; for items 4 to 7.9 inches, 15.5 percent; for items 8 to 11.9 inches, 29.6 percent; for items 12 to 15.9 inches, 32.3 percent; and for items over 16 inches, 41.0 percent.

What People Read

The Continuing Study of Newspaper Reading reveals the high attention-attraction of photographs and drawings. Picture pages led all other types of pages in readership, and stories illustrated with pictures consistently outranked non-illustrated stories. Although the first page is considered the paper's show window—the place where the most important news, expected to interest the greatest number of readers, appears—in over-all readership it ranked third, with comic pages ranking second to picture pages.

The information which the studies reveal about readership of news categories is so voluminous that it is hard to summarize. Two guides to understanding reading interests are the readership of items catalogued according to subject matter, and the readership of the widest-read stories.

In the Swanson analysis only one type of news had a mean average of above 30 percent—war news, which scored 34.6 percent. Readership scores of other content categories were, roughly:

between 26 and 30 percent: defense, fire-disaster, human interest, weather, and individual;

between 21 and 25 percent: major crime, social significance, consumer information, science-invention, popular art-music-literature, vital statistics, health-safety, private benevolence-charity, leisure time activities, accidents, loyalty investigations, and economic-social international relations;

between 16 and 20 percent: local government, national government, labor, entertainment features, politics, education, home-family, business-industry, civil-judicial affairs, taxes, social relations;

between 11 and 15 percent: fine arts-music-literature, sports, state government, minor crimes, religion-church-morals, country correspondence;

below 10 percent: agriculture, finance.

The Continuing Study's summary lists best-read stories of the prewar years of World War II, the war years, and the postwar years. Since they represent more recent and normal times, the 42 postwar listings give us the best clues to readership.

The best-read stories for men readers were:

STORY	PERCENT
Million-Dollar Fire Ruins Two Buildings of Historic Dunlop Flour Mills on James [Richmond (Va.) *News-Leader*]	90
Sioux City Blast Kills, Injures Scores [Burlington (Iowa) *Hawk-Eye Gazette*]	86
Judge Smith Dies Suddenly in Home [Lima (Ohio) *News*]	86
Mrs. Burritt, Awaiting Husband, Plans 'Private Detective Work' [Columbus (Ga.) *Leader*]	81
Dr. George W. Stoler Dies Unexpectedly in His 56th Year [Lancaster (Pa.) *Intelligencer Journal*]	81
*Mine Union Fined $3,500,000 [Rockford (Ill.) *Morning Star*]	81
Three Confess Tavern Stickup Here [Rockford (Ill.) *Morning Star*]	81
*Confession in Degnan Kidnap-Killing [Binghamton (N. Y.) *Press*]	80
Opera House Block in St. Albans Ablaze at Early Hour This A. M. [Burlington (Vt.) *Free Press*]	80
*Radio Actress Dead [Washington *Evening Star*]	79
City Council Hears Differing Views on Hotel-in-Park Plan [Centralia (Ill.) *Evening Sentinel*]	79

For women readers the best-read stories were:

STORY	PERCENT
Judge Smith Dies Suddenly in Home [Lima (Ohio) *News*]	91
Bednasek Had Motive Quite Some Time, Prosecutor Thinks [Burlington (Iowa) *Hawk-Eye Gazette*]	90
Mrs. Burritt, Awaiting Husband, Plans 'Private Detective Work' [Columbus (Ga.) *Leader*]	89
Dr. George W. Stoler Dies Unexpectedly in His 56th Year [Lancaster (Pa.) *Intelligencer Journal*]	86
*Confession in Degnan Kidnap-Killing [Binghamton *Press*]...	86

* Indicates non-local news story.

* Indicates non-local news story.

Although the two lists show some differences in the reading interests of men and women, they indicate that some types of stories have almost universal appeal for adults, since eight stories appear on both lists. As to differences in men's and women's reading, the Continuing Study summary mentions the following:

(1) Men favored front-page national and world news stories, although in considering national and world news as opposed to local news, regardless of position in the paper, men's attention was about equally divided between the two.

(2) Women showed a marked preference for local stories, regardless of where they appeared in a paper; individual studies of the best-read stories by women show that they appeared almost as often on inside pages as on front pages.

Another way of comparing men's and women's readership is by the news categories, where there is a marked difference in scores. In Swanson's analysis, those with differences of 5 percent or more for men and women are:

Men: war, science-invention, political international relations, local government, national government, labor, politics, taxes, and sports.

Women: popular art-music-literature, vital statistics, home-family, social relations, fine arts-music-literature.

In addition to sex, influences on the type of material read are age, education, and economic status. One of Schramm's studies showed, in general, that news reading tended to increase rapidly through the teens, reached a peak between the ages of 30 and 50, and thereafter dropped slightly, and that readership increased with education and with higher economic status. The type of news read corresponded roughly to these three factors. Young people, people with only a grade or high school education, and people on the lower economic level tended to be chiefly interested in the newspaper for entertainment, sensational news, and pictorial material. Serious news—public affairs, economics, social problems—was read more by the older, better educated, and more financially well off people.[6]

Why People Read

The newspaper exists today to satisfy what Frank Luther Mott calls "news-hunger."[7] It has existed, as he points out, since humankind formed social groups. People have always wanted to hear about their fellow creatures, and tales told by primitive men in their caves, tree-dwellings, grass huts, and tents were the essence of what we today call news.

As civilization developed, the gathering and dissemination of news became organized. The Greeks, for example, had runners who brought the news of battle; Romans in outposts of the empire were informed of events in the capital by newsletters; those in the city itself were informed by official bulletins called the *acta diurna*.

There are, of course, different kinds of news and variations in the kinds that satisfy news hunger. On one level, we have what Schramm calls immediate reward news and, on another level, what he calls delayed reward news.[8] Immediate reward news satisfies people's curiosity about what other people are doing and enables them to share vicariously the experiences of others. It thrills, surprises, shocks, titillates, creates sympathy or aversion; it is the news of crime, accidents and disaster, sports, society, human interest. Schramm allies this appeal to Freud's pleasure principle. Delayed reward news deals with such matterss as the foreign situation, business and economics, governmental policies and problems. Schramm allies this appeal to Freud's reality principle. It has an element of discomfort in it, because it forces people to consider matters that may have grim consequences; its reward lies in its informing people about, and preparing them to meet, the problems of life.

6 Schramm, "The Nature of News."
7 Frank Luther Mott, *The News in America*. Cambridge: Harvard University Press, 1952, pp. 1-9.
8 Schramm, "The Nature of News."

Whether or not we wish to accept Schramm's interesting theory about the pleasure principle and the reality principle, we can readily perceive that he has stated the basic truth about why people read news: they do so because they get something out of it. What they get, of course, may be essential or nonessential. Much, perhaps most, of what he defines as immediate reward news is not essential, since missing it would not greatly affect our lives. Much of what he defines as delayed reward news is probably essential, in that we can make practical use of it. Delayed reward news helps us to adjust to changes in our environment and to form our opinions and beliefs about matters affecting society, and therefore ourselves.

The Evaluation of News

Our concern with readership is due primarily to the fact that as news disseminators we want to reach as large a public as possible. Basically, this is a matter of financial revenue. The newspaper's income is based on the size of its circulation, a part coming from subscriptions, but a greater part coming from advertising. Circulation size is a factor in advertising income because space rates and the desirability of a newspaper as an advertising medium depend upon the number of readers.

But revenue is only one aspect of setting circulation as a goal in choosing news content. Another is that the newspaper has primary functions of informing, educating, and entertaining the public. Of these, the most important is providing people with information necessary to conduct their own affairs and form opinions about politics, government, international relations, and other matters of public concern. The more people the newspaper reaches, the more useful it is as a social instrument.

Readership studies generally support the traditional bases for evaluating news. We have believed that people are more interested in what happens in their own community and state than in what happens on the other side of the world. Hence, we have considered proximity an important element in news. We have also judged news by its significance, rated on the basis of the number of persons affected by an event. We have known that people are interested in famous persons, and have used prominence as a basis for judgment. But we also have known that people have an interest in other people as people—in their troubles, successes, idiosyncrasies—and have defined this element as one of human interest. Finally, we have felt that news should be new, and have considered recency or timeliness an important factor in our standards of evaluation.

But these are only rough guides, obvious oversimplifications. For example, we may be as interested in a strike of workers in Poland as in one in our own community. Its effects as a sign of trouble behind the Iron Curtain might be more important to us than a temporary shutdown of a plant in our own city. Again, perhaps the belief that everyone wants to read about the private activities of prominent people may be wrong. Elmo Roper, a public opinion analyst, found in 1950 that five times as many people wanted full details about government activity in Washington as wanted an equal amount about the affairs of Hollywood stars.

If we used readership surveys as our sole guide in determining newspaper content, we would increase our use of photographs and add more comic strips and cartoons, since these top all readership categories. We would print more items in the following categories: fire-disaster, human interest, weather, individual, major crime, consumer information, and science-invention. We would reduce space devoted to news in the following categories: finance, agriculture, country correspondence, religion-church-morals, minor crimes, state government, fine arts-music-literature, and taxes. Two of our major news departments would shrink—the women's pages and the sports pages.

These are some of the things we might do if we adhered closely to readership study findings. But no one has set out to tailor a newspaper to such findings, and no one is likely to do so. The findings are revealing as an indication of what people choose to read from material offered them. But the surveys do not find out what other material readers might prefer. They do not tell us why some items are read less than others, or why some are read more. They do not tell us what information and services readers expect of their newspaper. They ignore, also, the social responsibilities and functions of the newspaper. And they do not take into account the especial role of the newspaper in relation to the competing mediums of radio and television. We must look beyond the surveys for the answer to some of our questions.

In considering what readership studies tell us, we might be tempted at first to toss out the news categories with low interest ratings. To do so might be a mistake. While readership might appear to be shockingly low, the fact that we carry such information may be the reason for some people taking a newspaper. The newspaper, as a mass communication medium, is designed to appeal to all types of people, and as such should have something in it for everyone. Editors know that nobody reads everything in the paper, but they also know that almost everybody reads something.

Readership studies fail to tell us anything about the intensity of interest. While society and sports as general categories have lower reading scores than some other types of news, the disproportionate space devoted to them may be worth it. Those who follow society and sports are avid readers in their field of interest. While omission of an important scientific story, a category of news with fairly high readership, would result in no complaints from readers, let an editor omit an account of the country club's big dance of the year or the high school football team's victory, and his telephone will start ringing almost as soon as the papers begin rolling from the press.

Routine stories about local civic, welfare, fraternal, and other organizations form another news category with low readership. Interest hardly extends beyond the membership, but again, omission of this information might be a mistake. Members want to see items about their organization in the paper; they are eager for publicity. Moreover, notices of club activity are an important community service. For instance, in Pittsburgh, where the people were without newspapers for seven weeks because of a strike of mailing room employees, the annual Community Chest drive was delayed ten days: fund solicitors were deprived of the information and the stimulus to work ordinarily provided by the newspapers.

Just as omission of some types of news with low readership might not be a good thing, devoting more space to types of news with high readership might not be the answer to the problem of increasing the acceptance of a newspaper. Sensational news—fire, disaster, major crime—and entertaining news—human interest and personality stories—rank high in readership. But a newspaper devoted primarily to items of this type would be condemned by the people. They read it, to be sure, but they want more from their newspaper than mere sensationalism and entertainment. They can get the latter—more of it and better—from radio and television. If the newspaper meets the needs of the people for information, if it can be essential to their well-being, it need not fear that they will desert it for the two newer media.

In brief, the newsman must never let his standards of evaluation harden into a formula, for people and society change. People are better educated now than they used to be, they have more leisure time, they travel more, they have a greater variety of interests; they are, in short, different. The journalist, if he is to satisfy their news hunger, must at least keep up with them; he will be more successful if he stays ahead.

ASSIGNMENTS

1. As a class project, measure in inches the space devoted to the 25 categories of news given below in a single issue of a newspaper at the start or midpoint of each of the past five decades. Then write an article interpreting the findings.

Foreign news, international relations.
Washington news, federal government.
State government.
County government.
Municipal government.
Politics.
Business, industry.
Finance.
Agriculture.
Labor.
Social welfare.
Crime.
Health, medicine.
Education.
Science, invention.
Accidents, disaster.
Clubs, organizations.
Human interest, personality articles.
Sports.
Society.
Home, family.
Fashion, beauty.
Entertainment—movies, television, radio, etc.
Art, music, literature.
Pictures.

2. Using the same content categories, measure the space devoted to each in a metropolitan daily, a small-city daily, and a small-town weekly. Write an article interpreting your findings.

3. One of the basic functions of the newspaper is to provide people with information needed in performing their duties as citizens. What can be done by newspapers to increase readership of news of government?

4. Measure, in columns, the space in a daily newspaper devoted to advertising, straight news reports and comment, and entertainment, such as comic strips, puzzles, and features. From the standpoint of the social functions of the newspaper, do you find the space devoted to each disproportionate?

5. Judged by current performance, what are the strong and weak points of newspapers, radio, and television as mediums for communicating news?

CHAPTER 2

THE REPORTER AND REPORTING

The Role of the Reporter

WHEN JAMES H. RICHARDSON, city editor of the Los Angeles *Examiner,* got his first job on a newspaper, among his early assignments was an interview with Lord Strathcona, high commissioner for Canada. As he relates in his autobiography, *For the Life of Me,* Richardson was so awed by the dignitaries surrounding the great man that he slunk away instead of pressing forward to get his story.

Richardson received his first lesson in the responsibility of the reporter when he finally faced his city editor, who told him: "Kid, you're going to have to learn to walk different."

At Richardson's surprised exclamation, "Walk different!" the city editor replied: "Yes, walk different. I can always tell a newspaperman by the way he walks. A newspaperman always walks as though he had the right to be there, the right to go through any door. No matter where it is, he has the right to be there and he knows it. No matter what the door is, he has the right to go through and he knows it."

The first requirement for the reporter is to "walk like a newspaperman," to realize that he is performing a public service of immense importance, and that in consequence the right to get the news is protected by the Constitution and hallowed by long tradition.

It is a social responsibility that is becoming more, rather than less, important. Walter B. Lister of the Philadelphia *Evening Bulletin* has assigned to the reporter the key role in journalism. "Throughout a wide segment of the daily happenings which constitute news, the reporter is the man who first deals with the facts in the raw," he said in an interview. "On the accuracy with which these facts are reported depends the validity of the news story you read in your newspaper, the newspaper editorial, the radio broadcast, the conclusions of the syndicated columnist, the deliberations of legislators, and, eventually, the collective judgment of the world."

The Temperament for Reporting

Though a sense of responsibility to the public is a most important attribute of the reporter, there are other requirements of almost equal value. And not all people who wish to enter journalism can meet them. Samuel Johnson's statement of the difficulties in one of his *Idler* essays is something of an understatement: "To write news in its perfection requires such a combination of qualities, that a man completely fitted for the task is not always to be found."

Once, the minimum asked of a reporter was that he be able to write facts accurately and concisely. Now, he may also be required to explain the meaning of the facts in a world where issues and problems have become increasingly complex. Of all occupations, few demand as much knowledge, both general and specialized, as is needed for reporting.

While learning is a requisite for the journalist, it alone is not enough. In his wisdom as an editor, Charles A. Dana concluded that "the cultivated man is not in every case the best reporter." The reporter cannot be too high above his readers, a fact recognized by Lincoln Steffens who, in his *Autobiography,* attributed his success to the fact that his

> picture of the world as it seemed to be was much the same as my reader's. That made me a pretty good journalist; it is that that makes good journalism. The reporter and the editor must sincerely share the cultural ignorance, the superstitions, the beliefs, of their readers, and keep no more than one edition ahead of them.

Other major qualifications for journalism have been stated time and again. They include a "nose for news," accuracy, judgment, speed, initiative, perseverance, versatility, integrity, tact, nerve, and so forth. Such qualities do not call for extended discussion. But there are other factors that do. One of the most important of these may be called a temperament for newspaper work.

The reporter is frequently called upon to witness painful and shocking happenings. These arouse emotions which, as a newsman, he must be able to suppress in order to get at the story. The attitude is described by Steffens: "If a leading financier, at the end of a dark day of disaster, sat tight denying something I was sure of till, worn out, he fell across his desk, weeping and confessing, I picked up not the hysterical man but the confession."

Such events happen frequently, for the reporter, by the nature of his work, more often meets his fellowmen in moments of disaster and disgrace than in their periods of triumph and happiness. He interviews the wife of the absconding bank teller, the bereaved parents of a kidnaping victim, the children whose father died in an explosion. When people want to be alone with their grief or their remorse, the newspaperman must intrude. "Because he ceases for the moment to act humanly," says Helen MacGill Hughes in *News and the Human Interest Story*, "the reporter is able to create a human interest story."

What are the effects on the reporter? If extremely sensitive, he may conclude that he cannot for long play the role of vulture or ghoul. Or his work may make him callous, the hardened cynic that some reporters have been, or have posed at being. But sometimes, as Mrs. Hughes says, the reporter's work develops in him "an attitude approaching the aloofness from personal passion that marks . . . the philosopher and the artist."

The reporter should not let himself be overwhelmed by his experiences, for he must always be able to get the story. Nor should he become hardened, for he thereby loses his greatest value as a reporter—always to be able to encounter a happening for the thousandth time as though it were the first. "When," writes Stanley Walker in *City Editor*, "a reporter says, 'I've seen a big ship go down before,' or 'This is a fair obituary, but I liked best the one I did on Chauncey M. Depew,' or 'I can't see much point to this murder; you see, I covered the Rosenthal killing,' it is, perhaps, time for him to leave the city room forever." The true reporter must always be able to see "red at a fire," must never reach the state in which he looks upon murder as "only another crime."

As in his approach to news of human tragedies, the reporter must be able to maintain objectivity toward economic, social, and political questions. He should be able to write as fairly about the Republican party as he does about the Democratic though by principle he may be a Democrat. He should not let his religious beliefs color his account of another faith. He should avoid letting his knowledge of which side his bread is buttered on influence his handling of a story dealing with labor or economics.

Besides objectivity, another characteristic of the journalistic temperament is skepticism. Experienced journalists have found that most people fall into two types—those who want to get into the newspapers and those who want to keep out. On the one hand, the reporter must be on guard against people seeking publicity. When he meets a news source who appears over-willing to talk, he should become suspicious. Is the crusading minister more interested in getting his name and his picture in the newspaper than he is in correcting evils? Is the chairman of a congressional investigating committee more interested in the headlines than he is in finding the facts? On the other hand, the reporter must be suspicious of unwilling news sources. Is the highway commissioner opposed to divulging information about construction contracts because they are too technical and would not interest people, or has he something to hide about how they were granted? Is the police chief's refusal to release details about a criminal investigation due to the fact that it would interfere with catching the culprit, or is it due to the inefficiency of police efforts?

As the reporter's experience with misery and pain may tend to make him unfeeling, so his constant scrutiny of motives may incline him toward misanthropy. He may so often have to look for the worst in man that he may never be able to see the best in him.

Another aspect of journalism that may eventually disturb the reporter is the realization that he can seldom accurately quote Walter Duranty in saying, "I write as I please." He usually does not write as he pleases.

In the first place, the nature of journalistic work requires the reporter to write under the tension of having to make a deadline. Seldom does he have time to mull over his information and get it down on paper the way he feels it should be written. In the second, much journalistic writing is bound, by rules of style and structure, to a formula. These two conditions often inhibit originality and creativeness.

In another sense, the journalist writes not to please himself but someone else. City editors and copyreaders are at liberty to cut or changes stories as they see fit. This is one of the most infuriating aspects of journalism, especially for the writer who takes pride in the way he expresses himself. After laboring to produce a vivid bit of description based on painstaking efforts to obtain details, it is disheartening to find paragraphs deleted for lack of space in the newspaper.

Such matters, though irritating, may not prove to be serious frustrations. More important are the occasions when the reporter's inclinations may run counter to his newspaper's policy. A. J. Liebling in *The Wayward Pressman* says that he knew of few newspapermen who were forced to write things they did not believe, but that he knew of many who were prevented from writing what they did. Even such privileged persons as columnists have had their articles suppressed or badly mutilated in editing.

The news writer, then, must realize that he frequently has to subordinate his beliefs or ideals to what his readers or his employers will accept. He need not, as in the case of one nationally known editorial writer, consider his talent as something for hire, writing on one side of a question for a newspaper and on another for a magazine. But he must be cognizant of the realities of journalism.

The News Organization

In journalistic jargon, a reporter is frequently called a "legman." It is an apt designation. He cannot sit in an office or pressroom and expect news to come to him; he must go out and get it.

The organization of the news staff is based on this necessity. Working under the direction of the city editor, reporters are assigned to "beats" or "runs," the routine sources where the bulk of the news originates. Most of these are governmental offices and agencies, where, as Walter Lippmann has pointed out, "people's affairs touch public authority." Thus there are city hall reporters, police reporters, county building or courthouse reporters, and capitol reporters. Other beats may be business—the chamber of commerce, retail credit association, trade and professional groups, banks, industrial firms; labor unions; civic, service, and welfare organizations; and such specialties as sports, society, science, and agriculture.

Not all news, however, turns up in routine places, and consequently newspapers employ reporters called general assignment men. Their work consists of reporting meetings and conventions, doing interviews and features, and covering events which beat reporters do not have time to get. The police reporter, for example, sometimes cannot conveniently be pulled off his run to go out and get the details of a crime or accident. The city editor may send a general assignment man to do this upon a tip from the police reporter.

The general assignment reporter may also double as a rewriteman. The rewriteman, a fast and versatile worker, receives information from the beat reporters by telephone and writes the story. In the case of a major event, he may receive information from several reporters assigned to cover it, and weave all the facts received piecemeal into a general story. On occasion his work may consist merely of the routine chore of taking dictation on the typewriter from reporters who telephone complete stories composed mentally from their notes. When not handling material telephoned into the city room by reporters, he may rewrite publicity releases mailed or delivered to the newspaper or items clipped from other newspapers.

In addition to these reporters and writers, the newspaper may maintain district men or suburban reporters in its surrounding trade area and correspondents in more distant areas. These reporters cover all the happenings of any nature occurring in their area that might interest the newspaper's wide circle of readers.

While a reporter's effectiveness is shown in his dealings with his news sources and the public, his intramural relationships are also important. Getting out a daily newspaper is an immensely complicated task, calling for the best efforts of many people; one person who falls down on his job may upset the whole operation. Thus the reporter who fails to get to work on time or who does not know and meet deadlines can cause trouble. City rooms tend to be bustling places, and staff members have a duty to do their work quietly, to avoid disturbing other staff members with idle chatter, and to keep their friends and relatives outside the office.

Though the city editor supervises the work of reporters, he cannot be expected to know as much about the runs and beats as the men regularly assigned to them. The reporter, as one newspaper said in an instruction sheet to new staff members, should be a "self-starter." The instructions continue:

> Don't wait for your city editor to tell you what you are to do. Organize your own work in such a way that you produce your copy in time for the proper edition with a minimum of commotion. Your city editor has a list of your assignments. If he wants this story or that put ahead, he'll tell you so. Any reporter who

says he has nothing to do is blind to the potentialities of life as a source for news, and should pick out some other occupation. We can hire stenographers and statisticians to make copies of public records.

Your city editor is surrounded by four walls, you by the blue sky itself. You are his eyes, and you are his ears. He'll give you assignments, yes, but he also expects you to have ideas of your own. Check with him and proceed. A good newspaperman once described news this way: "Anything which in your day's rounds impresses you sufficiently to remark as you sit down to dinner with your family, 'The most interesting thing happened today . . .'— that sometimes is news. It is merely a challenge to the reporter to make it conform to good newspaper practice. A good reporter can make a story out of it, or a picture, or a cartoon, or all three.[1]

The reporter's task is to get all the facts about a happening and write a story that is fair, objective, and complete. He should not twist information to what he conceives to be the editorial policy of the newspaper. Gideon Seymour of the Minneapolis *Star* and *Tribune* instructed a new reporter in a memorandum:

> We are jealously proud of the freedom of our news columns from slanted stories and biased selection of news. Public confidence in the purity of our news columns is our greatest asset. Do not try to write or play news to conform with views expressed on the editorial page. It is the business of the news columns to tell the news, fully and fairly; it is the business of the editorial pages to advocate views and to publish opinions about the news for such readers as desire them.

If the reporter fulfills his obligations to the newspaper by doing his work accurately, honestly, and fairly, if he lives up to the accepted ethics of his profession, he should in turn be able to count on the backing of his newspaper, at least to the extent of being given a fair hearing when an influential news source threatens to get his job or when he is accused of inaccuracy.

Contacts with the Public

As one of the chief liaison men between the newspaper and the public, the reporter has a responsibility to make a good impression for the institution that pays his salary. A reporter discourteous in his dealings with the public can undo the work and the thousands

[1] Memorandum for new staff members prepared by the Oklahoma City *Daily Oklahoman*.

of dollars that the newspaper's promotion department spends in attempting to build up good will.

Some reporters, realizing that they have the power of the press behind them, may have a tendency to ride roughshod over opposition, demanding news instead of asking for it. There are times, of course, when the hard-boiled attitude may be necessary; but in the long run it is the quiet-mannered reporter who gets the news, while the cocky fellow, pretending to have all the inside dope and truculent toward his sources, will fail.

Yet the reporter covering a big run such as a courthouse cannot take time for the delaying formalities that a salesman or an applicant for a job has to go through. He must have ready access to offices, and in most public buildings he does. The reason for this is that most officials want publicity and will go out of their way to cooperate with reporters. The businesslike reporter who has specific questions to ask his news sources generally can develop a relationship with officials that will gain him admittance to those sources.

The reporter should not limit his cultivation of sources to the bureau chief or department head. While it is not to be expected that employees will betray the confidence of their superiors, they frequently are in a position to supply tips. Paul Fairleigh of the Memphis (Tennessee) *Press-Scimitar* has advised the inexperienced reporter:

> Tips on some of the biggest news breaks come from clerks, stenographers, the rookie cop and even janitors. Be friendly with everyone on your beat from the department heads to the most insignificant employee in every office you visit. In short time you can develop a close personal contact and train them to give you tips on what's going on in their offices or around their buildings.

But he warns that the reporter should not divulge the origin of such tips, since, if the word gets around that the reporter cannot be trusted, the sources will dry up.

Another reporter who has found subordinates valuable is Robert J. Donovan of the New York *Herald Tribune*. In his experience, he says, "a reporter probably will find that some obscure, quiet, white-haired gentleman hidden away in a corner of the department of finance, or the corporation counsel's office, or the department of public works knows more about what is going on in the city government than all the councilmen combined." It may not always be a quiet, white-haired gentleman, but there is almost always some such person in any office. The heads come and go with shifts in the political wind, but the public work goes on unaffected; the burden is carried by veteran employees, simply because changing administrations cannot afford to fire them.

Although making friends facilitates the gathering of news, it is not always possible, or desirable, to develop close friendships. They have inherent dangers, for the reporter may permit himself to suppress or gloss over disagreeable news about his friends. The occasion will always arise when he must write stories that will be bad publicity for them, and it is hard for him to do so if he has been on terms of close friendship. Obviously, his first duty is to his newspaper and to the public. He will have to get the news—even if it means hurting someone he likes.

Experienced news sources are aware of this problem facing the reporter, and they are not always reluctant to capitalize on it. The reporter, therefore, must be wary of people who are too friendly. If he is not careful, he may allow himself to be used by them, to become little more than a personal publicity agent for them.

The person planning on journalism as a profession has to consider many factors, some of them extremely subjective. Certain native attributes are essential—the usual listings of speed, accuracy, intelligence, and broad background. But it is necessary to consider other factors. Journalism may be an exciting experience, or it may be a deadening one. It offers the chance to see humanity at first hand, but it may result in the journalist's becoming fed up with people. It provides the means of doing a service for society, and yet there are circumstances which tend to obstruct such service.

The good journalist, it would seem, is one who trusts his fellow men, but does not permit himself to be taken in by them; who is tolerant of the evildoer, but not of evil; who finds satisfaction in the fact that his best efforts never satisfy him; and who loves his task, though he may sometimes hate his taskmaster.

ASSIGNMENTS

1. Write an article telling why you became interested in journalism and what you expect from it as a profession.

2. List in the order you consider them important the major requirements for a good reporter. How do you rate yourself as a potential reporter, according to your scale?

3. Study the news sources of your home town and determine what size reportorial staff you would need to cover the news adequately. List the runs or beats to which you would assign each reporter.

4. Imagine yourself the city editor of a newspaper interviewing an applicant for a reporting job. What questions would you ask him to find out if he seems fitted for newspaper work?

CHAPTER 3

TECHNIQUES OF REPORTING

The Local Background

THOUGH THE JOURNALIST needs a broad background in history, politics, economics, sociology, and other areas of knowledge in order to handle intelligently the variety of topics confronting him daily as a news writer, he also needs to know well the community in which he works. Managing editors say that a new man is not worth his salary until he has been some months on the job— until he has become acquainted with the people, organizations, geography, economy, and history of the area which the newspaper serves.

The reporter, therefore, should spend his spare time during his first weeks on the job seeing at firsthand every part of the city, reading the back files of his newspaper, browsing through the archives of the public library or local historical society, and talking about every aspect of the community at bull sessions with other members of the newspaper's staff.

The nose for news is oftentimes not something intuitive, but just simple knowledge. For instance, if a police report of a brawl at the Colony Club comes in, the reporter's background information gives him a clue to its news importance. If the club is a dark, dingy dive near the railroad station where brawls are common, the reporter knows he very likely can give the occurrence routine coverage. But if the club is a swank place with modern décor and a cover charge, he knows he had better get to the scene—the participants are likely to be prominent and therefore highly newsworthy. Reporters know that the appearance of certain attorneys at the courthouse means a big story is in the offing—these attorneys do not handle trifling cases.

It is important, also, for the reporter to keep informed about current happenings, not only on his own beat but in the entire city. This means that he should be a constant reader of his own newspaper; he should not be the reporter who looks at the newspaper only to see what play his own stories received or how much damage copyreaders did in editing. On any day he should be almost as well prepared to cover some one else's beat as he is his own. Knowledge of all beats is especially needed by general assignment men, who may not know from one moment to the next where they will be sent on a story.

Even keeping up with details of happenings on one's own run requires effort. If the newspaper has a good library or morgue, clippings will be available for the reporter or rewriteman to refresh his memory about earlier developments and to obtain names, addresses, and other facts. The city editor, also, generally has clippings in his future book or file for follow-ups. But if, as on many small newspapers, the morgue is inadequate or nonexistent, or if the city editor's clippings do not cover all the background needed, the reporter would do well to keep his own filing system of stories continuing over several weeks or months. He can thus prevent waste of time in checking through the newspaper files for earlier reports.

Communication Problems

No matter how well the reporter covers his beat or special assignment, his effort will be wasted if he cannot get his story into the office. This is an aspect of news work often slighted by schools of journalism and newspapers. For example, the Federal Communications Commission failed to assign any specific frequencies to newspapers in proposed allocations of mobile radio channels because only a few publishers had taken steps to utilize them.

It would seem obvious that automobiles and airplanes equipped with two-way radio should be of immense value in covering events and in relaying information to the newspaper office. The Boston *Herald-Traveler,* in an argument submitted to the FCC, described the mobile relay radio communication system as "the greatest single innovation in newspaper reporting since the invention of the telephone," explaining:

Use of the radio allows for a tremendous saving in manpower and permits reporters to meet deadlines which they would not be able to meet if they had to depend on other means of communication. In addition, editors are enabled to deploy the reporting forces quickly and in the most efficient way possible for coverage of a story.

Though somewhat belatedly, publishers fortunately awoke to the possibilities and won four frequencies in the 162-174 Mc range to be shared with motion picture service, and 20 frequencies in the 450-460 Mc range to be shared with other industrial services.

What this means for the reporter is that he must learn oral or spoken expression as well as written expression. It is not enough that he be able to sit down at a typewriter and compose a story; he must also be able to relay his information to a rewriteman in concise and comprehensible terms. Preferably, and this will come with experience, he must master the art of dictating a complete, finished story from his notes in the form it will appear in print.

Actually, however, the art of oral expression has been a requirement on some newspapers for many years, since it is a necessity in telephoning information to the office. Peter Kihss of the New York *Herald Tribune* advises:

> A few elementary points in telephoning will make any rewriteman's life happier. Know what you're going to tell him, and how. Summarize: "This is a fire story—fire and explosion, three-story building, first floor burned out, nobody inside." Sometimes it's better to telephone a story as if dictating the actual copy, lead first. Sometimes it's more comprehensible to give it chronologically, the way it happened.
>
> Remember the fellow on the other end is taking notes, and it's all new to him. Especially on names, and on quotes, be sure you understand each other. There are lots of variations of almost any name. Lewis might come out Louis, if you don't check.[1]

In respect to the last point mentioned by Kihss, reporters have adopted the practice of spelling out all proper names and words that might not come through clearly. They follow a code system, similar to that used in military communications, in which each letter of the alphabet is given a name. The standardized military designations—Able, Baker, Charlie, Dog, etc.—have not been adopted, however, and reporters use any word beginning with the

[1] Joseph G. Herzberg, *Late City Edition*. New York: Henry Holt and Co., 1947, p. 40.

letter that happens to come to mind. Adoption of the military code would probably facilitate telephoning information. Thus, in spelling out a name, the reporter would give it like this: "Smyth—S as in Sugar, M as in Mike, Y as in Yoke, T as in Tare, and H as in How."

In learning the art of dictation, the reporter should begin with short items. Before long his ability to organize facts logically into complete sentences will develop to the extent that he will find himself dictating longer and longer stories.

Since two-way radio facilities have not become universal, one of the first things the reporter should do when sent on such assignments as fires, explosions, storms, and floods is to make sure he has access to a telephone or other means of communicating with his newspaper. In fact, it might well be the first step in coverage. He might as well not get names and addresses, descriptions, and other information if he cannot relay it to his office.

The Art of Note-Taking

Ben Hecht, reminiscing in his autobiography about his days as a reporter and picture snatcher for Chicago newspapers, wrote that before leaving on an assignment he slipped into an overcoat pocket a pair of pliers, a jimmy, and a large file. Thus equipped, he was prepared to enact his role of "ruffian, picklock, and enemy of society." While his unorthodox approach to news gathering may be condemned, his preparation at least was praiseworthy. Too many reporters start on an assignment equipped only with a stubby pencil and a swatch of copy paper folded twice horizontally.

Poor note-taking is one of the principal reasons why reporters sometimes garble information and why, in direct quotations, people in news stories all talk alike in a hybrid language of journalistic clichés and headline punch words. "Some reporters," wrote A. Vernon Croop of the Rochester (New York) *Times-Union,* "make baseball players talk like the professors which they ain't, or make ward heelers sound like the gentlemen which they aren't."

There is, of course, a question as to whether people should be quoted exactly as they talk. Speaking off the cuff, few persons express themselves in complete sentences and they often ramble around a subject instead of coming to the point. For example, a reader of the St. Louis *Post-Dispatch* complained of a quotation attributed to President Dwight D. Eisenhower. Asked if he was

astonished by the total results of an election or individual cases, the
President said:

> Well, as a matter of fact, I was thinking really of a number of
> individual cases. Of course, I was pleased with all the reports I
> have seen as to the size of the vote. That I believe is—no—I asked
> the last minute for an estimate of the number of people who
> voted. I didn't get it. We haven't it, maybe you people have; but
> from what—I was quite astonished with that, and very pleased
> about that one.

The reader's objection was that he did not believe it possible for the
President to be so vague and incoherent, and that even if he were,
the newspaper should not have printed the quotation.

The passage was a verbatim excerpt from a press conference, but
in writing a straight news story about statements of news sources
other than the President, most reporters, if they take them down
complete, translate them into formal English, probably with quotation marks.

Such practice may be acceptable as long as the quoted remarks
are substantially in the words of the speaker, but on occasion it
may cause trouble. The Associated Press, for example, issued a cor-
rective when the playback of a tape recording of a speech by Vice
President Richard M. Nixon showed that he had been misquoted
because his actual statement was incomplete. The A. P. story quoted
him as saying the Eisenhower administration had "kicked the
Communists out of government not by the hundreds, but by the
thousands." The tape recording had him saying: "We're kicking the
Communists and fellow travelers and security risks out of the government, not by the hundreds but by the thousands."

Another question of quoting people exactly as they talk arises
over the use of dialect and accent. Undoubtedly such passages in a
news story would make it more readable, but objections immediately occur. Reproducing actual speech is so difficult an art that
even fiction writers, devoting years of study to it, often do not
master it. The reporter who tries to reproduce dialect, even in
interview and feature stories where it would be most appropriate,
may turn out something ludicrous. A Scottish reporter attempting
to show the American speech of Milton S. Eisenhower, for instance,
had the Kansas-reared brother of President Eisenhower talking in
a vernacular like that of a deep-Southerner. Another reason for
newspaper avoidance of dialect is that it may be prejudicial to the

person quoted. Editors feel that, in straight news reports, there is no justification for directing attention to a person's lack of education or his national or racial background.

When appropriate, however, a speaker's words, recorded exactly as he utters them, make a story more readable than one in which, because of the reporter's inability to capture the flavor, they are paraphrased. The following passage, for instance, gains in interest because the reporter used a realistic direct quote:

> A 15-year-old Beechview boy, captured by police twice in 10 days after auto chases, taunted officers today when they questioned him about district auto thefts.
> "Nyah, nyah, ya can't touch me," he sneered. "I'm a juvenile."
> —Pittsburgh *Press*.

Or the following, by Les Biederman, Pittsburgh *Press* columnist, giving baseball player Gene Freese's version of his being fined $50 for "inciting a riot" in an argument with umpire Augie Donatelli, when Freese could not talk clearly because he had given his denture to another player to hold:

> "I had gone through five games without a hit and popped up in the second inning that night," Freese explains. "Before I went to the plate the next time, I gave Eddie O'Brien my bridge to hold for good luck and I singled.
> "In the seventh inning, I gave O'Brien the bridge. I went out but hit the ball good. In the ninth inning, I handed over the bridge again and this time I singled.
> "So when I was called out, I tried to talk back to Donatelli but felt so silly yapping without my teeth, I just threw up my hands in disgust. He tossed me out of the game and then came the beer cans.
> "That was quite a riot I started for fifty bucks."

The point of all this is that the reporter must master the art of accurate note-taking, and this can best be done by learning shorthand. In this respect, British reporters are frequently better prepared than American reporters, for most British reporters have learned one of the conventional systems, whereas American reporters often rely on haphazard abbreviations they have developed on their own. But such hit-and-miss taking down of statements will no longer do, when tape recordings made by television and radio newsmen uncover, as they have too frequently in recent years, misquotations in newspaper stories.

In taking notes, American reporters may get off to a bad start by using folded copy paper, rather than a hard-backed notebook. But more and more of them, according to a poll by *Editor & Publisher*, are abandoning copy paper for stenographer's notebooks. The poll quotes Ed Wallace of the New York *World-Telegram and Sun:* "Twenty years ago no self-respecting reporter would have carried a notebook. I got the habit as a reporter in the army, when I wanted the greatest convenience, and wasn't worried about how it would look."

Sixteen respondents in the *Editor & Publisher* poll of well-known reporters said they wished they knew shorthand, two thought such knowledge might be helpful, and two felt it was unnecessary. Those who approved knowing shorthand gave such reasons as getting complete statements at trials, hearings, and interviews; capturing the idiom and flavor of a person's speech; and being able "to hang a man by his own quotes."

Actually, complete mastery of a system based on phonetic symbols might not be necessary, since a year or so of intensive study and practice is needed to develop speed. Perhaps a better plan would be to learn one of the simplified systems based on the regular alphabet. Even a complete mastery of it might not be necessary, if it provides the reporter with a systematic method of abbreviations to use in part, instead of the individual and unsystematic shortcuts he is likely to develop himself.

Shorthand, however desirable it may be, has drawbacks. The reporter is likely to rely too much on note-taking to the neglect of developing his memory; he may concentrate so much on getting down the speaker's exact words that he misses the meaning; and he may amass so many notes that he finds it difficult to untangle them in writing his story. Moreover, if he leans too heavily on written notes he is at a disadvantage in situations—and they are frequent— in which it is undesirable or not possible to pull out a hard-cover notebook and take down what is said.

An advantage of the notebook over copy paper is that it facilitates keeping notes. A reporter cannot burden himself by preserving all his notes taken in the course of a day's work, but often if kept for several days or a week they prove useful when the accuracy of a story is questioned or when they may be needed to refresh his memory for follow-up stories. And he will find a permanent file of notes valuable for that book he plans to write sometime in the future when he can get a month off.

The sound-recording industry has provided the present-day reporter with an important aid, not as yet in wide use, in the development of small-size tape recorders and portable dictation machines. Michael James of the New York *Times* uses a tape recorder that fits into a coat pocket for interviews and speeches, and Hilliard Schendorf, Associated Press radio feature writer, finds a portable dictation machine useful for interviews.

Valuable though these devices may be on occasion, it is unlikely that they will become standard equipment for reporters. James, for example, may use his tape recorder several times a week and then not use it for a month or more. Such portable machines seem most practical for arranged interviews or press conferences, and for speeches; articles based on such transcriptions probably should be magazine-length features, rather than regular newspaper items. Since the devices cannot be selective in what is recorded, the reporter, in writing his story, probably would have to listen to 30 minutes of talk to get a quotable paragraph; under the pressures of daily journalism, he would seldom make his deadline.

How to Be Accurate

One of the first lessons in journalism learned by Don E. Weaver of the Columbus (Ohio) *Citizen* was the need for accuracy. Starting as a cub in 1924, when Robert M. La Follette was running for President, Weaver wrote a short item about a campaign rally and, in his ignorance, gave the name as "Lafayette." The slip, as such slips invariably do, got into the paper.

A gagster clipped the story and put it on the bulletin board under the caption, "Lafayette, we are here!" But even more stinging in Weaver's memory than this ridicule was the step taken by his city editor to cure him of the habit of carelessness. Thereafter, the city editor made him recheck by telephone book or city directory all names in his stories, whether he was sure of them or not.

If there is one area of reporting where it would seem that error could be avoided, it should be in names, for the spelling can be verified. But nevertheless misspelled names are one of the most frequent newspaper errors. The Hartford (Connecticut) *Times,* in two tests of its accuracy, clipped news stories and sent them to the source, with a request that errors be pointed out: misspelled names accounted for 30 and 47 percent of the errors.

How can the reporter make sure that he has names correct? Apparently he cannot, but there are routines to follow that can prevent most mistakes. One, if the news source is not known to the reporter, is for him to start the interview by asking the person how he spells his name. The reporter should follow this protocol even for persons who apparently have commonplace surnames; unless the name is spelled out for him, the reporter cannot tell if it is Brown or Browne, or Smith, Smyth, or Smythe.

Another routine is to check all names appearing in public records, rosters of club officers or members, hospital records, and so forth, either by the persons concerned or by city and telephone directories. A survey made by the Yakima (Washington) *Morning Herald* and *Daily Republic* showed that hospital records, in particular, were a major source of misspelled names: people entering the hospital for emergency treatment are more interested in seeing a doctor than they are in getting their names spelled correctly. The survey also indicated that friends, and even relatives, of persons mentioned in news items are often unreliable authorities for the spelling of names.

Unfortunately, it is not possible to check all names. This is particularly true for arrests, police reports of accidents and crimes, and hospital emergency admissions, when the persons involved may not appear in the telephone book or city directory. Since these are frequently short items not worth a firsthand check, the reporter relies upon the public record version—often to his regret.

Reporters gather most news secondhand from public officials and from persons involved in an event or witnesses to it. As psychological experiments have shown, or as testimoney in almost any trial will reveal, the stories of participants and observers vary. Most of us are inexact observers, seeing things not as they really happen, but interpreting them from previously formed "pictures in our heads." Thus, many errors in news stories originate in the fallibility of the source of information. This situation emphasizes the need for the reporter to check his facts from more than one source. By obtaining details of a happening from several persons, the reporter is more likely to get the true story than if he relied on only one person's account. If the accounts vary greatly, the versions of all the sources should be given, at least in points where they differ.

Another reason for the unreliability of secondhand sources of information is that the person concerned may not wish the real facts to get out. He may suppress certain information or gild other information to give a favorable impression. It is not enough, then, for the reporter to present accurately what his news source tells him. He must, by persistent cross-examination, obtain more information than the source is willing, without prodding, to divulge. When the reporter cannot get the answers to questions that must be answered in the story, he can let his readers know that something is being kept back. He can do this by giving the questions asked and stating that the source declined to answer them. In a more general way, he can indicate evasiveness by such statements as that the source refused to comment or declined to give details. If the source becomes angry at being questioned, refuses to talk at all, or obviously avoids seeing the press, such information belongs in the news story. For the reporter to confess to the reader that he was unable to get the news, however, is not enough; when he cannot obtain the full story from one source, he should try to uncover the information from other sources.

In respect to the fallibility of news sources, the reporter may compound error under the theory that anything can be printed, so long as it is attributed to someone. Under this rationalization, anything that anyone says, especially if the individual is prominent or in public office, may get into the news story. When, to his own knowledge, the reporter is aware that a news source or speaker is making a misstatement of fact, he should raise the question of accuracy. If the news source insists on his version, the reporter should give opposing versions in the story. Though readers may not have the knowledge to decide which is correct among conflicting versions, they are at least warned that there is disagreement as to what the facts are.

While inability to obtain information, or to learn what the facts are, is a frequent cause of error, some avoidable practices in the profession contribute their share of mistakes. One of these is the emphasis on the "Gee whiz!" element in news: in the words of Raymond Clapper, "the pressure upon all newsroom workers, from managing editor on down, to whip up a lead that will knock the reader's eye out."

To attract readers and make them want to read a story, the reporter is told to get punch in his lead. Thus he builds up entirely out of proportion a minor incident that is dramatic or unusual, or he resorts to souped-up words and expressions. "Violence flared today" is used to begin a strike story in which the only clash was the arrest of a single picket for disorderly conduct. A robber is arrested after a "fusillade of shots," when a policeman fired his gun once or twice in warning. "The city faced a water crisis today," when officials merely requested that residents stop watering their lawns.

In the opinion of many editors, such leads, simply to make punch headlines, are obsolete today. Before radio, when newspapers were first with the news, such shock tactics may have been justified. But what readers want from the newspaper today, in the words of Frank Jenkins of the Klamath Falls (Oregon) *Herald-News*, "is an orderly presentation, in type, of the day's occurrences, so that they may sit down at leisure and review it and get the news straight, including names and places and who's who; no longer does a big headline bring to them much of a shock of surprise." And Paul A. Schrader of the Toledo (Ohio) *Blade* comments that "blazing headlines and the accompanying evil of loosely used action verbs and adjectives are more responsible for errors, ambiguities, and overplay than any other human frailties."

Deadline pressure is another major contributor to inaccuracy in the news. The reporter feels that he must get his story written, even if he has not had time to analyze his information carefully, to determine what it means, or to check additional sources to get the whole picture. For instance, in 1956, when segregation was one of the big stories of the year, the United States Supreme Court included in a long list of orders a notation that an appeal involving a South Carolina bus segregation case had been dismissed. Reporters jumped to the conclusion that the Court had upheld a lower court decision banning racial segregation on buses. Two days later the correct interpretation was made clear: the Supreme Court refused to consider an appeal because there had not been a final judgment in the trial court; its action was a procedural one, not a ruling on the merits of the case.

Robert U. Brown, in his "Shop Talk at Thirty" column in *Editor & Publisher* (May 12, 1956), blamed the error on the pressure of deadlines, and went on to say: "Newspapers will gain more in the end if they strive toward complete accuracy in reporting and background interpretation even at the expense of speed. Other media can get to the readers faster. Newspapers should get there in more complete and reliable fashion."

Besides careful checking and avoiding hurried assumptions, a reporter's general stock of information and his ability to write correctly and clearly are his surest protections against inaccuracy. Readers do not place much confidence in a news story that contains grammatical errors and misspelled words, that attributes a play or a book to the wrong author, or that misnames a well-known organization. Accuracy in small things every minute of the day may prevent a blooper that becomes a subject for legend.

ASSIGNMENTS

1. Listen to a speech over radio or television and attempt to take down verbatim the important passages. Compare your versions with a newspaper's report of the speech or the printed text, if it is published.

2. Take notes on the conversation of someone you know who has a colorful and idiomatic way of speaking, and write a report that catches the flavor of his talk.

3. Make a list of contractions, abbreviations, and other shortcuts you have found useful in taking notes.

4. Using the first page of the campus paper, make an accuracy check for all news items. Use the student directory, faculty directory, university catalogue, a book of facts, a book of quotations, and any other reference works required to verify information. Make a list of all errors found.

5. Find examples of news stories where reporters have gone to several sources to get different versions of an event. What inconsistencies do you find in the various versions? Which version are you inclined to accept? Why?

6. Compare the stories of the same event appearing in two different newspapers. What inconsistencies do you find? Which do you consider the more accurate version? Why?

CHAPTER 4

PROBLEMS OF REPORTING

Relations with Publicists

THE BEGINNING REPORTER will not be on the job long before he discovers that his news source may not be the mayor, the congressman from his district, or the president of the town's largest manufacturing firm, but their public information men. If the reporter has been indoctrinated with the belief that these people are "space grabbers" and "free publicity seekers," he is likely to be somewhat resentful. But as he learns more about his work, he will find them a help in gathering news. He will also find them a handicap, but he can overcome that.

Lambasting publicity men and press agents and their attempts to get stories into the newspaper is a popular pastime of editorial writers and speakers at press conventions—and rightly so. But in recent years the space-seeker has become a public relations man or public information man. The change in nomenclature reflects a change in practice and concept. Scott M. Cutlip of the University of Wisconsin sums up the new point of view:

> Public relations is, essentially, the adjustment of an institution or industry to its community. This involves fact-finding, policy-making, and public contacts. The first two are assuming more and more importance, the last less and less in the working definition of the trade. A growing body of public relations practitioners are concerned more with *what kind* of news their client gets rather than with *how much* news he gets in the press. And they realize the *what* must be defined by the acts and policies of the institution itself. In this concept there is no place for shoddy press-agentry.[1]

[1] Scott M. Cutlip, "The Press Versus the Publicist," *Nieman Reports*, 5:2, April 1951, p. 21.

While it is true that enlightened practitioners of public and press relations maintain they are performing a useful social function, their claims need not be taken at face value. To a great extent they may be, but the reporter should never forget that their first loyalty is to their employer and not the public.

The problem of dealing with public information or publicity men may be considered in three areas: (1) publicity for local organizations and institutions; (2) public information and press relations in government; and (3) public information and press relations in industry.

In the coverage of local groups such as chambers of commerce, service clubs, welfare organizations, churches, museums, and schools, the person in charge of publicity, whether a temporary appointee or a full-time paid employee, is of material convenience to the press. Much of the news of meetings, speakers, programs, and campaigns is routine, often of little interest to anyone outside the membership. The people who bring or telephone this information to the newspaper save manpower and time. In fact, many newspapers conduct training programs or issue information sheets to instruct these persons in what news is and how it should be prepared for publication.

But recently, editors have been giving this type of material a closer scrutiny than formerly. The standard for judging any publicity has been whether it is news and whether it serves a social purpose. Some editors have decided that oftentimes it does not amount to much as news. At one extreme we have L. T. Anderson of the Charleston (West Virginia) *Gazette*, who says in an article in *Editor & Publisher* (June 4, 1955):

> As matters now stand, this list of agencies is so large that a survey of most medium size dailies will show that about 30 per cent of the day's "news" output is devoted to them. These "stories" are necessarily dull. They interest no one except the individuals directly concerned. They don't help sell newspapers. They don't evoke public response. They are space consuming and worthless. They shouldn't be printed.

A public relations director for a welfare group has also challenged newspaper practice of printing without question much of the publicity of fund-raising drives. Walter W. Reed of Cumerford, Inc., Kansas City counselors on fund drives, suggests that appeals be reported objectively rather than publicized. Among his recommendations are that "canned" stories be checked with local news sources for facts, that activities of organizations be covered between campaigns, that inquiry be made into the distribution of funds, and that operating expenditures and budgets be scrutinized.

In government, the horde of public information people—most of whom are ex-newspapermen—also perform a helpful service to the press. In fact, it is hardly conceivable that the volume of news about government printed and broadcast today could be maintained without their assistance. Joseph Loftus of the New York *Times* says the reason is simply that government has become so large that newspapers, radio, and press services cannot cover it adequately by themselves.

Among the principal values of public information people is that they facilitate the gathering of news. Some governmental departments and bureaus are so large and perform so many services that nobody except a person on the inside knows what is going on. Thus activities, reports, and records that might never come to the attention of reporters are made known to the public through press releases. Public information officials who know exactly where to go to get information desired by a reporter can save him time and effort. They are also of assistance in arranging for interviews and conferences with heads of departments and bureaus, and can be questioned when people in the higher echelons are busy or unavailable. On occasion, they are helpful in setting up special facilities and newsrooms where the reporter can write his story and telephone or wire it to his office.

Most reporters prefer to write their stories from original reports and documents, but handouts of public information officials have their use. When the reporter is pressed for time or has a particularly complicated document to digest, the main points given in a news release help him write his story.

But perhaps the greatest value of public information officials is educating their chiefs in the importance of good public and press relations. Unfamiliar with what constitutes news and how it is gathered and published, department and bureau heads may adopt the attitude that their business is not the public's business. Information officials can help train bureaucrats to become less bureaucratic.

But if public information officials are an aid to the news-gatherer, they may also be a hindrance. They are a hindrance when their concern is primarily that of protecting their employer, instead of informing the public. In some departments and bureaus employees below the top level are instructed to refuse to give out material unless it is cleared through the information office. Some information officers conceive their role as a buffer between the press and their employer, and the reporter may be forced to conduct his interviews with top officials through an intermediary. "That kind of practice," says Loftus, "is channeling news, and channeled news comes close to being censored news." And he adds: "Multiply a condition like that in all government agencies and we won't need reporters. We'll need only messenger boys."

The reporter, however, probably has as much to fear from good public information officials as from bad ones. If he is kept well supplied with printable handouts, he may be tempted, especially if lazy, to rely upon them too much—to become merely a mechanical conveyor between newsroom and governmental agency.

The change in concept from publicity to public relations is best seen in business. Formerly, a business firm, when it employed a journalist to do publicity, did so because it wanted him to get advertising —disguised as news—into newspapers. This accounts for the low repute in which many editors today hold publicity and public relations. Getting the firm's name or product into news stories is still a goal of business publicists—many of the printed and mimeographed handouts that swamp the city desk are directed to this end but today, most publicists consider this only part of their job. What they are chiefly interested in is the good will of the public.

Few business leaders today would adopt the attitude of W. H. Vanderbilt, who told reporters seeking information: "The public be damned." Enlightened business leaders are more inclined to the viewpoint expressed in a brochure issued by General Mills, Inc., for the guidance of employees in dealing with the press:

> Honest, accurate publicity is good publicity and of great value to General Mills.
> It gives the reading and thinking public a true picture of a great modern industrial enterprise which is extremely valuable economically and socially.
> It fortifies the confidence built up among consumers by the quality of our products.
> It lends power to our advertising.
>
> *   *   *
>
> We have nothing to hide. The public is entitled to know everything about General Mills, with few exceptions. [A footnote

lists these items as details of confidential research, interim production and sales figures, detailed expense breakdowns, or costs
of new construction projects.] After all, our products help to feed
50 million people a day. We buy millions of dollars worth of
crops from the farmers each year. And in addition to our own
employees, we help make jobs for thousands of other men and
women in related industries.

Yes, the public has a big stake in General Mills. And the people
deserve to know the facts about us.

The "let 'em like or leave it" attitude never won friends for
any organization.

Hence, the reporter, when he must go to a large business firm or
manufacturing plant for news, finds a public relations man ready to
provide him with information or to guide him to the executive who
will answer his questions. The reporter very likely will get good
cooperation, even when the news is adverse. A Koppers Company,
Inc., publication, for instance, advises employees about press relations: "Bad news inevitably becomes known to the press. It is best
that it become known from company sources. In that way it escapes
secondhand exaggeration."

There remains one more problem of public relations and publicity for the reporter to consider, although it is also a problem that
may arise in his dealings with other news sources: it is the attempt,
too often successful, to buy his good will. It may range from the
practice of letting a news source pick up the check for a luncheon,
through the acceptance of gifts, to outright payments of money, but
in the words of Norman E. Isaacs of the Louisville (Kentucky)
Times, "It's bribery!"

Reporters are so often recipients of free meals, free drinks, gifts,
and gratuities that they may come to expect them. An instance is
cited by Robert U. Brown in his "Shop Talk at Thirty" department
in *Editor & Publisher* (November 20, 1954). Reporters were invited
to attend the first session of the National Committee for Repeal of
Wartime Excise Taxes. After the purposes of the organization were
explained, cocktails were served, but reporters were told that luncheon was strictly for members of the committee. One reporter was
quoted as saying: "They must be positive that these taxes will be re-
pealed—there could be no other reason for pushing the press around
that way." And another: "I thought the next thing that was going to
happen was that they were going to give us a handful of nickels and
tell us to go to the automat." Brown's comment on the incident was:

It has become part of the public relations technique to wine and dine reporters whenever there is a story to put over. We have never thought that the amount or quality of the food and drink had anything to do with how the reporter wrote his story. . . . We are hopeful that this specimen is rare among the denizens of the city room. For surely, it is just as bad for the public relations crowd to educate reporters to think a free meal will accompany such handouts as it is for reporters to believe they are being "pushed around" when they aren't entertained.

But as Isaacs asserted in a speech at the University of Minnesota, the problem of the bought press is more serious than the acceptance of free meals, small gifts, such as a bottle of Scotch at Christmas, or junkets sponsored by government or industry. He lists three major fields where the news columns are for sale: sports, entertainment, and women's news. Sports writers are frequently on the payroll of athletic promoters and race tracks; columnists and reporters who write about cafe society, the movies, and travel get their pay-off in free entertainment, gifts, and trips; and the damsels in the women's department receive their loot in the form of gifts from advertising agencies and manufacturers. "I think this whole sorry situation is one of the great shames of American journalism, circa the 1950's," Isaacs declared.

The Impulse to Secrecy

A good working definition of news might be this: If people want to get something into the paper, that's publicity; if they want to keep something out, that's news. If the reporter had to deal only with publicity, his job would be easy; but his best stories are likely to be those that for a variety of reasons the persons involved do not want printed.

Sometimes news sources are uncooperative because of the newspaper's editorial policy. The labor reporter may have difficulty getting news because of editorial-page attacks on unions. The police reporter may be shut out because of a newspaper campaign urging the ouster of the chief for incompetency and corruption.

In such situations there is no sure formula for getting news. The reporter's best asset is his reputation for fairness and honesty. If he has proved trustworthy in the past, news sources may be willing to continue providing him with information. The reader of Lincoln Steffens' autobiography, for example, is impressed time after time by the fact that he was able to get along with political bosses and ward heelers, although they knew the next issue of the muckraking magazine for which he worked might describe them as crooks and thieves. Steffens' reputation for integrity gave him entree with all sorts of public figures, from presidents down to precinct captains.

But there are other reasons why it may be difficult to get information from governmental and other sources, and they do not all have to do with the desire to cover up incompetency or graft. It has been described by J. R. Wiggins of the Washington (D.C.) *Post and Times-Herald* as "the impulse to secrecy." It reached such a stage after World War II that the principal journalistic professional organizations began campaigns "for the people's right to know" and "for freedom of information."

In part, the impulse to secrecy is a hangover from the censorship and controlled news of the war; in part, it results from the tensions of the cold war with Russia and the continuing need for protecting military secrets; in part, it springs from the massive growth of government that tends to separate officials from the people they represent. It is a situation that will take a long time to remedy. "Public officials at every level are asserting the right to withhold information with greater frequency," Wiggins wrote, "and private citizens have been more quietly acquiescing in the invasion of their right to know."

In the fight for freedom of information, the individual reporter has a role. He can zealously stand up for his right to get news, since this can be equated with the right of the people to know. The reporter is better able to do this if he is familiar with his legal rights and privileges. What these rights and privileges are occupies a broad field of law, difficult to summarize, but the reporter can familiarize himself with the general principles. In addition, the newspaper itself can demand access to public records on the basis of special pecuniary interest, since its sale could be harmed by the shutting off of information gathered from them.

Governmental proceedings and records open to the public, and therefore to the press, are set forth in statutes, court decisions, administrative regulations, and opinions of attorney generals.

Judicial proceedings are generally open to the public because of the constitutional requirement of public trials, and the press has a qualified privilege to publish fair and true accounts of trials. The right to attend trials and report them, however, is not absolute. There may be some restrictions in trials involving minors and in certain types of cases, such as divorce and sex offenses. Judicial proceedings other than trials—arraignments, preliminary hearings, and deposition hearings—are also open. Grand jury sessions, while of a judicial character, are not open, nor are trial jury deliberations. Court records are public records in the sense that they may be examined by the public and the press.

Legislative proceedings constitute another area of governmental activity generally held to be public. The reporter may attend and report sessions of Congress, state legislatures, and municipal councils. Rules, however, may provide for exclusion of the public and press during executive sessions held when confidential communications are received from the Chief Executive. Much of the work of legislatures is carried on through committee hearings and investigations, and these can be open to the public or closed at the whim of the chairman and members.

It is in the executive department of government that the rights and privileges of the press to obtain information are most in doubt. The principal problem here is access to public records and to proceedings of the numerous boards and commissions established to carry out specific functions. As for public records, the reporter must keep in mind that not all documents kept by the government are public in the sense that they are open to inspection. Generally speaking, the documents available to the public are those an official is required by law to keep.

In the federal government, access to records is controlled by a law that actually is an invitation for officials to suppress information rather than to publish it. The statute states that heads of executive departments are authorized to publish such information as they "may deem important to the public interest" or "so much" as they "may deem important and material." This statute has been a particular target in the struggle by journalistic groups for the right of the people to know.

Under the theory that a public record is any record that officials are required by law to keep, most records of state, county, and municipal governments are open to inspection. When officials deny a reporter access to them, he should point out the law and request that they cite legal authority for their refusal. If this tactic is unsuccessful, he should take up the matter with his city editor and managing editor. A threat to go to court may be all that is needed to open the books, and if it is not, the newspaper can file a mandamus action to force officials to make public records accessible.

Because premature publication of crime investigations and indictments might interfere with law enforcement and the apprehension of criminals, some records kept by police and sheriffs, as well as the findings of grand juries, cannot be published without permission. Generally, however, the police blotter, a record of persons arrested and committed to jail, is held to be a public record.

Access to public records, however, is not the complete answer to getting news of government. So much important and interesting news is made by boards and commissions that the major fight for freedom of information is directed toward opening their sessions to the press. The reporter, therefore, should seek entry to all official sessions of university regents, school boards, highway commissions, welfare commissions, utility commissions, and the scores of other such state and local governmental agencies.

Government news, unfortunately, is not the only news on which secrecy is imposed. Getting information from private individuals and organizations may at times prove extremely difficult—particularly when its publication would result in unfavorable publicity. The difficulty is compounded, since there is no legal recourse, as with the right of access to public records.

As with some other reporting problems, the newsman's reputation for fairness, integrity, and accuracy is oftentimes such that a reluctant news source is willing to talk. Where the public interest is involved, an appeal regarding the people's right to know may prove successful in getting news from a reluctant source. Another effective appeal is that the person, or group, should get his side of a story before the public. When the reporter has a few facts to go on, but not the complete story, he may be able to persuade the source to give him information by pointing out that, since the story is going to be printed in any case, it would be to the source's interest to have it correct rather than incomplete, and perhaps inaccurate.

Most of these devices were used by reporters to end a news blackout in 1956 during contract negotiations between the United Steelworkers of America and industry leaders. Regular briefings on each day's sessions were arranged after reporters signed and submitted to the negotiators the following petition:

> We the members of the press corps assigned to keep the public informed on the progress of these negotiations wish to protest the news blackout imposed by joint agreement of both parties. The contract talks are bound to have profound effect upon the

lives of 160,000,000 Americans. They are not a private matter of sole concern to the negotiating parties. The public, which has no direct representation within the conference room, is entitled to a regular and reliable flow of information about the progress being made by union and industry representatives.

It is not our desire to have to depend upon indirect "keyhole" gossip or to indulge in flights of speculative fancy, based on lack of factual reports. We do not feel that the interests of the industry, the union, or the country would be well served by such procedure.

Regular briefing sessions for the press are a feature of all international conferences. Certainly nothing less should be available here.

When a candid approach fails to get access to information, the reporter may have to use other methods. His first resort probably will be reliance upon friendly contacts made in the past. In any matter involving several persons, someone almost invariably can be found to leak information if his name is not used. And there are other methods over which, to use the journalistic cliché, perhaps a veil of secrecy should be drawn.

Off the Record

If there is an ethical rule of news gathering that has universal acceptance, it is that the reporter must not violate a confidence. The rule has two applications: one is when the information may be printed, but not attributed to the source; the other is when the information is not to be printed at all.

The attitudes of newsmen vary on the acceptance of off-the-record information. At one extreme is the belief that the reporter should accept nothing in confidence—that it is his job to publish information, not to conceal it. Norman E. Isaacs expressed this attitude in an article in *The Bulletin of the American Society of Newspaper Editors* (January 1, 1949) by describing instructions he gave his staff regarding news sources volunteering information with the understanding it was not to be printed: "When they say, 'This is off the record,' you just say you're sorry but you don't want to hear it, and walk out. You can always find out what it is they're trying to freeze up on. It's your job to go out and crack that story." On the other hand, Arthur Krock of the New York *Times* has defended off-the-record information on the ground that "it is in confidence that much important news is acquired which otherwise would be withheld from the public that has a right to know it."

The occasions are frequent when a reporter is given information only if he agrees not to divulge the source. Many exposé stories, such as those dealing with criminal activity and graft in government, could not be written unless tipsters were assured that their identity would not be revealed. Public officials also are often cooperative in giving information if their names are withheld.

One of the principal dangers of publishing news, but concealing the source, is that it may be denied. Walter Lippmann, in one of his columns, describes the situation:

> It is the rule of the game that an official cannot be held publicly responsible for remarks made off the record. He is entitled to repudiate his remarks even if he made them, even, indeed, if he agreed off the record that they could be used without attribution to him. A correspondent who attends an off-the-record press conference knows that in return for what he gets, he must pay a price—he must take the risk of having his story denied. This is the rule of the game which, like most human arrangements, has its advantages and disadvantages.

James Reston of the New York *Times*, in a discussion of background conferences at which reporters in Washington receive information they can print but cannot attribute, lists other dangers. One is that the "unimpeachable source," the "high administration official," the "usually well-informed source"—some of the expressions used to avoid naming names and at the same time to indicate reliability—may give not the official policy, but his own interpretation of what it is or ought to be. Another danger is that the backgrounding conference may be a way of avoiding responsibility for public information that could be, and ought to be, put out officially and publicly through the open press conference. A third is that reporters may be used, not as a vehicle for passing accurate information to the American people, but as an instrument of governmental diplomacy and propaganda. To these may be added the danger that off-the-record statements of policy are perhaps merely trial balloons and that the policy may be denied if the public reaction is unfavorable.

The reporter may be tempted to accept information in confidence as background for handling a story when it is ready to be announced publicly. It is dangerous for him to do so. Some other reporter may run across it and, not bound by a promise of secrecy, may break the story. Or the reporter may get the details from some other source but, committed to silence, be unable to publish the story unless he can get permission from his original source.

Public officials, aware of the way the press respects confidences, often use the off-the-record device as a way to tie the hands of reporters. Some talk freely to newsmen about policies and programs, and then at the end of the press conference or interview say, "Of course, my remarks were off the record." Or in a speech they may say that some of their remarks are off the record and not for publication, apparently willing to let people hear what they have to say, but unwilling to let them see it in print. The reporter should not permit himself to be victimized by these dodges. Nothing should be off the record unless he agrees to it in advance.

Rights of News Sources

Almost any dubious ethical practice in gathering news can be defended under the theory that whatever the reporter does is done in the public interest. But the argument does not hold up well under scrutiny: people who appear in the news and those in positions to give out information have rights which the reporter should respect.

Good ethical practice requires that, in most instances, the reporter get his news openly, not under cover. It is hard to conceive of deceit, even in the public interest, as a commendable way of getting news. In approaching someone for information, then, the reporter should introduce himself and give his newspaper connection. This may have the effect of shutting off information, but it is only fair to let people know that what they say may appear in print.

Similarly, information obtained by chance, when the people concerned do not know a reporter is present, should not be used in a news story unless permission is obtained. For example, the United Press killed a quotation attributed to President Dwight D. Eisenhower in a column, "Backstairs at the White House," by Merriman Smith. The quotation referred to Eisenhower's announcement that he was willing to seek re-election, a decision strongly urged by Republicans. He was quoted as saying: "I had to say yes because they told me they didn't have time to build up another candidate." Lyle C. Wilson, U. P. Washington bureau chief, said in explanation:

> On inquiry, I learned that the remark had been overheard as the President and several persons passed down a White House corridor.
>
> It was not possible to determine to whom the President was talking, nor what he had said just before and just after the quoted

remark. Whether that remark was facetious or serious was unknown. It was possible that Mr. Eisenhower was repeating something some other person had said. The remark was wholly out
of context.

   I killed it because we lacked the additional facts which would
have placed the remark in proper perspective.

It will be noted that nowhere in the explanation is the propriety
of printing an overheard remark questioned. The omission is probably due to the fact that public officials are, from the journalistic
viewpoint, in a different category from other people. They are always fair game for the press. As George Sokolsky has argued, it is
not necessary for the press to be gentle or even fair toward public
officials.

If the practice of entrapment, or getting information by any
means, fair or unfair, is ever justified, it is when the reporter has
evidence to show, or good reason to believe, that officials are sup-
pressing information of legitimate public concern. Many people do
not accept the principle that bad means should be used to achieve
a good end, but the reporter may sometimes be compelled to do so.

Even when the news source knows he is talking for publication,
there are occasions when the reporter may ask himself if he should
use a quotation he knows is likely to make a good headline. In
speaking off the cuff, a person may toss out a sensational remark
without realizing he is doing so, and is often astounded by the re-
percussions when the remark has been played up in the nation's press.
Granted that the quotation makes good reading, is it worth it?

In one sense, it is not, because it harms the press. The victim's
usual comeback is: "I was misquoted." Newspapers, because they
try to be fair and objective, print the denial. Which will the public
believe? Many people will believe the author of the quotation, and
the reputation of the press for accuracy suffers.

In another sense, such headline quotations may be undesirable
because they distract from more important matters. For instance, in
1956, Secretary of Defense Charles E. Wilson described as "a phony"
a Democratic move to increase funds for the Air Force over recommendations of the Republican administration. Incensed Democratic
senators took up several days of congressional time berating the
Secretary of Defense and calling for his removal or resignation.
Wilson was compelled to take time from important duties to explain
the remark. He did not deny the quotation, but said his description

was intended to characterize a reporter's question in a news conference, and not the stand of the Democratic senators. Accounts of the squabble made good reading for several days, but in the end nothing was gained.

It would seem to be a good rule, before rushing a striking quotation into print, for the reporter to make sure his news source means what he says or seems to say. Often the question, "May I quote you on that?" is all that is needed to make sure that the person realizes the significance of his remark. Sometimes the reporter may want to pursue the matter with further questions to make sure the remark accurately conveys the speaker's meaning and is not an off-the-cuff statement, publication of which will embarrass him and cause needless controversy.

Invasion of Privacy

In an article in the *Harvard Law Review* in 1890, Louis D. Brandeis and Samuel D. Warren proposed that legal safeguards be set up to protect the individual's right of privacy. They defined it as the right to be free from unwarranted publicity and unwarranted revelation to the public of matters with which the public is not concerned. Appearing in an era of sensational journalism, the article said:

> Of the desirability—indeed of the necessity—of some such protection, there can, it is believed, be no doubt. The press is overstepping in every direction the obvious bounds of propriety and decency. Gossip is no longer the resource of the idle and of the vicious, but has become a trade, which is pursued with industry as well as effrontery. To satisfy a prurient taste, the details of sexual relations are spread broadcast in the columns of the daily papers. To occupy the indolent, column upon column is filled with idle gossip, which can only be procured by intrusion upon the domestic circle.

Often cited in discussions of journalistic ethics, the article furnishes the basis for one of the rules in the Canons of Journalism adopted by the American Society of Newspaper Editors in 1923. The A.S.N.E. code states: "A newspaper should not invade private rights or feelings without sure warrant of public right as distinguished from public curiosity."

The right of privacy receives no legal sanction except in respect to unauthorized use of a person's name or picture in advertising and trade. As to news, Harold L. Cross, counsel for the A.S.N.E., sums up the legal status in the following two points in the Society's *Bulletin* (July 1, 1954):

(1) The right yields to matters of public interest and to matters of a private nature in which the public has a legitimate interest. Accordingly, there is in general no violation of the right in use of name, picture, or photograph in current spot news.

(2) In general, use of name or likeness is not a violation where it appears for purposes of illustration in educational, informative, or entertaining features such as travel stories, surveys of social conditions, historical narratives, reproductions of past news items, and the like.

In news gathering, the occasions when the reporter should ask himself if he is unwarrantedly invading the right of privacy are in interviewing and writing about the relatives or friends of persons figuring in spot news. Should he, for example, write a human-interest story about the wife of a man arrested for murder? Or should he describe the demonstrations of grief of a mother whose child has been killed in an accident?

In considering invasion of privacy, newsmen make a distinction between ordinary citizens and persons in public life. Those who live by publicity—actors, singers, entertainers, athletes, and politicians—may expect their private affairs to be public affairs. Political figures, in particular, cannot expect to be let alone. The prevailing press attitude toward them has been summed up by George Sokolsky: "The people have a right to know everything about their employees. If a man wants to live a secretive life, he must shun public office."

The Danger of Libel

Under the heading, "Correction on Heroin Raid," the New York *Herald Tribune* printed the following:

> Police and the district attorney's office in the Bronx said yesterday that they had made public an erroneous address in announcing last week a narcotics raid of a Bronx apartment where several young men were arrested as heroin addicts. In giving details of the raid they said several of those arrested were caught in a vacant apartment in a three-story frame dwelling at 734 E. 165th Street. This was the wrong address. Assistant District Attorney David S.

Blatt and Detective David H. Snipe, of the 11th Division, said that the raid took place at 728 E. 165th Street.

This correction, or "beg your pardon" as it is often called, illustrates the chief pitfall encountered by reporters in handling material likely to be libelous—inaccuracy.

Libel is one of the principal bugaboos of journalistic work, but it is neither so hard to understand nor so dangerous that it should be unduly frightening. It consists of anything, except for certain well-recognized types of material, printed or spoken in a broadcast over radio or television that would give a person a bad name or harm his reputation. A standard legal definition is this from the Oklahoma statutes:

> Libel is a false or malicious unprivileged publication by writing, printing, picture, or effigy or other fixed representation to the eye which exposes any person to public hatred, contempt, ridicule or obloquy or which tends to deprive him of public confidence, or to injure him in his occupation, or any malicious publication as aforesaid, designed to blacken or vilify the memory of one who is dead, and tending to scandalize his surviving relatives or friends.

The principal elements of libel are four: (1) a publication must be defamatory; (2) it must be false; (3) it must be malicious; and (4) it must be unprivileged. Spoken defamation has traditionally been defined as slander, a less serious offense than written defamation, which is permanent in form and susceptible to wider distribution. Court rulings, however, have considered spoken defamation by radio and television as libel rather than slander because of the large number of people who may hear it.

The news every day includes stories that are obviously damaging to reputations: reports of arrests, attacks made by politicians on their opponents, adverse criticisms of books and plays, exposures of the misbehavior of public officials. They are published because they do not meet the conditions that would permit the person who has been harmed to sue for damages in a court of law.

If the reporter is reasonably sure of his facts, that is, if he feels he could prove the truth of his statements in a law court, he need not hesitate about including them in a story. As the *Herald Tribune* correction indicates, a principal danger of committing libel lies in making errors in facts that are difficult to check—addresses, names, and identifications. This is the main reason for the journalistic insistence on meticulous accuracy.

The fact that a reporter did not intend to commit a libel—that he made an error inadvertently—does not protect a newspaper from a suit. An accidental error is presumed to be malicious under the legal definition of malice. In one sense, the word carries the popular meaning—any action motivated by ill will, evil intent, hatred, or deliberate intent to injure. But in law, the word also means negligence or disregard for the rights of others.

The protection afforded by privilege in libel suits is rather complicated. It includes publication, in the public interest, of fair and true reports of certain proceedings and actions: (1) by a public officer in the proper discharge of an official duty; (2) legislative and judicial proceedings, or any other proceedings authorized by law; and (3) the contents of public records, such as police blotters, court dockets, and other records that public officers are required by law to keep.

In the public interest, newspapers and other communication media also have the right to comment adversely on and to criticize public officials, candidates for public office, writers, musicians, actors, athletes, and others who, in effect, invite public attention. This is the right of fair comment and criticism. Such comment or criticism must be made with a good motive, must not be actuated by malice, and must be based on fact. Attacks on moral or personal character must have a bearing on the individual's qualifications to hold office or do his work.

Another protection in libel is the right of reply and consent. Frequently a victim of an attack by someone consents to publication of defamatory statements about him so that he may defend himself subsequently by issuing a denial or giving his side of the story. Such consent, given either directly or inferentially, is a complete defense in a libel suit.

In guarding against libel, the reporter must keep in mind that his newspaper is responsible for any defamation it prints. Attributing harmful information to another source is no protection unless the source is privileged. Thus, a libel uttered by a political candidate in a campaign speech would not be privileged, nor would a libel reprinted from another newspaper. Such attributions and qualifications as "alleged," "it was charged," "police said," and "it was reported" offer little protection. Their chief value would be as evidence of lack of malice in a trial for libel.

ASSIGNMENTS

1. Clip from a newspaper stories and articles that you consider publicity. Do you think they were worth printing from the viewpoint of reader interest and social benefit?

2. Most stories based on information from a public relations or press relations source do not specifically indicate the origin. Find examples of stories which do attribute information to the public relations man or department. Why do you think this was done? Would you recommend that this be done in all stories? Why?

3. Prepare from the compiled statutes of your state an abstract of all laws relating to public records and those making governmental proceedings open to the public.

4. Conduct an informal poll of ten citizens to find their attitudes toward the following questions:

   a. Should newspapers be allowed to print the names of persons arrested for traffic violations?

   b. Should newspapers be allowed to criticize individual members of the city council?

   c. Should newspapers be allowed to print accounts of divorce trials?

   d. Should newspapers be allowed to name persons and firms found violating fire and sanitary regulations?

   e. Should the school board be allowed to bar reporters from its sessions when the newspapers have been critical of the board's conduct?

   f. Should newspapers be allowed to print the contents of a will filed for probate?

   g. Do newspapers print too many stories finding fault with public officials?

   h. Are newspapers fair in their reporting of political campaigns?

   i. Are public officials the victims of bad publicity in newspapers?

   j. Are radio and television fairer and more accurate in their news than newspapers?

Pooling your findings, do you find support from the public for "the people's right to know" or for "freedom of information"?

5. Clip news stories which clearly are damaging to the reputations of the persons named in them. What defenses could the newspaper employ if sued over the stories?

PART II

The Art of News Writing

CHAPTER 5

FUNCTIONAL NEWS WRITING

Evolution of a Formula

IN THE VERNACULAR of journalism, reports of events are called stories. Actually, however, they are seldom written as stories. Conventional narratives begin with minor details—the presentation of a character or situation, a description to indicate setting or tone; events are told in such a way as to build to a climax. This procedure is reversed in the straight news story: the most important or most interesting information appears in the first paragraph, details, in dwindling order of importance or interest in later paragraphs.

Raoul de Roussy de Sales, a French journalist, in contrasting French and American news writing, wrote that the French reporter leads his reader dramatically to the climax in such a way that when he gets there his "pulse will be up around 120," while the American reporter knocks his reader out "cold" in the first sentence. "The French reporter *tells* a story," De Sales said; "the American *covers* it."

The American method of news writing evolved in the decades after the Civil War. One influence, no doubt, was the practice of press association correspondents, in telegraphing news, to give important details in brief dispatches comparable to the bulletins of today. These were printed in the order of receipt. For example, the New York *Times* in its issue of April 15, 1865, printed the following Associated Press reports of the assassination of President Lincoln:

Washington, Friday, April 14—12:30 A. M.
The President was shot in a theatre tonight, and is, perhaps, mortally wounded.

Secretary Seward was also assassinated.

SECOND DISPATCH

Washington, Friday, April 14
President Lincoln and his wife, with other friends, this evening
visited Ford's Theatre for the purpose of witnessing the performance of the "American Cousin."
It was announced in the papers that Gen. Grant would also be
present, but he took the late train of cars for New-Jersey.
The theatre was densely crowded. . . .

The second dispatch continued for almost two columns, giving
details about the shooting and the reactions of the people in the
audience and throughout the capital. If it had been printed as a
continuation of the first, without the label and the new dateline,
the Associated Press report would be almost a model news story
according to today's standards.

Another factor in the evolution of the news story form probably
was competition and the growth in size of newspapers. Since type
was set by hand and publishing processes were slow, it was often
necessary to give the gist of a story in the first sentences, because
time did not permit printing the full account. Thus, by the 1870's,
such an editor as Samuel Bowles of the Springfield *Republican* was
instructing young reporters: "Put it all in the first sentence." Bowles
had also learned that readers did not care to read a column of
material to get at the news, and he would advise: "Don't suppose
that anyone will read through six lines of bad rhetoric to get a
crumb of news at the end."

This practice had hardened into a formula when E. L. Shuman
published the first textbook in journalism in 1894, titled *Practical
Journalism*. He wrote that "the style followed almost universally in
large American newspaper offices at present" was to give the "mar-
row of the whole story" in the first paragraph. In an enlargement of
his text in 1903 he introduced the formula of the Five W's—Who?
What? When? Where? Why?—which had to be answered in what
we now know as the lead of a news story.

Thus, the general theory of the way to write a news report has
had an almost three-quarters of a century acceptance. It applies not
only in the processes of gathering, writing, and publishing the news,
but also in the habits of the newspaper reader. Nevertheless, its
utility should be carefully questioned by today's news writer.

Benefits to the Reader

For the reader, the formula is advocated on the grounds that it is the natural way to divulge information, immediately satisfying his curiosity about the nature and significance of an event, and that it enables him to select quickly from the scores of items printed those that are of interest or concern to him. The formula, as Frank Luther Mott says in *The News in America,*

> may seem a tortuous and unnatural structure, but the reasons for it are clear. Most newspaper readers want it that way. They want to be able to glance at a headline; and if it seems to indicate subject matter of interest, to skim the cream off the story by reading a summary; and if interest still holds, to read most or all of the story. The time is long gone when anyone can be expected to read the paper thoroughly from end to end; in this era of impatient readers and forty-page papers, skimming is not only common but the almost universal rule. The structure of the modern news story is suited to the skimmer.[1]

Convenience to the reader may be a rationalization for preserving the formula today, but it is certainly a logical reason in view of the fact that surveys show Americans spend only about thirty or forty minutes a day in reading the newspaper. The formula, of course, discourages reading to the end of a story; possibly the reader, had he not developed the habit of hit-and-skip reading, would spend more time with the newspaper if the stories were written in such a way as to sustain his interest. Weekly news magazines, with a generally narrative treatment of events and with information that newspapers ignore about personalities and locales, apparently satisfy a demand that newspapers fail to meet.

Mott comments that "having indulged the reader in his skimming habit (and helped teach it to him), the newspaper is now faced with the necessity of making its stories shorter and shorter." He says that "the contemporary pursuit of brevity, with its inevitable consequence of fragmentation," harms the newspaper's function of providing full access to the day's news, and adds that "if the newspaper asks its reader to await the issue of the weekly magazine for adequate treatment of affairs, it is selling its birthright for a mess of bulletins."

[1] Frank Luther Mott, *The News in America*. Cambridge, Mass.: Harvard University Press, 1952, p. 159.

Benefits to the Newspaper

For newspapers, the formula is justified on the ground that it is necessary in order to meet certain production conditions. One of these conditions is described in a special number of *Nieman Reports* (April, 1950) devoted to problems of writing the news. The formula, says an article on "The Shape of the Story,"

> enables editors to throw a newspaper together faster. If an edition is going to press—and one usually is—the editors cannot wait for all stories to be complete. Often they can get only the first part of a story in type, maybe only the first paragraph to use as a bulletin. So they demand that in writing important news the main facts be placed near the top. Besides, they are constantly forced to cut stories to fit certain holes or to make way for other stories. The easiest and quickest method is to lop from the end upward. So they demand that in writing important news *no* main facts be placed near the bottom.

A similar condition exists in wire transmission of news by press services. Stories sent by leased wire are received by newspapers in typewritten form on a teletypewriter. Because the agencies serve a great number of newspapers going to press at different times, and it is therefore necessary to get as many different stories as possible into editorial offices within a short space of time, the major stories are sent piecemeal by takes instead of by complete articles.

These conditions—the need for speed in transmitting the wire news stories and in getting matter into type to make editions—plus the need for shortening stories from edition to edition to fit type into the forms constitute a plausible defense of the formula. But it must also be pointed out that they apply to relatively few newspapers. Only big-city newspapers issue numerous editions during the day; smaller-city newspapers issue only one. And the conditions apply also to only a small proportion of the news stories written—those about events that occur near the deadline.

As for wire transmission of stories to newspapers with varying deadlines, the argument for the hind-end-foremost news formula has only theoretical validity. It was disposed of in 1951 when the press services began teletypesetter transmission of news on their state wire circuits. Although still providing typewritten copy, the new method also punches a tape which can be fed into a typesetting machine for automatic setting of type. Serving primarily smaller newspapers with only one daily edition, the new method permitted a change in the system of moving stories on the wire. Early stories sent are those not likely to need revision because of new developments; reports of changing situations are held back until later in the day, when they too can be sent in one piece. Thus there are few new leads for stories and little need for revision every hour or so to catch an edition, since the smaller newspapers publish only one edition a day. The wonder is that this sensible arrangement had to wait for the perfection of the teletypesetter before it was adopted.

Criticisms of the Formula

In the past several years the top-heavy structure of the news story (it is usually called an inverted pyramid) has been frequently attacked. For instance, Carl E. Lindstrom, managing editor of the Hartford *Times*, wrote in an article in *Editorially Speaking,* a publication of the Gannett group of newspapers:

> Just about everything that is wrong with news writing today can be traced to the pyramid lead. In itself it is bad enough with its primitive, out-of-breath, hit-'em-in-the-eye approach. But to its crudity can be traced many other sins: incoherence, inaccuracy, loss of the unities of time and place, poverty of expression and, finally, the story's death through sheer exhaustion and general debility. Most newspaper stories come to an end like a guttering candle finally blown out.
>
> I don't particularly like the term pyramid lead because, even though it is standing on its apex, the word pyramid carries the connotation of solidity which the device does not have.
>
> Consider instead, please, the term jackpot lead. Let me explain: Your reporter hurries back from the scene of an accident, the fire, the carnival or the caucus and on his way mentally churns up his facts in the business of finding a beginning. Usually he has it by the time he reaches his typewriter, but sometimes, especially if the deadline isn't breathing on his neck, he will sit and ponder, chew a pencil end or chain smoke. He may make a try or two, ripping out the copy paper and giving it a crumpling toss in the general direction of the waste basket.
>
> Suddenly he has it! The lead—it's done!
>
> The rest is easy. The typewriter pours out a cascade of clattering, clanking facts in a fearful disorder which continues until the last feeble fraction of a datum has been accounted for.
>
> What is this marvelous device? You have pulled some sort of trigger; you have tripped an escapement; you have hit the jack-

pot and the payoff is at your feet in a glut of disorder, a plethora
of confusion followed by a vacuum.
This is the jackpot lead.

As a form of writing, the faults of the inverted-pyramid structure
are fairly obvious. It often results in distortion and inaccuracy because of the reporter's desire to bowl his reader over in his first
sentence; it is frequently hard for the reader to get the facts in
sequence, since the emphasis is on the result rather than what led
to the result—and newspaper practice of piling new lead upon new
lead as an event develops merely compounds this difficulty; the
reader is confused by the news account which twists events out of
their natural time sequence or hopscotches from topic to topic
because of the writer's attempt to conform to the theory of diminishing importance. And, since it is designed to make it unnecessary
for a person to read a story through, it makes it unlikely that he
will do so.

These inherent faults have been exaggerated by rules laid down
from time to time as additions to the general formula. One of the
most pernicious was that the first paragraph of the story must answer the five W's, to which was later added the How? This was done
so that the reader might obtain all the information he desired from
the first paragraph alone. The result was a sentence monstrosity—
too long for the reader to grasp all the facts presented and too
involved for him to figure out the relationship of the parts.

Another dictum, called the rule of block paragraphing, was that
each paragraph must stand as an independent unit, deletable from
the story without affecting the sense. The block paragraph, of course,
eliminated the transitions formerly used to create continuity.

The rules reached the point of absurdity when, in conformance
with the belief that the most important or interesting fact must be
played up, that is, put first in the lead, it was decreed a story could
not begin with the articles "a," "an," and "the." The effect of this
last rule can be encountered frequently, even in the body of news
stories where the articles are dropped for no apparent reason, as:
"Principal reason for the action was that . . . ."

Fortunately, in the past several years, editors have become increasingly concerned with the problem of improving news writing. Readability studies, such as those of Rudolf Flesch and Robert Gunning,
showed that news stories were harder to read than popular magazine
articles and books. The sentences were too long, too many big words
were used, and the appeal of human interest was lost because of

failure to report events in terms of people—the makers of most news. As a result, many of the straitjacket rules that formerly bound the reporter have been relaxed.

Another factor in the crumbling away of the inverted-pyramid structure has been the recognition that the-lead-that-tells-all is no longer necessary: radio and television are now first with the news of importance. Hence, better ways of telling the news are needed. As Lindstrom said in his attack on the inverted pyramid:

> Why should there be a limit on the time the reader spends over the newspaper, a limit on its pulling power?
>
> That pulling power is in our hands. You will never increase it if you assume that the reader has so little time for newspapers that you must pack all the information into the first paragraph.
>
> That's what radio and television are doing. They are the bulletin media; they will never be anything else. But they are beating us to the punch as bulletin media. Once upon a time we could win with that technique; we were Johnny-on-the-spot, first with the news. We flung the news at the man in the street in flashes and headlines.
>
> You can't stop him on the street any more. He is sitting at home in a comfortable chair and he's got all the time in the world to read our story—provided we know how to tell it.

In the frequent discussion of the inverted pyramid, the one fact which seems to have been entirely ignored is this: the headline for a news story gives a summary; it lets the reader know what the story is about and it furnishes enough information for him to decide whether the report would be of interest. Why, then, should the lead repeat this information? And why, then, should details be presented in disorder in the body of the story? To some extent, the convenience of shortening the story from the end upward answers these questions.

But is this a valid answer? It is not, in the experience of the Philadelphia *Evening Bulletin* and other newspapers. For a number of years the *Bulletin* has disregarded the inverted-pyramid formula by printing stories written in chronological sequence. For example:

Numbers Writer

Trapped at Hospital

Patrolmen Jack Kelly and William Reice went to the Philadelphia Hospital for Contagious Diseases, 2d and Luzerne, in work clothes yesterday and posed as new employes at work on the grounds.

They were there at the invitation of hospital authorities, who complained that someone was taking numbers bets at the institution.

Shortly after noon, Obie Lumpkin, 36, Fitzwater near 12th, a hospital laborer for the last year and a half, went to the phone in the guardhouse at the gate. The policemen followed.

Kelly told Magistrate Donnelly today they found Lumpkin phoning numbers bets. The disguised policemen tapped him on the shoulder and said they wanted to place bets. He took their quarters and phoned in their selections. When he hung up, they arrested him as he was noting down their numbers.

Lumpkin had six slips listing 690 bets, the policemen said. He had $5.40 in change. Asked where the rest of the bet money was, he said it was owed him.

Lumpkin was held in $500 bail for court.

In explanation of this treatment of the news, Walter Lister, managing editor, says:

There is nothing formal about our frequent avoidance of inverted-pyramid leads. We do preach effective writing, sometimes successfully, sometimes not.

In general, we leave it to each writer how he should begin a story. The only thing approaching a formula is that we flatly instruct our people not to write a lead on a short. About five years ago, when I first came to the *Bulletin* as city editor, I discovered that because we had told our reporters to keep their leads short we were getting a lot of three-paragraph stories which would begin something like this:

"A 75-year-old woman was injured today in a freak accident on Broad Street."

This keeps the lead short, but it is also sheer waste. It is more effective to let the headline say:

Freak Accident Injures

Woman, 75, on Broad St.

and then let the story be immediately specific, as:

"Mrs. Carrie Jacobs, 75, broke her left arm today when she tripped over an adding machine on Broad Street at Lehigh."

Regarding the practice of shortening stories to fill the holes in make-up, Lister says: "We don't mark stories told chronologically for special handling in make-up because we just don't let make-up editors bite anything. On long stories a make-up editor will sometimes ask the news editor if he can get a trim of so many lines, but otherwise each story is expected to go in the paper the way it was written."

It is unlikely that the inverted-pyramid convention, so completely ingrained in newspaper journalism by long acceptance and practice, will be abandoned immediately, or even ultimately. In fact, as has been pointed out, it solves several problems of high-speed daily journalism and assists the reader both in surveying the day's multitudinous events and in finding stories that particularly appeal to him.

But it should not be used as a strait jacket to constrict the writer—it should be loose enough for him to move around in. Nor should it be conceived of as the only way to tell a story—even spot news reports. When the facts of an event, no matter how arranged, are not of impelling importance in themselves, the reporter may tell the story in the most effective way he knows to create sustained reader interest.

ASSIGNMENTS

1. Take one issue of a daily newspaper and study the stories from the standpoint of structure, omitting columns and non-news material and departmental news, such as sports and society. How many stories conform to the inverted-pyramid structure? How many do not?

2. Paste one story on a sheet of copy paper. Analyze it to see if it conforms to the formula in giving details in dwindling order of importance.

3. Paste one of the non-formula stories on a sheet of copy paper. Explain why you think the reporter avoided the inverted-pyramid structure.

4. Rewrite the story from the Philadelphia *Evening Bulletin* in this chapter to make it conform to the formula.

5. Interview ten persons not engaged in journalism and obtain the following information.

> a. Explain to them that newspapers have adopted a method of writing news stories to make it easier for them to get at the gist of the news quickly. Ask them if they know what the method is.
> b. Explain the inverted-pyramid formula to them and get their opinion of it.

c. Find out how much time they spend each day reading newspapers and tuning in to radio and television newscasts.

d. Find out which medium most nearly satisfies their desire for news, and why.

e. If they read a news magazine, such as *Time* or *Newsweek*, find out what they especially like about the magazine. Ask such questions as: Are the articles more interestingly written than newspaper articles? Does the magazine report the news more fully than the newspaper? Are the magazine articles easier to understand than newspaper articles?

Write an article summarizing your findings and interpret them in the light of the chapter discussion of the news writing formula.

CHAPTER 6

THE NEWS STORY LEAD

Analysis of a Story

THE NEWSPAPER'S AIM of presenting news so that the reader has little trouble in quickly informing himself about current affairs is achieved by the headline and the inverted-pyramid formula for telling the story. The headline, in big type, gives the main facts in a few words. It is almost always a complete statement with a subject and a predicate: *Mayor Backs Charter Revision;* it is not a mere label or title: *Mayor's Attitude on Charter Revision.* In the inverted-pyramid formula the main facts are given in somewhat more deail in the lead.

Since in current practice the headline is not considered an integrated part of the news story, it is clear that the opening, or lead,[1] is the most important part of the story. It is sometimes a single sentence, although in describing a complex event the reporter may require several sentences or paragraphs. It is essentially a summary, with amplifying details given in the body of the story. Ordinarily, the opening answers the Five W's and H: Who? What? When? Where? Why? and How? But they should not be crammed into an opening omnibus sentence, since such a sentence is too big a bite for the reader to swallow.

The following story illustrates these fundamental principles of formula news writing:

---

[1] The custom is to refer to the first paragraph of a news story as the lead, although it may not perform all the functions expected of a lead. Actually, the term has a loose meaning. For example, in revising a story to bring it up to date with new developments, all new material preceding the old, even if it runs to several pages, is called a new lead.

Suspect Is Slain
Resisting Police

Victim Felled After Firing
3 Shots at Officer

A narcotics squadman fatally wounded a suspect during a chase yesterday afternoon after the man three times had attempted to shoot him.

Police identified the victim as Lester Smith, 28, of 300 E. Park Street. He was pronounced dead at 1:25 p. m. after being wounded by Patrolman James Arthur.

Chief Thomas Peters said Arthur and Patrolman Homer Williams saw Smith riding a bicycle in the vicinity of E. Park and N. Fifteenth Street and called to him to stop so they could question him. The officers had arrested him on other occasions.

Instead of obeying the officers' orders, Smith jumped from his bicycle and started to run.

Arthur alighted from the police car, fired one shot in the air, and ordered the man to halt. He said he called out: "Stop, Lester, or I'll have to shoot."

Peters said that Smith produced a .32 caliber revolver and pointing the weapon at Arthur, who was about 25 feet away, pulled the trigger three times. The gun, however, failed to fire.

Arthur said he fired one shot in Smith's direction and the bullet struck him in the side. Smith ran about a quarter of a block and collapsed.

Robert Adams, special investigator for the coroner's office, said an

Headline gives only bare facts of event.

The first paragraph of the lead gives the *what* and *when;* the *who* is given only in a general way; the *where,* other than that the event obviously took place locally, is not specified; the *how* is indicated briefly.

If the *who* had been explicitly set forth in the first paragraph, the paragraph would have been too long. Hence a second paragraph of the lead is needed to complete the *who.*

The specific *where* of the event is not given until the third paragraph, which may be considered as starting the body of the story.

In accordance with the news story formula, amplifying details of the event summarized in the two-paragraph lead are presented in dwindling order of importance. After the first two paragraphs, the story could be cut at any paragraph without great loss to the reader unless he really *wanted* to learn all the details.

The student will note that the story does not answer one essential question: *Why?* Why did Smith fire at the officer? Why did the officer apparently shoot to kill? Since Smith is dead, why he fired can only be surmised. Ap-

autopsy would be conducted to-morrow.

Peters said Smith had a long arrest record and had served time in the state penitentiary. He said a full investigation of the shooting was being made.

parently the officer's fatal shot was not intentional, but this is not made clear in the story.

Playing Up the Feature

In order to answer the important questions which will immediately satisfy the reader's curiosity, the lead ordinarily must play up, or feature, the one that is most important, most interesting, or most unusual. In the sense used here, "play up" and "feature" mean to emphasize by position, that is, whatever is played up or featured must come at the very beginning of the sentence.

This means that most stories start with the *who* or the *what,* since they are the essential ingredients of any news. The *when* and the *where,* except for events scheduled in the future, are seldom of first importance; the student may have to look through several issues of a well-edited newspaper before finding a lead beginning with either. In fact, they are often indicated only generally, as "yesterday," "last night," "here," or "in the southeast part of the city." Any lead written in the past tense, however, *must* contain an indication of the *when* by such designations as "yesterday," "last night," or "this morning." If more precise designations of the *when* and the *where* are required, they most often come after the first paragraph.

How and *why* openings are also infrequently encountered. When used, they are likely to be unusual, and therefore serve the purpose of quickly capturing the interest of the reader. The student checking for examples of *how* and *why* beginnings will find that they frequently are placed first in the sentence in a subordinate clause or a phrase.

The choice of the featured element depends primarily upon the nature of the event the reporter is describing. Many events that he covers—accidents, robberies, burglaries, and fires—have only routine interest; mere factual reporting of these according to the formula will suffice. But if there is anything exceptional about an event, it belongs in the lead—perhaps at the start—even though it is not the most important factor in the event.

When a prominent person is involved, his name is newsworthy in itself and normally should be used to start the story:

> John L. Simmons, president of the Chamber of Commerce, was grabbed by two men, dragged into an alley, and robbed of $75 this morning in the 100 block of E. First Street.

If the victim were not well known, another type of beginning could be used:

> Two men grabbed Jerome T. Smith, 48, 200 N. Elm Avenue, as he was walking along the 100 block of E. First Street this morning, dragged him into an alley, and robbed him of $75.

Or the reporter might omit the name in the interest of brevity and write:

> Two robbers grabbed a man as he was walking along the 100 block of E. First Street this morning, dragged him into an alley, and took his billfold containing $75.

Here, the identity of the victim would be given in the second paragraph. The deferred naming of the person is better for a metropolitan newspaper than for a small-city newspaper, since in the small community the victim would be known to a relatively larger number of people. The axiom that names make news is more often true in the small city than in the large one.

While the circumstances of this robbery are not especially unusual, they are sufficiently so that the reporter would be justified in writing a *how* lead:

> Grabbed and dragged into an alley as he was walking along the 100 block of E. First Street, Jerome T. Smith, 48, of 200 N. Elm Avenue, was robbed of $75 by two men this morning.

Under appropriate circumstances, the robbery might be of such a nature as to warrant beginning the story with the *where*:

> The alley in the 100 block of E. First Street was the scene of a second robbery in two days when two men grabbed a man walking by this morning, dragged him into the alley, and took $75.

Or a time element might be emphasized:

> Ten minutes after securing a loan of $100 this morning, Jerome T. Smith, 48, of 200 N. Elm Avenue, was penniless—the victim of two robbers who dragged him into an alley in the 100 block of E. First Street and took his billfold.

Other Lead Requirements

In addition to giving the gist of an event and answering the questions asked in the Five W's and H formula, the opening of the news story must provide sufficient identification of persons, organizations, places, objects, and even the event itself for the reader to orient himself immediately. The most fundamental rule of identification is that, usually, first mention of persons in a news story must designate the full name and give some sort of appositive explanation as to who or what he is—address, title, position, or occupation.

Note the identifications in the following leads:

Person

> Dr. Peter A. Taylor, professor of history at Middletown University, will speak on "Turning Points in American History" in a lecture at 8 p. m. Friday in Town Hall.

Organization

> The Interstate Gas Transmission Co., one of the nation's major pipeline operators, opened its case for increased wholesale rates today before the Federal Power Commission.

Place

> The Rampart Hotel, built in 1830 and long considered one of the city's most important historical sites, will be torn down to make way for a 20-story office building.

Event

> An enrollment of 10,500 students, the largest in the university's history and 500 above that of last year, was reported yesterday by Registrar Thomas A. Arbor.

Another frequent requirement of the lead is that it must give the source of information, if it is not obvious from the context. Reporters often are not witnesses of events they cover, and consequently must get their material from by-standers or participants. Since the newspaper, obviously, cannot vouch for the authenticity of material obtained at secondhand, it gives the source to enable the reader to evaluate the information. This is known as attribution.

In the lead below, for example, the charge made by the speaker is unproved. It would be an unwarranted assumption for the newspaper to print it as a statement of fact without the qualification of indicating who made the charge. And since the source is necessary if the reader is to evaluate the material, the reporter quite properly emphasized it by putting it first in his story.

> Charles L. Adams, candidate for police commissioner, declared last night that he had evidence of 58 instances in the past year of brutal third-degrees conducted by police in attempting to force confessions from suspects.

Simplifying the Lead

As has been pointed out, one of the dangers inherent in the Five W's formula is that the reporter may crowd too much information into his beginning sentence, as in the following lead:

> Literally buried in his automobile in a collision in which a 10-ton truck forced the car against an embankment, then overturned and dumped a load of crushed stone on it, Peter Moran, 67, of 200 E. First Street, was trapped for half an hour yesterday in Temple township until police and state highway workers dug him out.

Containing fifty-eight words, the lead is typical of those published in newspapers until just a few years ago. It would, however, be unacceptable in most newspapers today, for one of the outstanding recent developments in news writing has been the emphasis on short opening sentences or leads.

The trend can be illustrated in a word-count of leads in the New York *Times* of front-page stories printed in 1945 and 1955. In the 1945 issue, the paper had twelve stories on the first page, and the leads ranged in length from 25 words to 56 words—an average of 43.2 words. Ten years later, the leads of thirteen stories on the first page ranged from 14 words to 37 words—an average of 24.9 words.

In many newspapers, and in press association dispatches, the length of the leads is frequently less than that of the *Times*. For instance, a recent front page of the Chicago *Daily News* contained nine stories. The leads ranged in length from 10 to 23 words—an average of 18.6 words.

Typical of the short leads demanded by newspapers today are these from the Chicago *Daily News*:

> A silent, well-dressed robber casually walked out of the Michigan Avenue National Bank of Chicago, 30 N. Michigan, with $1,550 in loot shortly before noon Friday. *(27 words)*

> Partly concealed by a tombstone, top mobster Tony Accardo watched from a distance Friday at graveside prayer services for his old ally in crime, Louis "Little New York" Campagna. *(30 words)*
>
> City Treasurer Morris B. Sachs lopped two employes from his payroll Friday, saying their jobs were "superfluous." *(17 words)*
>
> Police investigating the fatal stabbing here of a Catholic priest from India had apparently conflicting clues Friday. *(17 words)*

Instead of answering all the Five W's in a catch-all opening sentence, the practice today is to scatter them through the first several paragraphs. Devices for doing this include the following:

(1) Deferring names and identifications of the people involved in an event.

(2) Deferring specific details about the time and place.

(3) Deferring the statement of the source of information.

(4) Deferring or omitting minor details.

As has been pointed out, the name of a prominent person is newsworthy in itself and belongs in the lead, but in a case where the person is less well known and the news interest lies in the event itself, not in who is involved, it is frequently better to omit the name in the lead, as in the following:

> A father who admitted teaching his two teen-age sons how to be "real burglars" was named in two true bills Monday by the grand jury.
>
> He is Taylor L. Adams, 41, 200 N. First Street. His sons are James, 14, and Harold, 16.

A fault of a general rather than a specific *who* designation in the lead is that monotony is likely to result if too many stories begin with such wordings as "a Northside man," "a school teacher," or "a city real estate man" "was injured," "was robbed," or underwent some other mishap. Worse, the abbreviated lead has resulted in an aberration that might be called the "age lead": A 30-year-old housewife was robbed; a 41-year-old man was arrested; a 35-year-old woman was injured, etc.

Except for advance stories of scheduled events, the time and place can be frequently delayed in the news story. For example, in the following story this information appears in the third paragraph:

> The Red Cross got better than 100 per cent backing from people in the Middletown area during its fund drive, some 500 volunteer workers were told yesterday.

Charles P. Taylor, chairman, said the campaign brought in $325,000—or 103.6 per cent of the goal.
Tayor addressed the workers at the Middletown chapter's annual meeting at the Rampart Hotel.

Similarly, the attribution or indication of the source can be deferred. Instead of letting it dangle at the end of the first sentence, it is better to use it to start the second paragraph. If the attribution is absolutely necessary because of doubt as to the reliability of the information, it should be used to start the story.

Below is an example of the unemphatic dangling attribution followed by a strengthened version in which the attribution starts the second paragraph:

John T. Taylor, twice an all-American back at Middletown University, has been chosen coach for the high school football team, Dr. Clayton D. Donald, principal, announced yesterday.

*   *   *

John T. Taylor, twice an all-American back at Middletown University, was named yesterday as coach for the high school football team.
Dr. Clayton D. Donald, principal, said he was chosen over four other well-known football players considered for the job.

Which details can be considered as trivial or minor, and therefore omitted from the lead, is often a matter of judgment. As has been indicated, the time, the place, and the source are frequently delayed in the story. Often the surplus of details is due to wordy statements about the obvious, as in the following:

Twelve persons, destitute and without transportation back to New Jersey as the result of a traffic ticket given when the driver was found without a driver's license, were transported back to New Jersey Wednesday by the Rev. Thomas A. Rogers, 200 E. Fifteenth Street, an officer of the American Rescue Workers, and his son, Joseph.

This can be simplified to:

Twelve persons stranded here when the driver of the car in which they were traveling was arrested for not having a driver's license were provided with transportation to their home in Brunswick, N. J., Wednesday by a minister and his son.

In trying to be brief, the reporter may run the danger of producing meaningless leads. The purpose of the lead, in theory, is to give the gist of an event, and this purpose is not achieved when the lead is so short that the reader has no idea what the story is about. Rudolf Flesch, engaged as readability adviser for the Associated Press, labeled these "empty leads" and cited the following examples:

> BELGRADE, Yugoslavia (AP)—Mrs. Emma Dobeljak, a native of the United States, went on trial today.
> CINCINNATI (AP)—Ohio river men still had their fingers crossed today.
> WASHINGTON (AP)—Politics had a different look in Congress today.

"These are not leads but sounds of someone clearing his throat," Flesch commented.

Accent on the Interesting

In the discussion of the inverted-pyramid structure, it was pointed out that the news story form seems designed to discourage the reader from finishing the story. But an important function of the lead is to serve as a baited hook to capture the reader's interest and to get him to swallow the whole story, or most of it. This function has resulted in an addition to the Five W's of the lead that some newsmen call the sixth W, or "wham," element.

Interest may be engaged by the facts that the reporter emphasizes in the lead, or by the way he phrases his material. Even within the formula, it is possible to turn out lively and readable copy, as in the two examples below:

> University of Pittsburgh researchers are going to help Uncle Sam find out how well you perform when the heat's on.
> The Pitt Graduate School of Public Health has been awarded a $39,875 contract by the Army Quartermaster Corps to study "physiological effects and heat uptake in clothed men exposed to infrared radiant heat sources."—Pittsburgh *Press.*

> * * *

> One-arm drivers may not have to use any arms at all (for driving) in a few years.
> In fact, they wouldn't even have to watch the road at all if devices now available were put into use on cars, an electronics engineer said here Wednesday.
> "A car that drives itself wouldn't be at all hard to make," said Conrad H. Hoeppner, chairman of the National Telemetering Conference, in the Morrison Hotel.—Chicago *Daily News.*

There are many opportunities in news writing to bypass the formula, as in the feature story, and in the suspended interest story where the climax or point is held back until the last paragraph, but the writing style of the adept and imaginative reporter can create the same effects within the standard conventions.

ASSIGNMENTS

1. (a) Clip newspaper stories with leads that illustrate the featuring of each of the Five W's and H. Label them and state whether you think the reporter chose the right element to feature.

(b) Rewrite each of the leads to play up another suitable feature.

2. (a) Write a lead that plays up the most interesting element in the following information:

> R. N. Black, a dairyman in Potter Township, went to his barn at 5:45 a. m. today to milk his cows. When he entered, he found six of them dead in their stalls. "They were just lying there—six of them," Black told the reporter. "Three of them were all right. I got an electric shock as I walked around in the barn. I thought that's what killed them." However, Peter A. Clinton, inspector for the Midstate Electric Corp., tested the pipes and lines in the barn and couldn't find anything wrong. Dr. Arthur L. Dane, a veterinarian, was called. He said laboratory tests would have to be made to find out the cause of death. He took specimens from the cows' hearts, spleens, kidneys, and livers and also of their food to test for poisoning. Black said his cows were worth $400 each.

(b) Write two other leads that you think would be suitable for a story based on the above information.

3. Clip from a newspaper examples of crowded leads and write simplified and shorter versions of them.

4. Obtain examples of a newspaper story of a local event and of a press association report of the same event. Analyze them to note differences in the writing, and account for the differences.

5. (a) Clip five newspaper stories with leads that you think are especially interesting—"bait" that would attract readers.

(b) Clip five stories with uninteresting and stereotyped leads. Rewrite them in a lively and readable way to make them appeal to readers.

CHAPTER 7

ORGANIZING THE STORY

Single-Incident Stories

EVENTS WHICH CONSIST of a single incident offer the writer few difficulties in deciding on his lead and in presenting amplifying details in the body of the story to conform with the principle of diminishing importance or interest.

The news writing formula is suitable for most simple happenings. Readers get the main facts quickly and, if interested, can continue their perusal of a story either to the end or to the point where their desire for information is satisfied. Ordinarily, too, the conventional order of giving details does not do violence to unity or coherence.

Suppose, for instance, the city council appoints a new city manager. What should go into the lead of the story about the appointment is hardly debatable—it is the name of the man and who he is. The lead might be written:

> John A. LaFonda, a veteran of 20 years' experience in municipal administration, was named city manager last night at a salary of $15,000.

Most readers would probably want next to know more about the new city employee and his qualifications for the job. The second paragraph, therefore, should give a brief account of the highlights of his experience. Subsequent paragraphs would give additional biographical details bearing on his fitness to manage the city's affairs. After these main points are given, reporters might differ about what details to present. Some might continue with more biographical information; others might prefer to give such information as the date the new city manager will begin work, or statements by council members about the appointment.

Unless there are unusual circumstances, most automobile accidents can be reported as simple incidents. Because human casualties are the most noteworthy factor in most accidents, information concerning those injured or killed belongs in the lead. Next in the normal order of a presentation which will satisfy the reader's desire for information is an account of how the accident occurred. The less important facts, which taper off the story in accordance with the formula, probably are biographical details to amplify the identification given in the lead or second paragraph.

Though the formula is used in writing most news stories, it is not as easily followed as a recipe for baking a cake. The cake baker is told exactly how much flour, sugar, milk, and other ingredients to use, and exactly in what order to mix them. The news writer must use his own judgment about the ingredients to include in his story and the order in which to put them.

Multiple-Incident Stories

Choosing the most important or most interesting information for a lead and organizing details in the body of a story become a somewhat complex problem in reporting events with a number of diverse elements.

The problem arises in such stories as reports of proceedings by city councils, school boards, and legislatures, which may transact a half dozen or more items of business; or in such stories as reports of storms, fires, and disasters, which may involve loss of life, property damage, rescue work, and other factors. It also arises in a type of story known as a roundup, in which several happenings of the same sort, such as minor automobile accidents or burglaries, are combined in one story.

If one element of a multi-angled or multi-incident event is of overwhelming importance, it may be written as a separate story and the minor elements written as sidebars printed with their own headlines under a spread head of several columns placed over the main story. A variation of this is to write up the minor elements as dash matter, to be printed as separate items under small headlines trailing the main story.

If each element is of sufficient importance to require a long story to relate it fully, several separate stories may be written, the main story appearing perhaps on page one and the others on an inside page. In this case, the main story will likely have an editor's note directing attention to the related news on another page.

But most events with diverse elements or multiple incidents can be handled in a single story. Suppose, for instance, a city council met and did the following:

(1) Amended an ordinance to increase the fine for jaywalking.

(2) Amended the traffic code to prohibit parking of vehicles on one side of a downtown street.

(3) Approved installation of sanitary sewers in an outlying part of the city.

(4) Appointed a new city engineer.

Within the inverted-pyramid formula, or minor variations from it, this report could be handled in several ways:

(1) A summary or comprehensive lead could be written, with the details of each separate action reported in the body of the story in the order of importance.

(2) One of the actions considered the most newsworthy could be described in the first paragraph and the other actions summarized in the second paragraph; the body of the story would give details of each action according to the outline in the two paragraph lead.

(3) The action considered the most newsworthy could be described in the first paragraph, with all amplifying details following immediately. Then would come the paragraph summary of other actions, with amplifying details of each following in order. In effect, this story would have two leads—a main lead forming the first paragraph of the story and a secondary lead coming in the body of the story.

(4) The action considered the most newsworthy could be described in the first paragraph, with amplifying details following immediately; then would come the action considered second in importance, with details; then the action considered third in importance, with details, and so forth.

The Summary Lead

The summary lead may take several forms. It may enumerate the separate actions in clothesline fashion:

> The city council last night amended an ordinance to increase the fine for jaywalking, restricted parking to one side of Grand

Avenue in the downtown area, named a new city manager, and voted to install sanitary sewers in Highland Addition.

If this lead is used, details of each action are presented in the body of the story in the order of listing in the lead. The opening paragraph serves as an outline of the story, making it easier for the reader to get a complete picture of what went on at the council session, and to follow the details in a coherent and orderly manner.

A drawback of the clothesline lead is that it may throw too many ideas at the reader at once. It can be made easier to comprehend by by breaking it up into two paragraphs:

The city council last night increased the fine for jaywalking and amended the traffic code to restrict parking to one side of Grand Avenue in the downtown business area.

In other action, the council named James J. Becker, former city engineer at Parkerville, city engineer to succeed Arthur Blake, who resigned last week, and voted to install sanitary sewers in Highland Addition.

Another variation in the summary lead to help the reader assimilate the news quickly is a short general statement in the first paragraph giving the gist of the story, followed by the more detailed statement of action impossible in the clothesline lead. If this plan is used, the lead may run to several paragraphs:

The city council in a three-hour long session last night took action to relieve the traffic situation in the downtown business district and filled the vacant position of city engineer.

In taking up the traffic problem, the council debated several proposals and finally ended up by amending the traffic code to restrict parking to one side of Grand Avenue between First and Tenth Streets. It also amended the jaywalking ordinance to increase the fine for violations from $5 to $10.

James J. Becker, former city engineer at Parkerville, was appointed city engineer to replace Arthur Blake, who resigned last week.

The council also voted to install sanitary sewers in Highland Addition at a cost of $100,000.

This type of beginning presents all the information that most readers would want to learn about the council meeting. Persons with a greater interest in municipal affairs would go on to read the details in the remaining part of the story.

A frequently-used device to emphasize the main factors in an event is a 1-2-3-4 listing following a comprehensive lead:

The city council in a three-hour long session last night took action to relieve the traffic situation in the downtown business district and filled the vacant position of city engineer. It:

1. Restricted parking to one side of Grand Avenue between First and Tenth Streets.

2. Increased the fine for jaywalking from $5 to $10.

3. Appointed James J. Becker, former city engineer at Parkerville, to fill the city engineer post left vacant by the resignation of Arthur Blake.

4. Voted to install sanitary sewers in Highland Addition.

In presenting details about each of the factors that make up the news report, the reporter should follow the outline in his introductory paragraph or paragraphs. He should not, in other words, skip back and forth from topic to topic in an attempt to follow too slavishly the formula of giving details in the order of declining importance or interest. If he does, his story will be an incoherent mish-mash.

Main-Feature Leads

When one angle of an event with diverse elements or multiple incidents is of greater newsworthiness than the others, the reporter should play up that feature in his lead. Thus, for the city council story he might decide that the ban on parking was the most important, since it would affect more readers personally than any of the other council actions:

The city council took action last night to relieve traffic congestion in the downtown business district by banning parking on one side of Grand Avenue between First and Tenth Streets.

This could be followed by a second paragraph of the lead enumerating other action:

The council also moved to discourage jaywalking by increasing the fine for the offense from $5 to $10. In other action, the council appointed a new city engineer, James J. Becker of Parkerville, and voted to install sanitary sewers in Highland Addition.

The body of the story would start with details of the topic featured in the lead—the ban on parking—and continue with details of the other topics in the order of listing in the second paragraph.

A variation in treatment would be to follow the first paragraph announcing the ban on parking with a paragraph giving more details about the traffic situation, and then to give the summary of other action in the third paragraph. The organization of material in the body of the story would be the same as that described for the preceding treatment.

Another possibility would be to follow the first paragraph with several paragraphs narrating in full the council's consideration of the traffic situation, then to give the summary of other action taken in a secondary lead in the body of the story. The story would continue with details of topics summarized in the secondary lead in the order of listing there.

Still another variation would be a string-of-beads arrangement, with the separate topics strung along one after another. If this order were used, the lead about the ban on parking would be followed by several paragraphs of details. Then the second most newsworthy action or topic—perhaps the appointment of the new city engineer—could be introduced, with details given in several paragraphs. These would be followed by introduction of the third most newsworthy topic, the increase in the fine for jaywalking, with details given in subsequent paragraphs. The story would end with the information about the Highland Addition sewers.

In accordance with the theory of newspaper writing that most readers want only the main facts about an event, the preferred story organization is one that gives those facts in the first two or three paragraphs. Thus, for most events, a first paragraph that reports the major feature, followed by a second paragraph summary of other features, is better than one in which the summary appears later in the story, or one in which separate topics are strung along one after another. The pattern that the writer chooses, however, should be the one best fitted for the events and subjects he must cover.

The method of organizing material in a roundup story of separate but similar incidents is the same as that for the report of a session held by an organization or governing body.

For example, a summary lead can be written for a roundup of automobile accidents:

> Six persons were killed yesterday in highway accidents in the Middletown area as the death toll over the long Memorial Day weekend continued to rise.

The organization after this lead would give details of each accident in the order of newsworthiness, followed by a recapitulation or summary of the accidents and casualties reported the day before.

Or, a main-feature type of lead can be written if one accident has aspects that makes it stand out from the other accidents of the day:

> Planning to beat the heavy Memorial Day traffic by getting an early start, a Middletown woman drove only to the outskirts of the city yesterday when her car crashed head-on with another car and she was killed instantly.

This lead could be followed with additional details of the accident, then a summary paragraph or secondary lead, and finally an account of other accidents. Or it could be followed by a summary account of other accidents, then the details of the accident reported in the lead, and finally the details of other accidents in order, with the end devoted to the summary account of accidents and casualties previously reported.

The Chronological Report

Whenever the reporter covers an event in which there has been considerable action, he may find that, after a beginning in which the main points are sketched in, the best way to give the details is as a chronological narrative.

Many sports events are reported according to this formula. A football story, for example, usually begins with several paragraphs telling who won and giving the high points of the game. Then follows a play-by-play account, beginning with the kick-off and continuing until the end of the game.

The chronological narrative may be employed in many other stories. Here is one printed in the Chicago *Tribune*:

> An outraged Chicago transit authority bus driver yesterday locked 35 belligerent, defiant and disorderly students from the Montefiore social adjustment school, 653 W. Fourteenth Street, inside the vehicle and drove them to the Maxwell police station, 943 Maxwell Street, for detention.
>
> The incident recalled the arrest 18 months ago of 30 young hoodlums, most of them from the Montefiore school, after they took possession of a Halsted street car and manhandled a 63-year-old conductor.
>
> Yesterday the driver-conductor, R. W. Watzke, 28, 11031 Eberhart Avenue, and several CTA officials wrestled with the hooting, jeering students for 20 minutes before Watzke took the lot to the police station.
>
> The action commenced at 4 p. m. when Watzke's bus, northbound in Halsted Street, stopped at Fourteenth Street. The boys,

ranging in age from 14 through 18, crowded aboard. One kicked
Watzke's change pouch into the aisle.

Watzke jumped from his seat and tried to push through the
milling boys to retrieve it. Jamming against him, they kicked the
pouch to the rear of the vehicle, spilling coins over seats and
floor, and then picked it up and passed it from one to another to
keep it from the lunging driver.

Because of past troubles with Montefiore students, the CTA
had several of its detectives nearby. These men blocked entrance
and exit doors of the bus and tried to help Watzke. The boys,
pulling, shoving and holding the detectives, prevented them from
entering the coach.

Watzke fought his way back to his seat, slammed the doors and
started the bus. He drove one block north to Maxwell Street and
turned west to the station at Morgan Street, taking the bus off its
normal run.

Even in front of the police station the pupils were defiant.
When police demanded surrender of the money pouch, they
replied with Bronx cheers. After trying for 15 minutes to quiet
the boys, policemen surrounded the vehicle and removed them,
one by one, to the bull pen in the station house, where they were
locked up.

At 5:30 p. m. they were being questioned and telephone calls
were being made to parents. Juvenile officers at the station took
charge of the investigation. Montefiore school officials were called
to verify identifications of the young prisoners.

There are several advantages to the chronological narrative. It
often is the easiest method to use in organizing details; once the
reporter reaches the point at which he can start his narrative in time
sequence, the rest of the story practically writes itself. The method
also prevents confusion to the reader; he is never befuddled as to
when something happens, as he would be if there were a skipping
back and forth in time. And last, it keeps the reader interested
because he is carried along by the momentum of the story itself.

Use of Transitions

In the foregoing discussion of the news story form, an attempt
has been made to show that, even within the inverted-pyramid convention, information can be presented logically and coherently.
Fundamentally, it emphasizes the following three aids to the reader:

(1) It is easier for the reader to follow the reporter's account if
he is told where he is going. The lead or introductory part of the
story amounts to a concealed table of contents, or to the prefatory

statement of a speaker who says: "In my discussion of my topic I shall make the following points."

(2) It is easier for the reader to absorb information if related ideas are kept together in the same part of the story.

(3) It is easier for the reader to understand what took place and to place himself upon the scene if events are narrated in the order in which they happened.

But unity in a story cannot be achieved completely by such rough devices. They are merely building blocks; they become a structure only when they are cemented together. In writing, the cement holding the blocks together consists of verbal transitions and connectives.

Unfortunately, certain conditions of newspaper writing have to a great extent resulted in frequent omission of the cement. The practice of shortening stories by leaving out whole paragraphs and inserting new paragraphs to bring them up to date has resulted in a tendency to leave out transitions and connectives.

This omission is one of the main criticisms of newspaper writing made by Theodore Morrison, adviser to Nieman Fellows at Harvard University. In a special number of *Nieman Reports* (April, 1950) devoted to an analysis of news writing, Morrison said:

> A good prose writer can be defined as one who has learned skill enough to get along with a minimum of formal or conspicuous transitional sentences or phrases. But the minimum is indispensable. Good expository writing is a tissue of general and particular, principle and fact, thesis and illustration. A skillful and needed transition is not a mere formality. It distributes emphasis, makes a distinction, sets relative importance in order, puts a rib in the skeleton, or generalizes the particulars and illustrations. In a good deal of newspaper writing, transitional sentences seem to be forbidden. Anyone who has watched a reporter trying to recover the lost art of transition will understand what I mean by the effect of his working conditions on him as a writer, will understand my emphasis on the *habits of mind* apparently bred by the business as the source of much lamentable newspaper expression.

Transitions are especially needed in newspaper writing because of the conventions of the inverted pyramid. When a story is told chronologically, it contains an inherent progression that carries the reader along. But when, as in the news story, the report begins with the end rather than the beginning, interpolated temporal transitions may be required to enable the reader to keep the time sequence straight. Thus, such expressions as "earlier," "later," "two hours before," and "subsequently" may be needed.

In the multiple-incident story, transitions are needed to indicate a shift from one topic to another—signs that definitely state: we are now leaving this topic and taking up a new one. Examples of such transitions follow:

In other action, the council voted . . . .

Turning from the question of taxes, the speaker declared . . . .

In addition to its decision on parking meters, the council . . . .

Transitions and connectives may be needed for the following oc-casions:

(1) To indicate an addition to something that has been said previously: again, also, and, and then, besides, finally, in like manner.

(2) To indicate a comparison: in like manner, in the same way, likewise, similarly.

(3) To indicate a result: accordingly, after all, as a consequence, finally, hence, therefore.

(4) To indicate differences: but, conversely, however, neverthe-less, on the contrary.

(5) To introduce an illustration: for example, for instance, in this way, namely, to illustrate.

(6) To indicate repetition: as has been said, in fact, indeed, in other words, to repeat.

The following story from the New York *Herald Tribune* would have been hard for the reader to follow if the reporter had not beer careful to orient him by means of transitions:

> WASHINGTON, June 28—Just two days before the Selective Service law was to expire, the House and Senate approved today a bill extending the regular draft for four years and the doctors draft for two years. President Eisenhower reportedly is prepared to sign it quickly.
>
> *In another development today,* the House Armed Services Com-mittee approved by a 29-to-1 vote a compromise version of the administration's compulsory military reserve program.
>
> Rep. Carl Vinson, D., Ga., the committee chairman, said he will seek a "show-down" vote Thursday *on this measure.* It has become extremely controversial because of efforts by Rep. Adam Clayton Powell jr., D., N. Y., to attach an amendment that would forbid segregation in the National Guard.
>
> The draft extension bill, as worked out in joint conference, was approved in the House by a 388-to-5 vote after considerable

parliamentary maneuvering and a bitter debate over coupling the doctors draft provisions to those of the regular draft.

The Senate accepted it by an overwhelming voice vote *minutes after the House had acted.*

The regular draft affects men aged 18½ to 25. They must serve two years in one of the armed forces, unless deferred, in which case they are liable to induction until they become 34.

Today's measure differed from the law that expires Thursday in two respects.

The new bill requires a man who joins the National Guard before he is 18½ to serve until he is 28 instead of 34.

The maximum age for doctors, dentists and veterinarians inducted under the doctors draft provisions was lowered from 50 to 45 years.

During the debate, Rep. Joseph W. Martin jr., Mass., Republican House leader, stated repeatedly that President Eisenhower not only was for the bill's passage, but also wanted it known that he felt the regular and doctors draft should be in one bill.

On a key vote by which the measure could have been killed, *however,* 127 Democrats and 91 Republicans favored the President's position, and 88 Democrats and 83 Republicans opposed it.

In the debate, Rep. Walter H. Judd, R., Minn., said the services did not really need to force doctors into the military organizations. He charged military leaders simply would rather have the draft than make the services more attractive to medical men as a career . . .

ASSIGNMENTS

1. Clip newspaper stories that illustrate the methods of organization of material discussed in the chapter and paste them on a sheet of copy paper. At the side explain or diagram the story to make the method of organization clear.

2. Rewrite two of the stories using another method of organization.

3. Clip an inverted-pyramid story that you think could be better told in chronological sequence after the lead, and rewrite the story.

4. (a) Clip two stories that you think make good use of transitions and connectives and paste them on sheets of copy paper. Underline the transitions and connectives.

(b) Clip two stories you think would be improved if more transitions and connectives were used. Supply those you think are needed.

5. From the information below, write news stories to illustrate three of the methods of organization discussed in the chapter.

As a reporter, you attend the monthly meeting of the Board of Education at 7 p. m. in the Board of Education Building. All members are present, and William B. Roberts, president, presides. The minutes are read and approved. Thomas T. Foster, secretary-treasurer, gives a report that $100,882.31 is due for salaries for the month and recommends that warrants be drawn to pay them. A motion that the salary claims be allowed is approved.

Foster presents bills for $23,202.80 for current expenses. A motion that the claims be allowed is approved.

Superintendent Homer A. Bodkins reports that he has received the resignation of Oscar B. Johnston as principal of Emerson Junior High School. He explains that Johnston, principal for the past five years, wants to resign to go into private business. He proposes that Miss Abbie L. Perkins, head of the English department at the school for the past five years, be appointed the new principal. He adds, upon the request of members for details about her background, that she has taught in the school system for ten years. She holds B. A. and M. A. degrees from the state university. He says that as head of the English department she has shown administrative ability and is thoroughly qualified to head the school. The Board votes to accept Johnston's resignation and to approve the appointment of Miss Perkins as principal.

Peter A. Coburn, chairman of the buildings and grounds committee, reports that the city's increasing student population can be taken care of with the construction of a new grade school in Hillcrest Heights and by additions of classrooms at the high school, at Emerson and Webster Junior High Schools and at Longfellow, Irving and Washington grade schools. He says that a bond issue of $800,000 will be needed. The Board approves a motion to ask a bond election for the new construction.

Superintendent Bodkins reports that the Northern Interscholastic Athletic Association has asked permission to hold its annual basketball tournament in Middletown, using the gymnasiums of the high school and junior high schools. He explains that there are 20 schools in the association and that the tournament from April 3 to 9 will bring several hundred visitors to the city. The Board votes permission for use of the school gymnasiums.

After the meeting, you seek more information on Johnston's resignation from Superintendent Bodkins. Bodkins suggests that you call Johnston. From Johnston, you find out that he is resigning because he cannot support his family on his $4,850 salary. "I've been working in a supermarket at nights," Johnston says. "But I find that it interferes with my school work and home life. I think teaching is the most wonderful profession in the world, but I just can't afford to stay in it. My wife has been sick and I have two girls that are ready for college." He reveals that he will take over the management of a filling station. He holds B. S. and M. S. degrees from the state university and began teaching in Middletown High School ten years ago.

CHAPTER 8

OBJECTIVITY AND THE NEWS

Growth of an Ideal

AMONG THE CHARACTERISTICS of the American newspaper as a chronicle is that it *is* a chronicle—that it records facts insofar as they can be obtained. In recording information, the newspaper's standard of practice can be summed up, somewhat inaccurately, in the word "objectivity." The standard requires that the reporter have no bias in his selection of facts, that he omit comment on the facts, and that he keep himself out of his report

Newspapermen prize highly the ideal of objectivity. Herbert Brucker, editor of the Hartford *Courant,* says, for example: "The tradition that the news must be reported objectively is beyond question the most important development in journalism since the Anglo-Saxon press became free from authority." And Alan Barth, editorial writer for the Washington *Post and Times Herald:* "The tradition of objectivity is one of the principal glories of American journalism."

But the goal, if not the practice, of objectivity is much older than its American development. It was set forth in the first issue of the first daily newspaper to be published in London, on March 11, 1702, when the editor promised to cite the names of foreign newspapers from which he reprinted news, adding: "Nor will he take upon himself to give any Comments or Conjectures of his own, but will relate only Matter of Fact; supposing other people to have Sense enough to make Reflections for themselves."

Throughout much of the history of American journalism, however, there was little objectivity in the presentation of news. Most newspapers in the early years after the founding of the Republic were political party organs, and printed news with the principal aim of helping the party. Even after editors had learned, with the success of penny papers in the 1830s, that news itself was a commodity that could be sold and that newspapers could support themselves without party subsidies, the partisan press continued to dominate journalism. Editors editorialized not only in the editorial columns, but also in the news columns.

Gradually, though, the belief that the news function and the editorial function should be kept separate prevailed. Influential in the development of this belief, no doubt, were the practices of the press associations. Though speaking only of his own work for the Associated Press, for which he was Washington agent, Lawrence A. Gobright described the principles that ultimately became accepted in reporting:

> My business is to communicate facts; my instructions do not allow me to make any comment upon the facts which I communicate. My dispatches are sent to papers of all manner of politics, and the editors say they are able to make up their own comments upon the facts sent them. I therefore confine myself to what I consider legitimate news. I do not act as a politician belonging to any school, but try to be truthful and impartial.

The word "objectivity" has been called a somewhat inaccurate description of the standard for news communication. Actually, of course, objectivity, in the sense of a scientist conducting an experiment, is an impossibility. Nor do editors themselves claim such objectivity. One of the most objective and impartial of newspapers, the New York *Times,* for example, carries the slogan: "All the News That's Fit to Print." The slogan clearly implies that personal judgment enters into the evaluation of news.

And this personal judgment is involved in all the processes by which information is obtained, written up, and edited for publication. It begins with the reporter who gathers the facts. He is faced with a multiplicity of them, and he must make a choice, omitting some and arranging those selected for his story in accordance with what he considers their importance and interest. Similarly, editors exhibit a personal judgment when they decide what play to give the stories; their judgment is carried out in determining how much of a story to print, the size of the headline, and the position on the page.

These considerations, however, do not invalidate the theory of objectivity. An attempt is made to present all the news that might conceivably interest readers, to present all sides of a controversy to go to all sources of information and name them in the story, and to use public interest as the basic principle in selecting the material to be printed.

In reporting and writing news, the reporter must be concerned with the following journalistic practices:

(1) Attribution: indicating the sources and identifying them.

(2) Editorializing: avoiding comment on the news and steering clear of evaluating expressions.

Use of Attributions

The editor of the first daily newspaper in London stated that he would relate only matter of fact, "supposing other people to have Sense enough to make Reflections for themselves." But how could he, or anyone, be sure that what he printed was fact? No editor today, despite careful efforts to insure accuracy, can be sure that what he prints is fact. He tacitly admits that the report might be wrong by insisting that the source be given not once only, but often several times, in a story.

Thus, the newspaper leaves it up to readers not only to "make Reflections for themselves," but also to decide for themselves the extent of confidence they place in a report. This does not mean that editors follow completely a policy of *caveat emptor*. They do seek to find the facts and omit information that is, so far as they know, false. But they cannot possibly be sure of all the so-called facts that they print. There are too many of them to verify, even if they could be verified—about 5,000 of them, it has been estimated, in a single issue of a newspaper. And most of them came to the newspaper secondhand, and not from personal observation or experience by reporters. Attribution is, therefore, a necessity.

The principles underlying strict use of attributions are well expressed in the *Associated Press Reference Book:*

> Proper attribution—naming the source—is a basic requirement in AP writing. This is not only a matter of placing responsibility where it belongs; it is a first principle of accuracy and objectivity.
>
> Every statement that is not an acknowledged fact or that we, of our own knowledge, do not *know* to be a fact should be attributed to a qualified and authoritative source.
>
> That does not mean that every sentence in a crime story must begin with "Chief of Police Whozis said x x." There are techniques known to every experienced reporter by which stultifying,

formula phrasing may be avoided and yet leave no doubt in the
reader's mind as to the source of the information.

The reason for this emphasis should be obvious. An examination of any single day's report shows that the bulk of the copy
recites what people *tell* us. What they tell us may or may not be
a fact. Until the statement is proved or disproved beyond question, it is only sound, objective reporting to say where the statement came from.

In any case, the Associated Press must not be put in the position of standing as authority for something which it does not of
its own knowledge know to be a fact. This applies to paragraphs
as well as to whole stories, to sentences as well as to paragraphs, to
individual words and phrases as well as to sentences.

In deciding whether an attribution is needed, the reporter makes
a distinction between a mere recital of facts and statements calling
for an interpretation, opinion, or conclusion about the facts. For
example, in a fire story he may without attribution describe the
scene, tell what firemen did to put out the blaze, and report what
the occupants of the building did—even though he was not a witness
himself. Any reader would realize that the reporter had gathered
his facts from firemen and others involved. But speculation as to
estimated damages and the cause of the fire, if not definitely determined, would be attributed to the owner or officials.

Thus, in a news story such as the following, every statement does
not need to be tied to the source. It is clear that the information
was obtained from police, and the attribution appears only once.

> The 500 block of Elm Avenue was awash with prune juice and
> grapefruit juice this morning after a truck-trailer upset at 2:11
> a. m.
> The driver, George A. Adams, 25, of 238 E. First Street, told
> police that he mistook street light reflections for an oncoming car
> as he drove north on Elm Avenue.
> He swerved his truck and it jumped the curb, snapped a utility
> pole, and upset on the lawn of James B. Matthews, 525 Elm
> Avenue.
> Bottles of fruit juice in the trailer were broken, and their con-
> tents, mixed with shattered glass, spilled into the street.
> Police detoured traffic around the scene until 7:30 a. m., when
> one lane was cleared.
> Adams was treated at Samaritan Hospital for bruises and shock.

On the other hand, when the news story content is mostly opinion, allegation, prediction, or other material of a non-factual character, attributions may be required throughout the story. Statements

made by people in speeches, trials, hearings, reports, articles, affi-davits, court petitions, and similar occasions are examples of stories in which nearly every sentence may be tied to a source.

> WASHINGTON—Public water and sewerage facilities must be increased by 70 per cent in the next ten years to meet the demands of a growing population, according to the Associated General Contractors of America.
>
> In the March issue of its official magazine, the association cited a government survey of such needs.
>
> The survey estimated that an outlay of $25,000,000,000 would be required in the next ten years. The 1954 value of the systems was estimated at $42,000,000,000—$23,000,000,000 for water supply and $19,000,000,000 for sewers.
>
> Of the $25,000,000,000 total needed, the survey recommended slightly more than $10,700,000,000 for water supply requirements and $14,600,000,000 for sewers.

At first glance, the above story might appear to be a very factual one, dealing for the most part with sums of money. But examina-tion shows that it is not factual at all; the apparent facts are merely what someone thinks are facts.

Newspapers ordinarily do not like to publish stories based upon anonymous sources. But frequently informants divulge material to reporters only on the agreement that their names not be used, and often definite information is hard to get. In such instances, the attribution may be something as vague as "a usually well informed source," "a spokesman for the administration," or "a high adminis-trative official." Very often, too, the reporter cannot get statements from persons involved, and must rely to a great extent on guesswork and his background knowledge of a situation to surmise what is actually happening. In such a circumstance, he must carefully qual-ify his story.

Note the attributions and qualifications used in the following story sent out by a press service:

> DETROIT—Tense negotiations between the Ford Motor Co. and the CIO United Auto Workers reportedly centered Friday on how much Ford would pay to supplement unemployment com-pensation of laid-off workers.
>
> Informed sources said supplementation of jobless insurance has been accepted at least in principle by Ford. But there were two different reports on how far Ford offered to go.
>
> Whether General Motors also had accepted the principle officially was a secret.

The Detroit Times said, however, that General Motors had topped in at least two instances Ford's negotiations-opening offer, which the union quickly rejected as failing to meet its demand for a guaranteed annual wage.

The Times said GM offered to increase pension benefits from $1.75 to $2.25 for each year of service, compared with Ford's $2 offer.

At the same time, it said, GM offered to raise the "annual improvement factor" from 4 to 6 cents an hour, where Ford offered 5 cents.

(This "improvement factor" is an annual pay raise designed to compensate for technical improvements and manufacturing efficiencies which displace workers.)

GM also reportedly offered a stock purchase plan in which it would pay half the cost, with workers being allowed to invest 10 per cent of wages in stock.

Ford and UAW negotiators took a recess Friday morning. Both sides said they planned separate caucuses, which often in the past have been a prelude to fast action on contract settlement.

There are only two facts in this story: the negotiations for a contract were going on and the negotiators took a recess Friday morning. Every other statement in the story is either attributed to a source—the Detroit *Times* apparently being considered reliable— or qualified as being a report.

The straight-faced reporting of what someone said, leaving it up to the reader to evaluate, has its serious dangers. As Elmer Davis says in his book, *But We Were Born Free,* such "objectivity often leans over backward so that it makes the news business merely a transmission belt for pretentious phonies." He continues:

> Publish everything that is said on both sides of a controversial issue and let the reader make up his mind. A noble theory; but suppose that men who talk on one side (or on both) are known to be lying to serve their own personal interest; or suppose they don't know what they are talking about. To call attention to these facts, except on the editorial page, would not, according to most newspaper practice, be objective. Yet in the complex news of today how many readers have enough personal knowledge to distinguish fact from fiction, ignorance from knowledge, interest from impartiality?

The problem has seriously disturbed responsible newspapermen, and they have not arrived at any real answers. For the fact is that many statements of public officials, to name a group which has had much to do with creating the problem, cannot be ignored. The newspaper theory is this: the statement may be false, but Senator

So-and-so said it; it must be printed as news. The reader is the victim. He is expected to know enough to evaluate the statement, but of course he does not. As a matter of fact, reporters themselves more often than not do not know. Or, if they are suspicious, they do not have the time to check. Davis frankly admits this in a discussion of the free-wheeling charges of Senator Joseph R. McCarthy:

> Most people may remember that McCarthy said there are 205, or 57, or 81 Communists in the State Department. But this is only one of McCarthy's many self-contradictions; who can keep track of them all? I have a stack of his speeches two feet thick on my office shelf; but when he says something that stirs a vague recollection that he once said something different, I seldom have time to run through his speeches. I can't afford to hire a full-time specialist to keep up with what McCarthy has said; and if I had a McCarthy specialist I should also have to hire a Louis Budenz specialist and a Harold Stassen specialist.

Though there may be no complete answer to this problem, the following steps can be taken: (a) if a person or organization is accused of some wrongdoing, he or it should be given a chance to answer in the same story in which the charge is made; (b) the originator of the charge should be identified sufficiently to indicate his bias or lack of it, or his reliability or unreliability; (c) the reporter should make an independent check of the facts and include this information in his story; (d) the reporter should omit dubious details not necessary to understanding the statement; and (e) the reporter should write the story to avoid sensationalism and bury unfounded allegations in the body where they will not be emphasized.

Editorial Expressions

Louis M. Lyons, curator for the Nieman Foundation at Harvard University, in telling one of his first lessons in objectivity, described an assignment dealing with the quarterly report of the old Boston Elevated transit system. The system for years had had an unbroken record of deficits, but the report Lyons was given to write up showed a profit. No one needed to tell him this was extraordinary, and therefore news. He began his story: "The Boston Elevated had a remarkable record for January, showing a profit . . . .

"The old night editor brought my copy back to my typewriter,"

Lyons wrote. "He knew I was green. In a kindly way, quite uncharacteristic of him, he spelled out the trouble:

" 'Remarkable is not a reporting word,' he said. 'That is an editorial word. We just tell the facts. Tell the story so that the reader will say, "That's remarkable." ' "

One type of editorializing has, through long condemnation, almost disappeared from newspapers except for small-town dailies and weeklies. It consists of puffs and boosts such as the following:

He was an outstanding player on the football team. Instead of the adjective, it is better to give the player's record and let that speak for itself.

One of the most terrible crimes . . . . A description of the crime is all that is needed; the reader can judge for himself how terrible it is.

An interesting program has been arranged. What is interesting to one person may bore another; the adjective is not needed.

All residents are urged to contribute. Urged by whom? It is better to attribute such statements, if used at all, to the news source; the newspaper should not be an exhorter in the news columns.

Reporters are urged to use strong verbs, but these may color the story and result in inaccuracy. Verbs can be as dangerous as adjectives in conveying a personal opinion. For example, many verbs used in reports of speeches—where speakers are pictured as rapping, flaying, or lashing out at something or other—usually do not accurately describe the delivery.

Advice against using hopped-up verbs and adjectives was given by Alan J. Gould, executive editor of the Associated Press, in a memorandum to reporters on writing political stories:

> Politics are rough and will get rougher before November—so we take this opportunity to warn against misuse of verbs and adjectives.
>
> Remember: There never was a verb better than "said"; there never was an adjective that really improved a controversial political story.
>
> We have seen some horrible examples this week, all of which could have been avoided by simple verbs, or elimination of fired-up adjectives.
>
> One story called Senator McCarthy a "fiery senator." Some people dispute that. We've had phrases like "stinging attack," "stinging rebuke," and the verb "noted," which connotes truth.
>
> The prize of them all (not AP) was this lead: "Canton, Ohio—

Senator McCarthy disclosed today the Democratic party was the party of treason x x x."
Which re-emphasizes: There never was a verb better than "said."

Another danger of evaluating words and expressions is what Elmer Davis calls "loaded words." He cites as an example, "named," as when a person has been "named" by a Congressional investigating committee as a Communist. Davis points out that the word means nothing without corroboration and adds: "Yet if that man keeps appearing in the news the tag will stick to him; he has been named."

Another type of this unconscious slanting is cited by David E. Lilienthal, a former chairman of the Atomic Energy Commission, in a letter of protest to the New York *Times*. Lilienthal took issue with the journalistic practice of identifying members of the Commission as Republicans or Democrats or as appointees of a Republican or Democratic President. He pointed out that the Commission was established by Congress as a nonpartisan, and not as a bipartisan, body and declared that it was dangerous for newspapers to thus associate in the public mind "the political affiliations or obligations of its members."

The use of loaded words is a well-established technique of propagandists, and reporters should, in the interest of objectivity, prefer the neutral word to one that might prejudice a reader for or against something. For example, the defeat of a government health insurance program may have been in part due to newspapers' calling it "socialized medicine," a label thought up by propagandists for the American Medical Association, which opposed the program.

ASSIGNMENTS

1. Paste a clipping of a newspaper story on a sheet of copy paper and underline the attributions. Note places where the attributions seem to be unnecessary and state why you think so. Note also unattributed statements that you think need attribution and state why.

2. Clip an editorialized story from a small town newspaper and rewrite to conform to the journalistic standard of objectivity.

3. Find five examples of statements in news stories that in your opinion give a false or biased picture because of the use of loaded words or evaluating expressions.

4. In 1954 and 1955 Fort Monmouth, N. J., was the object of a series of security investigations of workers by the Army and a Senate subcommittee headed by Senator Joseph R. McCarthy. The Army had found no evidence of espionage or Communist activity, but McCarthy, conducting his inquiry at closed sessions, made sensational charges in regard to spies and Communist associations of workers at the Fort. His charges were headlined daily throughout the nation, despite the fact he had been found very unreliable on many previous occasions.

Among newspapers that carried front-page stories of McCarthy's charges about Fort Monmouth was the New York *Times*. Later it made an independent investigation and printed a series of articles showing that McCarthy's charges were false or exaggerated. It commented editorially on the series:

> For the newspapers Fort Monmouth has been a lesson that will not quickly be forgotten, but the reading public should understand that it is difficult, if not impossible, to ignore charges by Senator McCarthy just because they are usually proved exaggerated or false. The remedy lies with the reader. If the Senator should hit upon something genuine there will be corroboration, but until there is the intelligent reader should refuse to accept a McCarthy charge as valid. Perhaps the Fort Monmouth case will prove valuable in the end as a typical example of McCarthyism that could be exposed. (New York *Times,* January 14, 1955.)

In view of McCarthy's known record of exaggeration and distortion, do you think newspapers should have printed at face value his charges about Fort Monmouth? If not, how might newspapers have handled the charges to put readers on guard? Do you agree with the *Times* that the remedy lies with the reader, or do you think it lies with the newspaper? Discuss your answer. Do you think that even "intelligent" readers were in a position to judge the truth or falsity of McCarthy's charges? What do you think of the *Times'* suggestion that readers should wait for corroboration before making up their minds?

5. Write a news story based on the following information:

> District Attorney William A. Harmsworth informs you on your regular visit to his office for news that he plans to petition the district court for a special grand jury investigation of the Board of Education.
> "The Board has mulcted the school district out of thousands of dollars through illegal purchases of equipment and supplies,"

Harmsworth says. "The only way we can get at the bottom of the matter is for a grand jury probe."

In answer to your inquiries, Harmsworth makes the following allegations against the Board:

1. It has evaded a state law requiring that bids must be asked for all purchases over $500. This has been done by purchasing supplies in small quantities instead of by bulk. In some instances warrants of $495 have been drawn to pay for purchases. One example was the payment of $495 to the Wadsworth Lumber Co. for lumber.

2. It spent more than $75,000 last year with the Laine Supply Co. The Laine company is owned by Porter Laine, brother-in-law of the Board's president, Theodore B. Atkins.

3. Individual Board members have received kickbacks from firms which have received big orders for school maintenance supplies and equipment.

"The Board's financial records are in such a mess that nobody can make heads or tails of them," Harmsworth says. "We'll have to get a firm of auditors in there before we know how much of the public's money has been squandered recklessly or gone into the pockets of individuals in the form of graft."

To get the other side of the story, you call on some of the Board members.

To the charge that the Laine Supply Co. is owned by his brother-in-law, Atkins says: "Why, there's nothing wrong about that. The Board was buying from him years before I was elected a member. He's a local business man and we try to throw business to local firms. If we didn't buy from the Laine company, we'd have to go out of town. It's the only firm here handling some things."

Jerome Atherton, Ward Three member, says: "Harmsworth is just playing a political game. There's nothing to his charges. He's just sore and wants to cause trouble because some of us opposed him in his race for district attorney. The Board's affairs have been carried on in a perfectly businesslike manner. We're not afraid of any sort of investigation."

Mrs. Hazel Durbin, Ward Four member, says: "I'm utterly shocked that the district attorney would come out with something like that. Why, his wife has been a good friend of mine. I never heard or saw anything out of the way. The only thing we're interested in is giving the children the best education possible."

Alex A. Wadsworth of the Wadsworth Lumber Co. says there was nothing out of the way in billing lumber bought from him. "The bill for what the Board wanted came to $495, and I charged that amount like I would anybody else. It's all on the records. Anybody can see my books."

You report the result of your inquiries to Harmsworth and ask him if he has anything else to say. He replies:

"From what I have been able to learn there have been a lot of shady things going on in the school Board. We'd been hearing a lot of rumors before I decided to investigate. The only way to clear things up is to have a full-fledged probe. If the Board is in the clear, the grand jury investigation will show it."

He adds: "The only thing I'm interested in is good government. We can't afford to have any graft or maladministration in public affairs. There's nothing personal in what I'm doing in asking for the grand jury investigation."

CHAPTER 9

IDENTIFICATION OF PEOPLE

Names in the News

THE NEWS MAY BE about damage wrought by a tornado, the city's new budget, a tax bill before the state legislature, the fall of a foreign government. But always it is about people. Every news story has its cast of characters, and they must be presented to the reader.

When a character makes his first entrance in a news story, he is almost always identified, no matter how well known. Even the President of the United States is given his title.

A fundamental rule in handling names of people in the news is that there must be no possible confusion as to identity. Journalistic practice, therefore, is to give the full name—first name, middle initial, and last name—accompanied by an identification. This practice should be waived, however, if the person has a particular way of writing his name. Thus, if Jupiter William Smith prefers to be known as J. William Smith, the newspaper should heed his wishes. The person is the best authority on how his name should be spelled and written. Other authorities are city directories and telephone directories and such special guides as official government directories, *Who's Who in America, Who's Who in Labor,* and so forth.

There are some occasions, however, when the full name may be omitted. Since there is only one prime minister, one president of a country, one secretary of state, one governor, and one mayor, and since all appear frequently in the news, some newspapers omit the first name. This is a matter of individual newspaper policy, and the reporter should follow his newspaper's rule. On the question of

the using of full names, the New York *Times* style book says:
"One reason for more meticulous recording of full names is that
many of the figures in the current news will pass from the pages of
newspapers in a few years, but the New York *Times* remains as a
permanent record which will be searched for its accounts of events
long after the principals of those events have gone from memory.
Another reason is that this method has long been a sound journalistic practice."

In recent years, newspapers have tended to omit identification in
the lead of a story for the sake of brevity, with the identification
quickly produced in the second paragraph. Examples of deferred
identification follow:

> Police today charged James T. Tanner with using a hatchet,
> sledge hammer, and shears to wreck his home after a quarrel with
> his wife.
> Tanner, police said, went to work on the furnishings at 100 E.
> First Street while his wife was at work.

> The United States bears the major responsibility for clearing up
> its misunderstandings with the free countries of Asia, Paul G.
> Hoffman said Tuesday.
> Hoffman, chairman of the board of the Studebaker-Packard
> Corp., addressed delegates to the golden anniversary of Rotary
> International.

In the use of the honorifics *Mr., Mrs.,* and *Miss,* newspaper practice varies. *Mr.* is not used when the title precedes a full name,
except on the society pages and in combination with *Mrs.,* as *Mr.
and Mrs. John B. Smith.* Rules vary on the use of the title when
only the last name of a person is given. Perhaps the most widespread
practice is to omit it. Some newspapers insist upon the title for all
men of good repute. Others use it for local persons in the news but
omit it in press association dispatches.

The titles *Mrs.* and *Miss* are prefixed to all women's names, with
the exception of those well known in public life. Actresses, singers,
sportswomen, writers, and public officials may be named without
the title on first mention in a story when the full name appears, but
the proper title is invariably used in subsequent reference when
only the last name is used. Professional names of actresses, writers,
and others, when different from the married names, take the title
Miss.

Although in social usage a married woman is known by her husband's name, there are numerous instances when this propriety is violated by newspapers. Instead of saying that Mrs. John T. Jones was injured in an accident, the newspaper will refer to her as Mrs. Sylvia Ann Jones. The practice apparently derives from the fact that public records carry a woman's given name rather than her husband's. When there is a chance of making a mistake, or when the husband's name is not known, the reporter should use the version that appears on the record; otherwise, it is preferable to call her by her husband's name, since it is probably better known.

By the time a girl reaches the age of eighteen, the legal age in most states, she should be given the title of *Miss*; previous to this time the title is usually omitted. On second and subsequent mention in a story, young girls may be referred to merely by their given name; in informal stories—such as features—the given name, rather than the last name prefixed by *Miss,* can be used even for girls who have reached their teens.

With the decline of social formality in recent years, there has been a growing tendency to refer to people by nicknames and first names. Such practices should be avoided. The style book of the St. Louis *Post-Dispatch* advises: "As a rule, don't assume the familiarity of calling persons by their first names. A first name sometimes is permissible where to use a last name or full name would be awkward— for example, stories of brothers, sisters or other persons with the same surnames."

There are places where first names and nicknames may be appropriate—on the sports pages and in feature stories—but in formal news reports it is best to avoid them. They often appear in headlines where the last names are too long to fit, but headlines should not be taken as models of the best prose.

In some instances, where a person is best known by a nickname, his designation may be by both his given name and his nickname, in quotes or parentheses, before the surname. If the nickname is used alone with the surname, however, it should not be in quotes. Thus: *Michael D. "Mike" Thomas,* but: *Mike Thomas.*

Methods of Identification

Since there are numerous ways by which a person can be identified, the reporter must make a choice. The following three rules will serve as a general guide:

(1) Use the identification by which the person is best known.

Such identification will broaden interest in the story, for more people recognizing a person means more people reading the news report. A John J. Adams of 200 E. First Street injured in an automobile accident might not mean much to readers. But call him John J. Adams, president of the First National Bank, and the story takes on added news value; it will interest not only those who know him personally, but also most people who do business with the bank.

(2) Use the identification that is most pertinent or appropriate to the story.

In a report of activities of an organization it is usually sufficient to identify a person only through his connection with the organization. If Thomas T. Perkins, president of the Chamber of Commerce, makes an announcement about the organization, identifying him by that title and office is sufficient. If he appoints a committee and the members are listed, the names do not necessarily have to be followed by an identification.

(3) For a person of good reputation, use an identification that does not tend to embarrass him or lower him in the esteem of others.

If a person is a street sweeper, garbage collector, or day laborer, or holds any job that would indicate he is a member of a low economic group, the newspaper should not gratuitously draw attention to the fact by identifying him by his occupation. His home address is a preferable identification, unless his occupation has a bearing on the news. If a laborer is injured in a cave-in while digging a cellar, his job is a part of the story; if he is injured in some other sort of accident while not at work, his job is irrelevant in the story.

In identifying people, the reporter has the following possibilities from which to choose:

Address. For local people the street address is probably the most frequently used identification, since many who appear in the news have no other more meaningful identification.

It is one of the most precise identifications and prevents confusion with other persons of the same or similar name. Thus, it is almost always used for people involved in accidents, law suits, arrests, and so forth, where a mistaken identity might have serious effects.

Age. The age as a part of the identification is customarily given in stories about persons involved in accidents, law suits, and arrests, since it is a very particularizing addition to a name. It is also used in obituaries and in stories in which biographical details are an important part of the news. It is considered an essential part of the news in stories about children or old people.

Occupation. A person's vocation is usually one of the first things about him that one wants to know, and identification by vocation helps to satisfy the reader's curiosity about the sort of person involved in a news event. In addition, a person may be more widely known through his occupation, especially if it requires his dealing with the public, than through any other identification available.

Title. If a person holds an office or position carrying a title, the title is usually the best identification, since it is the one by which he is probably best known. Thus public officials, institutional heads, and office-holders in organizations are ordinarily given their titles. On occasion, however, it may be undesirable to use an institutional or organizational affiliation for identification. If the president of the Rotary Club, for example, is arrested for drunken driving, there is no good reason for the newspaper to connect his transgression with the organization in which he happens to hold office.

Reputation. If a person is widely known in any field of endeavor, his reputation is probably his best-known identification. Frequently the identification is accompanied by an adjective, such as well-known attorney, famed atomic scientist, noted authority on Aztec civilization. Some typical identifications emphasizing reputation are: civic leader, city sportsman, popular sub-deb, noted educator, and wealthy philanthropist.

Achievement. A person may be most widely known not for a reputation built up over a period of years, but for a single achievement. An athlete who sets a world record is likely to have such an achievement tagged to his name for the remainder of his life, as will the girl who wins a Miss America title, a man who invents a new device, or a woman who is the first to climb Mt. Everest.

Connection with Past News. Some persons derive their news importance from being mentioned in connection with some past news event. This identification is required for immediate understanding of any currently developing story—a tie-back recalling earlier developments: *John T. Jones, arrested yesterday for robbing the Broadway Supermarket, will be arraigned in magistrate's court at 10 a. m. today.* Many people drop out of the news for years, only to have their past notoriety or fame recalled to mind when their obituary is written.

Relationship. The most frequent occasion for identification by

relationship is when children figure in the news; they are invariably
identified as being the son or daughter of so-and-so, who in turn
must be identified. Many people owe their news value to the prominence of relatives or friends. Members of the family of the President
of the United States may be of no particular importance in themselves, but their activities are frequently newsworthy because of
their connections. This concept of news value sometimes involves
questions of ethics. Should a newspaper, for example, make a bigger
story out of a drunken driving case because the person arrested
happens to be related to a famous person? Is it fair to a famous
person to bring his name into a news story over an event with which
he had nothing to do? Or, is a newspaper justified in writing stories
about the immediate family of a person arrested for an atrocious
crime?

Other Identification Problems

In addition to choosing the best identification for a person on first
mention in a news story, the writer must determine how to write it.
This may involve a matter of precedence—whether the name should
come first followed by the identification, or whether it would be
better to characterize the person first and then give his name.

Commonly used titles of address precede the name. These include
governmental titles (president, secretary of state, governor, mayor);
military and naval titles (general, colonel, captain, lieutenant,
ensign); a few professional titles (professor, attorney, coach, Dr.);
and ecclesiastical titles (father, canon, dean).

Such titles are always capitalized when they precede a name. They
may or may not be abbreviated, depending on the newspaper's own
style rules. It is best to avoid long, cumbersome titles preceding a
name: *President of the First National Bank John J. Adams.* Whether
the title should be repeated on subsequent mention of the person
in the story when only the last name is used also depends upon the
newspaper's style rule. If the newspaper uses *Mr.* before last names,
it is likely to insist that a title or a shortened version of it be
repeated every time the name appears.

Epithets indicating professions, occupations, and positions not
commonly used as titles may precede the name, but they should not
be capitalized, nor are they separated from the name by punctuation. Usually, also, the article is omitted: *halfback John Smith,
actor Adam Jones, violinist Peter Adams.*

A distinction must be made between the use of these terms as epithets and the use of them as nouns in loose apposition. In the latter, the definite or indefinite article is usually needed and the proper name, used as a noun in apposition, is set off by commas, as: *A grocer, John Smith, was injured.* But this is not an invariable rule: *The violinist Peter Adams will appear.* The commas are required with two expressions in loose apposition (nonrestrictive) and not required with two expressions in close apposition (restrictive).

In all cases, identifications following the name must be set off by commas, and titles and positions are not abbreviated. Whether they are capitalized depends upon the newspaper's style rule; perhaps the prevailing practice is not to capitalize. Examples: *John Smith, 200 E. First Street, was injured. Dr. Arthur A. Jones, professor of history, will speak.*

Sometimes the identification is a feature of the story and may precede the name. This is especially true when a person's achievement, reputation, or appearance in past news may be remembered after his name has been forgotten, as:

> PLUCKEMIN, N. J.—Memorial Day had a special meaning for a Presbyterian minister who coined the famous World War II battle slogan, "Praise the Lord and Pass the Ammunition."
>
> For the Reverend Howell M. Forgy, it was a time for solemn remembrance of those who fell before Japanese guns and bombs during the 1941 sneak attack at Pearl Harbor during which he uttered the inspiring words.

In many instances a single identification may not be sufficient. A double identification, for example, is often required for members of state legislatures and Congress. Party affiliation is almost invariably given, usually following the name, set off by commas or parentheses: *Senator James J. Smith (R., Clay County).* The official's role in a particular news story may also need to be indicated. *Senator James J. Smith (R., Clay County), chairman of the Senate appropriations committee.*

Frequently the news story needs, besides the identification, some biographical details to refresh the reader's memory about a person, or to make his appearance in the news more meaningful. News writers usually try to slip in this additional information unobtrusively by referring to the person by some other title or designation in subsequent mention, or by interpolating background at various places in the story. For example:

Former Senator John J. Smith, 75, who retired from politics last year after serving four terms in Washington, died at his home last night.

The author of many bills to increase social security benefits was stricken by a heart attack when he returned home after addressing a union meeting in Labor Temple.

Smith, who won his first Senate seat after serving three terms as mayor of Middletown, was taken to St. Anthony Hospital, where he died at 11:30 p. m.

Both these practices, however, have their dangers. If too many synonyms are used, the story may sound grotesque. The practice of working in identification material by interpolated clauses in the body of the story may produce awkward irrelevancies, as: *After his preliminary hearing, the youth, who quit high school before the end of the last school year, was returned to the county jail.*

When the reporter wants to supply additional information beyond the brief identification in his lead, it would seem better to devote a paragraph to it early in the story or defer it to the end. Giving extra details piecemeal and irrelevantly throughout the story frequently distracts and confuses the reader.

The identification need not be confined to the bare mention of a title or occupation. In feature articles and interviews, the story takes on life and color through the use of descriptive identifications of the sort used by *Time* magazine. Examples follow:

Pretty in skirts and pert in slacks—that's Mildred Miller, size 12 mezzo-soprano with the Metropolitan Opera Company.

Daisy Miller, 32, pistol packin' redhead, and her three Afghan hounds will be evicted Tuesday from her home on Sanitary District property near the Des Plaines River.

Such identifications, however, may be entirely out of place in a straight news report where the emphasis is not on the personality of the individual. For example, the fact that the man in the following story is handsome has no bearing on his being in the news; in fact, in the tragic news event reported the description is in bad taste.

INDIANAPOLIS—Handsome Bob Sweikert of Indianapolis drove his big new John Zink Special to victory today in the bloodiest 500-mile auto race in 25 years—a bitter contest that cost the life of two-time winner Bill Vukovich of Fresno, Cal.

A descriptive identification can also help reveal the significance of an event involving a person whose background or attitude may be unfamiliar to the reader. For example, the biographical details in the following story help the American reader assess the importance of the event:

> ROME—A rightist minority in his own Christian Democrat party forced pro-Western Premier Scelba to resign today and plunged Italy into a governmental crisis.
>
> The resignation came just two months after Scelba made a triumphal tour of the United States, where he was received by President Eisenhower and hailed by thousands of Italian-Americans as a stout friend of the United States.
>
> It was a bitter day for the little Sicilian, who has become known as Italy's leading postwar foe of communism.

ASSIGNMENTS

1. Check three different newspapers and note their policies on the following: the use of *Mr.*, or its omission, when only the last name is used; the use or omission of first names after a title on first mention of prominent public officials in stories; capitalization of titles used as identifications after a name.

2. Clip examples of each of the methods of identification given in the chapter.

3. (a) Consult reference books and make a list of the forms of address or designations for the clergy in the Catholic, Jewish, and principal Protestant faiths.

(b) Compile a list of organizations that appear frequently in the news whose officers are designated by other than the standard titles of president, vice president, etc. and give the proper titles used.

4. Find a story in which identification and biographical material are awkwardly distributed throughout the story. Rewrite to give it all in one place.

5. Write a 400-word news story on the announcement of the program for an artists' or lecture series sponsored by an institution or organization. Assume that the series will consist of five numbers. Make up details as to the name of the sponsoring group, the source of the announcement, the dates, ticket costs, and the persons appearing on the program. Obtain biographical information needed for the entertainers or speakers from standard sources.

CHAPTER 10

EXPLANATION AND THE NEWS

How Much Do People Know?

ONE OF THE BOASTS of newspapermen is that the American people are the best informed people on earth. Very likely this is true, but recent public opinion studies show that the people's stock of information is something less than ideal.

One of the most famous American documents is the Bill of Rights: in one public opinion poll 28 percent of the respondents said they had never heard of it. A key American foreign policy in recent years has been the reciprocal trade program: only 10 percent of the respondents in one poll could give a correct explanation of it. Guam was a strategic island in the U. S. campaign against Japan in World War II and is an important Far East bastion now: in one poll 72 percent of the respondents could not locate it on a map.

Such findings emphasize the importance of the journalistic rule that reporters should not overestimate the knowledge of their readers. This dictum has frequently been voiced, but little of a concrete nature was done to follow it through until 1949. That year the Associated Press Managing Editors Association set up a committee on explanatory writing to find out what could be done to make the news more meaningful to the reader. In its first report the committee said: "The work of the APME committee on explanatory writing has been one of pioneering. Born just this year, it had no charted course, no experience of others, to guide it. Also, it had no tradition, no rules, to restrict it. It did not even have a definition of the term explanatory writing."

The committee decided to make a distinction between explanation and interpretation. It said that explanation might extend to "a series of background articles about a complex news situation," but it found that explanation primarily belongs in regular news reports. The APME reached the following conclusions: (1) organizations may need to be identified; (2) geographical places may need to be located and described; (3) words, expressions, and names may need to be defined; and (4) events themselves may need to be reported in such a way as to show why they are news.

Editors, questioned on how explanatory material should be given in a news story, indicated a preference for integrating it in the report rather than inserting it as parenthetical matter or giving it in specially written stories to be printed as sidebars or inserts. The committee's report said:

> There should be no attempt to disguise explanatory or background material. Don't try to sprinkle it throughout the story in an effort to make it look like fresh material. Put it boldly right where it belongs in the story, whether it is the second paragraph or dash matter to follow the spot news. A few words of background dropped here and there may be disconcerting and irritating. Editors and readers will thank you if you give it to them in a chunk they can easily understand. You don't have to try to fool them about it or apologize for talking down to them.

Identification of Organizations

Many organizations in the news do not require identification if they are widely known or if their nature is plainly apparent from the name. If they are not, the reporter may have to identify them by one of the following methods:

By Purpose: Senior Achievement, Inc., a new corporation financed by a grant from the Wieboldt Foundation to assist retired people.

The U. S. Committee for the United Nations, designated by the government to promote nationwide observance of United Nations Day.

By Membership: The American Federation of Television and Radio Artists, representing 25,000 performers in the two mediums.

The Baker Street Irregulars, a club made up of Sherlock Holmes fans named for the street-boys who aided the fictional detective in some of his investigations.

By Institutional Affiliation: The World Health Organization, a specialized agency of the United Nations.

The Newman Club, an organization for Roman Catholic students.
By Type: Phi Beta Kappa, national honorary scholastic society.
The Eagles, a fraternal organization.

By Reputation: The American Civil Liberties Union, long a
defender of traditional American rights.

The National Council of American-Soviet Friendship, listed as a
subversive organization by the attorney general.

Frequently the identification tag after the name is not enough to
explain an organization. Its importance or nature may require a
sentence or two telling who supports it, who are its leading members, what its announced purpose is, how many members it has, and
where its headquarters are located.

For example, the New York *Herald Tribune,* in a story on the
election of new directors to the Fund for the Republic, printed this
paragraph of background:

> The fund, at 1 E. 54th St., is an independent, non-profit organi-
> zation founded in 1952 for the purpose of "eliminating restrictions
> on freedom of thought and inquiry and to develop policies to
> protect these freedoms." Robert M. Hutchins is president.

The Chicago *Daily News* carried this background in a speech on
slums made before the South Side Planning Board of that city:

> The SSPB devotes its attention to the seven square miles of
> Chicago bounded by Roosevelt rd., the lake shore, 47th st. and
> the Pennsylvania tracks.
> Business firms, institutions, neighborhood organizations and
> individuals make up its membership.
> In its nine years of activity, the board estimates that $225 million
> of public and private money has been invested in redeveloping the
> area.

Many times, in reports of conventions, the action taken will be
more significant if some information is given about the size of the
membership. The Associated Press included this paragraph in a
report of the American Baptist Convention at Atlantic City attended by about 10,000 delegates: "The convention represents 6,000
churches with 1,600,000 of the nation's 18 million Baptists. The
convention is one of 26 Baptist groups in the country."

An example in which background was needed to make a story
meaningful was cited in the Associated Press Managing Editors
Association report on explanatory writing. It was a story from
Denver about an attack by the American Council of Christian

Churches on a plan for Brotherhood Week sponsored by the National Conference of Christians and Jews. One editor commented: "Without some hint of the make-up of this group it is difficult to judge the weight or importance of the story." The story did include some information about the American Council—that it represented 15 Protestant denominations with a membership exceeding 1,500,000. But is failed to indicate how the size compared with the nation's total and what the particular group stood for. The committee report recommended the following paragraph of explanation:

> The American Council of Christian Churches represents 15 relatively small Protestant denominations with a membership of more than 1,500,000. Believing in the second coming of Christ, it is vigorously opposed to the Federal Council of Churches of Christ in America, dominant Protestant body of about 29,000,000 members.

A journalistic practice often confusing to readers is that of designating organizations by the initial letters or coined words formed from them. The practice was not unknown before the first administration of Franklin D. Roosevelt (Y.M.C.A. and G.O.P. are familiar examples), but it mushroomed with the establishment of a multitude of New Deal "alphabetical" agencies: WPA (Works Progress Administration), CCC (Civilian Conservation Corps), and PWA (Public Works Administration). These abbreviations were written without periods, and this practice is the general rule now. The growing tendency to use initial-letter designations has resulted in such terms as UMT (universal military training) and GAW (guarteed annual wage).

The journalistic rule for these designations is to write out the organization or agency in full on first mention and to use the abbreviation on subsequent mention. Thus: *World Health Organization* when first used in a story, but *WHO* for later reference. A more recent practice that facilitates recognition by the reader is to give the abbreviation in parentheses immediately after the name on its first use in the story: *the World Health Organization (WHO)*.

Perhaps the initial-letter designations should be dropped altogether in the interest of readability and clarity. They are not necessary, since the generic term can always be used, as it has in the past. As an example, the full name, the *Federal Communications*

Commission, should be used on first mention in a story; thereafter it can be referred to as *the commission.*

On occasions when the initials form a new word, called an acronym, the name does not appear in capital letters. The United Nations, Educational, Scientific and Cultural Organization frequently, for example, appears as *Unesco.*

Greek-letter societies in colleges and schools usually require an identification. There are several types—social, professional and honorary—and a distinction must be made among them. A men's social group may be given this way: *Phi Kappa Sigma social fraternity.* A women's social group is popularly designated a sorority: *Pi Beta Phi sorority.*

In recent years, especially in college newspapers, the custom has developed of labeling all the non-social groups as "honoraries." This is incorrect in two ways: all the groups are not honorary, and the word is an adjective, not a noun. Sigma Delta Chi, men's professional journalism fraternity, in its own publications has taken exception to the organization's being designated as an "honorary" on the ground that, while it is considered an honor to belong, the society nevertheless is a professional one.

Some groups are both honorary and professional, a circumstance that adds to the difficulties of correct designation. The only safe way to make sure of an identification is by consulting an authoritative listing of these orders, or their own publications or members. But it is usually safe to call any of them, including the orders for women, a fraternity or society, omitting the description of professional or honorary: *Sigma Delta Chi, men's journalism fraternity; Theta Sigma Phi, women's journalism fraternity.*

Identification of Places

In local happenings, elaboration as to locale is seldom needed. The locations of principal buildings, institutions, business and industrial concerns, parks and other structures, organizations, and places presumably are well enough known to residents to obviate the need for statements on their whereabouts. A street address usually suffices for locating places likely to be unfamiliar to many readers.

Occasionally, however, if a place has figured previously in the news or if it has a historical significance, some background will add to the story's interest. For instance, the lead in a Buffalo (New York) *Evening News* story on an automobile fatality called the site of the accident "dead man's curve," and located it on East Hill near the town of Warsaw. Later in the story, it gave this additional information: "The curve is on Route 20-A. It has been the scene of numerous accidents in recent years. The two-lane highway winds from a high plateau under a railroad trestle into the valley where Warsaw lies."

Many news stories would be improved by the addition of such descriptive details to help the reader visualize the scene and put him on the spot as if he were an eyewitness.

The committee on explanatory writing of the Associated Press Managing Editors Association noted that the need for explanation increases as a story gets farther from its point of origin. Rudolf Flesch, the A. P. readability consultant, stated: "The most obvious rule for explanatory writing concerns facts of geography; they must be explained to any reader who doesn't live right there."

Flesch cited a press association dispatch that contained this explanatory paragraph: "The Columbia river discharges into the Pacific and is the borderline between Oregon and Washington. Its basin reaches into Montana, Idaho and Canada." He said that this information would not be needed for readers in Washington and Oregon but that it would be for readers in other parts of the country.

Perhaps one of the reasons many people do not follow events in remote areas of the world—Indonesia, Iran, Pakistan, Guatemala, Vietnam, and other trouble spots in the post-World War II years— is that they know little about the geography of the areas, the people, and their history. Stories concerning such places would be more widely read if they gave the regions' geographical and historical background.

Explanation of Terms

Readers often have only a vague understanding of events because expressions and terms are used which they cannot define. Many of the terms which occur almost daily in the newspaper are used by editors and reporters in the belief that the public is so familiar with them that no explanation is needed.

For instance, we might assume that the expression "farm subsidy," which has appeared in the news so much in recent years, would be clear to anyone. Yet in a public opinion poll only 35 percent of the respondents understood its meaning, while 65 percent either said they could not define it or gave incorrect definitions. A similar result was obtained in a poll in which "bipartisan foreign policy" appeared on a list of common newspaper expressions. Only one in four persons could give an approximate definition.

In giving rules for the guidance of the Associated Press, Rudolf Flesch said: "All terms that are *possibly* unfamiliar to the reader must be explained, except those that have become part of our general everyday language."

Vague though it is, the rule probably will serve as well as any other. Generally the news writer, from his own knowledge and experience, has a fair idea as to which expressions need a word of explanation and which do not. When in doubt, he should supply the explanation. Certainly he cannot explain *every* expression that might *possibly* be unfamiliar to readers. Although newspapers and press associations did not explain the term "farm subsidies" because it seemed a part of everyday language, they have been careful to explain the expression "parity prices." Despite the evidence of the public opinion poll, journalistic practice might be justified in this respect.

Perhaps the situation is not so bad as it appears. Oftentimes the meaning of an expression is self-evident from the context in which it is used, and people frequently know and use words they would have difficulty in defining. Thus, the fact that 65 percent of the people polled about farm subsidies could not frame a definition does not necessarily mean that, encountering it in a news story, they would not know what the story was about. Similarly, many people probably could not explain exactly such legal proceedings as arraignments and preliminary hearings. But they have a general idea, and a newspaper would be foolish to insist that the terms be explained every time they appeared in a news story.

Why the Event Is News

The journalistic rule of objectivity states that all the reporter need do is to collect the facts about an event and record them in his story. But very often these surface facts do not add up to anything very meaningful. As a result, there has been a growing movement in recent years for news writers to interpret the event—to explain its significance. As has been pointed out, very often all that is needed to show the significance is to include explanatory material in the story.

One of the most frequent occasions for adding explanatory material is when a current event hinges upon a previous event. Thus, reports of events in which there were previous developments must contain some background material. The following story from the Pittsburgh *Post-Gazette* contains two paragraphs of such background:

> The first suit as a result of the school bus-train crash that killed four students and injured 44 others at a fog-shrouded Collinsburg crossing in Westmoreland County on September 17 was filed here yesterday in Common Pleas Court.
>
> Norma Jane Wiley, 15, one of the passengers in the bus load of Rostraver Township High School students, and her parents, Wayne and Norma E. Wiley, of Belle Vernon, are charging the bus company and the Pittsburgh & Lake Erie Railroad with negligence in two suits asking in excess of $5,000.
>
> The accident happened about 8:10 a. m. after the bus driven by Edward Steiner, 22, and operated by the Doernte Bus Lines, had made its next-to-the-last stop at Collinsburg to pick up 10 students.
>
> Minutes later as the bus rumbled across the tracks at the Collinsburg crossing a freight train struck the bus, tearing it off the chassis and sending the body hurtling along the highway.
>
> Miss Wiley, who was taken to Mercy Hospital, alleges in the suit that she received a brain concussion, contusions and abrasions of neck, head, body and arms, a broken wrist, internal injuries and shock.

In such follow stories the people involved are usually identified in the lead by a tie-back:

> James T. Smith, 28, arrested yesterday after he held up a First National Bank messenger in the midst of a noon-day crowd on Main Street, pleaded guilty at a hearing in magistrate court today and was bound over to the District Court for trial.

Sometimes the newsworthiness of an event is made clearer by comparing it with other similar events. Thus, a news story about a plane or train wreck in which there are a large number of deaths may be made more significant by mention in the story of how the number ranks with the number in other wrecks. Flood damage on a river can be made more meaningful if the story gives figures on damages from previous floods. The magnitude of an event is often the measure of its significance, and this should be indicated in the story.

Quite often the news value of an event is not in the event itself but in its significance. A Pittsburgh newspaper printed a story that began:

> The Yellow Cab Co. yesterday bought the strike-bound Airlines Transportation Co.
> The transaction appeared to pave the way for a resumption of limousine service between downtown and the Greater Pittsburgh Airport. That service has been halted since July 16 when 40 drivers and mechanics belonging to Local 128, AFL Teamsters Union, went on strike.

Many newsmen would contend that the real news is not the purchase of the Airlines Transportation Co. by the Yellow Cab Co. but the *effect* of the purchase on the airport limousine service. They would recommend, therefore, a lead something like the following:

> Resumption of limousine service between downtown and the Greater Pittsburgh Airport appeared closer yesterday with the purchase of the strike-bound Airlines Transportation Co. by the Yellow Cab Co.

The Associated Press dispatch below reports the significance of an event and shows how such handling broadens interest in it. If the writer had considered the news as solely in the event itself he might have produced the following lead:

> TIPTON, Ia.—A motion of the Tipton Golf and Country Club and the Tipton Moose Lodge to dismiss indictments for permitting mixed drinks to be served on their premises was denied today by District Judge B. J. Maxwell.

But the A. P. writer saw that this was not the real story and wrote the following account:

> TIPTON, Ia.—Private clubs which hold beer licenses apparently are under a legal cloud if they permit members to make mixed drinks on the premises.
> This was the indication Tuesday when District Judge B. J. Maxwell overruled defense demurrers of the Tipton Golf and Country Club and the Tipton Moose Lodge in a liquor case.
> The defense argued that the court should dismiss indictments based on raids against the clubs early in May. The raiders seized mixed drinks from the bar and tables of the two clubs.
> In arguing in favor of the demurrer, the defense said it was the

clear intent of the 1955 legislature to permit mixing of drinks in private clubs which also hold beer permits.

The new law permits club members to keep liquor on the premises of clubs which hold beer licenses.

Under the interpretation on which the Tipton indictments were obtained, it apparently is legal to drink liquor straight in such clubs but not to mix it with any other beverages.

Judge Maxwell did not rule specifically that mixing of drinks in private clubs is illegal. But he did hold in a 14-page decision that there is a sufficient question that a jury should pass on it.

The defense did not immediately indicate whether it will appeal to the supreme court from the overruling of its demurrer. If no appeal is taken the case will be eligible for trial in September.

The problem arises because the legislature, in granting a measure of special dispensation to private clubs, did not change another section of the law which forbids Class B beer permit holders to "allow the mixing or adding of alcohol to beer or other beverages."

The penalty, upon conviction, is revocation of the beer license and ineligibility for a new beer license later.

ASSIGNMENTS

1. Clip examples of stories in which additional information is needed about an organization to make the reports more meaningful.

2. Clip examples of stories which have place descriptions that help the reader visualize the setting.

3. Compare a newspaper report and a *Time* magazine report of the same event. Does the *Time* report contain descriptive detail and background information that the newspaper report lacks?

4. (a) Make a list of ten terms or expressions frequently appearing in the news that you think readers may not be able to understand. Test them on ten persons drawn from various walks of life.

(b) Frame brief explanations that would be suitable for inclusion in a news story.

5. (a) The U. S. Department of Agriculture reports that during the year turkey raisers of the nation produced 60,228,000 birds. They sold 1,004,546,000 pounds for a total of $337,093,000, an average of 33.6 cents a pound. What other information is needed to make these figures meaningful to the reader?

(b) The writer of the following story buried the real significance of the information; rewrite the story to play up the significance.

Officials of two state agencies operating installations in New

Orleans claimed Monday their vehicles are clearly marked with emblems or letters indicating they are state owned.

Capt. Thomas L. Lewis, assistant general manager of the Dock Board, said all of the board's 50 to 60 vehicles are marked with the Dock Board emblem.

And Olaf J. Fink, secretary of the Levee Board, said the same is true of all board automobiles and that the trucks are marked with letters.

They were queried on the markings following the disclosure Sunday that a state car had been used by members of the family of a wildlife and fisheries commissioner for personal errands and that the vehicle, a station wagon, was not marked as specified in the revised statutes of 1950.

Section 121 of part six of chapter one of title 49 says that state-owned vehicles shall bear the name of the state agency in letters not less than two inches in height and not less than one-quarter inch wide.

Capt. Lewis said that the Dock Board has been using its emblem to mark its vehicles since 1940 and that this marking "satisfies in spirit" the statute. He said he did not anticipate any change in the present markings.

Fink said that all the Levee Board's lakefront vehicles are marked in letters more than two inches in height and that the board's automobiles all bear the Levee Board seal.

CHAPTER 11

CLEAR NEWS WRITING

Readability and Readership

THE ESSENTIAL PROBLEM of news writing for any medium —the newspaper, the news magazine, radio, or television—lies in making the information instantly comprehensible to large numbers of people. It is not to delight with clever phrases, to charm with the mellifluous flow of language, or to transport beyond the real world to an imagined one: the art of news communication is the art of clear writing. Whatever other values the writing may have, it is bad writing from the viewpoint of the news communicator if it is not immediately clear.

For many years journalists believed they were doing a good job of communicating news. Had they not always followed the preachments of clarity, simplicity, brevity? But along about 1945 their pride in how well they were doing their job was deflated when newly developed ways of grading readability showed that news stories were hard to read.

For example, in 1945 the United Press employed Robert Gunning, director of Readable News Reports, to analyze its wire output. The analysis showed that many stories, instead of being easy to read on the mass level, were actually harder to read than articles in the *Atlantic Monthly,* a magazine not designed for popular reading. Discussing the findings, Earl J. Johnson, general news manager, wrote:

> The remedy can be described briefly as shorter sentences, fewer unfamiliar or complex words, and more human interest.
> That's the traditional U. P. style and it's older than the U. P. itself. Looking back over form letters that I've written from this

office in the last 15 years I find that I've preached simple writing more than almost anything else.

But, as the Gunning analysis showed, writers had somehow left the path of simple, direct writing and gone astray in a prose jungle of semantic obscurity and involved sentences.

Gunning's readability yardstick measures what he calls the Fog Index of a passage.[1] Through a mathematical formula he has equated the Fog Index with the grade level of school students. A Fog Index of 12, for example, corresponds to the level of understanding of a high school senior and a Fog Index of 17 to that of a college graduate. The procedure for obtaining the Fog Index consists of three steps:

1. Obtain the average sentence length in a passage by counting the total number of words and dividing by the number of sentences.

2. Obtain the percentage of words of three syllables or more per 100 words of the chosen passage. Omitted from this count are capitalized words, combinations of easy words like bookkeeper and butterfly, and verb forms of three syllables created by adding the suffixes -ed and -es, as in created and trespasses.

3. Add these two figures together and multiply by the constant .4 to get the Fog Index.

According to Gunning's formula, passages with a Fog Index of 10 or below are easy reading. Indexes of 11 and 12 are on the danger line, and indexes 13 and above are difficult reading.

Another widely used readability formula was developed by Rudolf Flesch, who has served as a consultant for the Associated Press and many newspapers and magazines. His formula measures the difficulty of words by the number of syllables they contain, and the difficulty of sentences by the number of words. He also scores an article's interest by the number of personal words (pronouns, nouns that have masculine or feminine natural gender, and collective nouns like people and folks) and the number of personal sentences (direct quotations of spoken sentences, questions, commands, requests, and exclamations).

His yardstick, abbreviated, follows:

Standard: not more than 150 syllables per 100 words; not more than 19 words per average sentence; at least 6 personal words per 100 words; and at least 12 personal sentences per 100 sentences.

[1] Robert Gunning, *The Technique of Clear Writing.* New York: McGraw-Hill Book Co., 1952, pp. 35-39.

Fairly poor: 151-162 syllables per 100 words; 20-23 per average sentence; 3-5 personal words per 100 words; 5-11 personal sentences per 100 sentences.

Poor: 163-186 syllables per 100 words; 24-27 words per average sentence; 1-2 personal words per 100 words; 1-4 personal sentences per 100 sentences.

Very poor: more than 186 syllables per 100 words; more than 27 words per average sentence; no personal words; no personal sentences.[2]

Both the Gunning and Flesch formulas, and others similar to them, have been misused. "Many people," wrote Gunning in an article in *Editor & Publisher* (September 13, 1947), "have picked up an inkling of readability principles and then have scurried to wrong conclusions."

Perhaps the most popular wrong conclusion is that all sentences should be kept below twenty words. The formulas state that the *average* sentence length should be not more than twenty words. An article made up only of short sentences would be monotonous—like the regular click of train wheels passing over the rails. Sentence length should vary according to the number of words needed to convey the thought intended. Some sentences may be short (five to twenty words), and others may be long (twenty to fifty words).

Other widespread misconceptions are that striving for a simple prose style means writing down to the level of children or morons, and that such qualities as flavor and individuality will be lost. The fallacy in these beliefs is shown in the fact that many highly acclaimed writers—Twain, Dickens, Hemingway—are easy to read according to readability tests.

A natural question arising from the consideration of reading ease is: Does an article scored as readable really attract more persons? The answer is "yes," according to some studies that have been made.

The Birmingham *News* compared the readership of stories, scored in a survey by the Continuing Study of Newspaper Reading, with their readability, scored by the Flesch formula. It found that stories rated easy to read attracted from 20 to 75 percent more readers than stories rated hard to read. The State University of Iowa carried out an experiment to test readership by printing two editions of a laboratory paper exactly alike, except that one carried a difficult

2 Rudolf Flesch, *The Art of Readable Writing.* New York: Harper and Brothers, 1949, pp. 213-216.

version of a story and the other an easy version. A readership study showed more readers for the easy story than for the difficult story.

The general principles of readability—short, simple sentences, everyday words, and human interest—are easy to grasp. But understanding of the principles does not tell a person how to write readably. Some of the techniques are discussed in the following divisions of this chapter and in the next chapter.

Clarity in Sentences

Long before the readability experts went into business, young writers were urged to use short, simple sentences for clarity. The advice is excellent—if not followed unthinkingly, for if such sentences alone were the answer to good writing, a child's primer would be a model to imitate. But no writer is foolish enough to write in primer sentences for adults, and no one would read him if he did.

A variety of sentences—some long and some short, some complex in form and some compound—will avoid the monotony induced by simple sentences. And, just as sentences should vary in length and form, so should passages change in pace, hurrying the reader along here and slowing him up there. Some ideas are so important that they deserve a sentence to themselves, while some are so insignificant that they should be subordinated in a dependent clause of a sentence.

The stumbling blocks to clear writing in sentence structure occur in simple sentences as well as in complex and compound ones, though they are less likely to do so. They include obscure pronoun reference, misrelated modifiers, improper subordination, and discontinuity in thought.

Pronoun Reference. News writers seem, at times, to have taken too much to heart warnings against obscure pronoun references. They tend to avoid pronouns as if they were communicable diseases. Their tendency to use a synonym, oftentimes a farfetched one, instead of a pronoun where one is suitable creates as much confusion as the use of a pronoun with an obscure reference. For example: "The union officials went into session at 9:30 a. m., and two hours later the labor leaders had not decided on a course of action." Many readers might be momentarily puzzled by this sentence because of the apparent distinction made between "union officials" and "labor leaders." The pronoun "they" in the second clause would cause no trouble at all.

But obscure pronoun references are more often a hurdle to quick understanding than are unnecessary synonyms. For example: "The detective said that he had carefully checked the suspect's alibi and that he was convinced he could produce witnesses to substantiate it." The third "he" in this sentence could refer either to the detective or the suspect; the reader has no way of telling which is meant.

The rule for clearness should be: Watch those pronouns but don't be afraid of them.

Misrelated Modifiers. Relative clauses and verbid phrases made with participles, infinitives, and gerunds should be placed next to the word or expression they modify. When they are not, they frequently seem to modify a word that they could not apply to. The results are sometimes amusing, as in the following:

> Her father will clasp the perfectly matched string of pearls about her neck which was once her mother's before he escorts her to the church.

But while we may enjoy such slips, we are not enlightened. The hurried news writer, if he wishes to be understood quickly, must take the time to check his clauses and verbid phrases to make sure they modify the right word.

Perhaps the most common type of misrelated modifier is the dangling participle. It occurs when the reader is led to believe that the participial phrase will modify one subject, only to find that another has been substituted:

> Darting in and out among the crowd, the police were unable to fire their guns to halt the fleeing bandit.

Here, of course, it is the fleeing bandit who darted in and out among the crowd and not the police. Other examples of misrelated modifiers follow:

> The bleeding bellhop was discovered by night clerk Sylvester Paine as he crawled down the stairs in a dazed condition.
>
> The post office now refuses to handle mail for students at the college which is addressed wrong.
>
> Besides checking on prices, Morgan said his agents will see whether dealers are complying with provisions of the new car orders.

Although not grammatically wrong, a long modifying phrase or clause intervening between a subject and its verb delays comprehension. It is a fault especially prevalent in news writing, because of the need for identifying people when first mentioned in a story:

> John A. Parker, president of the Committee on Constitutional Liberties who was arrested yesterday on a charge of inciting a riot, was freed today at a hearing in justice of the peace court.

The identification and the tie-back may be so essential that such a lead sentence must stand, but on occasion it can be reworded to avoid the interruption. Delaying the identification to the second paragraph is sometimes possible:

> John A. Parker was freed today at a hearing in justice of the peace court of a charge of inciting to riot.
> Parker, president of the Committee on Constitutional Liberties, was arrested yesterday. . . .

Improper Subordination. A pernicious development from the recent campaign for simplicity in writing is a new rule being propounded in some news rooms: Use only one idea to a sentence. The rule has its utility, when applied to first paragraphs, in discouraging marathon sentences that answer all the Five W's. It also may be true, as one editor has written, that one-idea-one-sentence writing speeds reading, but it does not necessarily follow that it assists comprehension. The rule implies that every idea is of equal importance, and this simply is not so. The reader can grasp material more easily if important ideas are placed in main clauses and minor ideas are placed in the dependent clauses where they belong. The following, for example, would be clearer if at least one of the subordinate ideas had been properly subordinated:

> The new directive was disclosed yesterday. It was issued under the signature of the chairman of the board. It stated that bids must be obtained on all purchases of more than $250.

All the ideas here are not of equal importance; an improved wording would be:

> The new directive, disclosed yesterday, was issued under the signature of the chairman of the board. It stated that bids must be obtained on all purchases of more than $250.

Reporters addicted to clauses beginning with "as" furnish frequent examples of improper subordination:

> The basketball squad opened its second week of preseason prac-

tice yesterday as the floormen prepared for their opener with
Washington and Jefferson December 5.

The main idea in this sentence is apparently that the team began
practice for the game with Washington and Jefferson, but the
statement of this is in the wrong clause. The sentence should read:

> The basketball squad, starting its second week of preseason prac-
> tice, prepared yesterday for its opener with Washington and
> Jefferson December 5.

Another common type of improper subordination consists of
thoughts of unequal value stated in two independent clauses joined
by a coordinate conjunction:

> The conference ended at 3:30 p. m., but none of the negotiators
> would divulge the nature of the proposals discussed.

The time at which the conference ended hardly seems important
enough for the emphasis given it. Placing it in a subordinate clause
would improve the sentence:

> None of the negotiators would divulge the nature of the pro-
> posals discussed at the conference, which ended at 3:30 p. m.

Discontinuity in Thought. When the reader has been led to expect one type of construction or has been carried along in one vein
of thought, he is disturbed if there is a sudden switch to another
mode of expression. Such shifts may involve failure to follow a
parallel grammatical construction, failure to keep a consistent enumeration or listing, and failure to maintain categorical unity.

The rule for parallel construction states that in pairs or series the
same grammatical forms and parts of speech must be used. The
following, for example, creates difficulty:

> Action of the city council last night included acceptance of
> sealed bids for construction of a new warehouse, voted to recon-
> sider a resolution establishing Fifth Street as a one-way through-
> fare, and refusal to approve a petition for rezoning two districts
> for business.

The first and third items are noun forms, the second a verb form.
Parallelism requires that all three have the same grammatical form.
Other illustrations of this fault are:

> The chairman said he would appoint a committee to study the
> rate situation and another for investigating employment practices.
> He earned his college expenses as a part-time clerk in a campus
> book store and working during the summers in a steel mill.

He denied that he was familiar with the procedure and knowing what hours the workers came on duty.

H. W. Fowler in his *A Dictionary of Modern English Usage* described faulty enumeration, or listing, as one of the most common
marks of "journalistic and other hasty writing." His name for the
blunder was "bastard enumeration." The blunder occurs when a
writer is unable to distinguish between the separate items in a listing and omits a necessary "and" or "or." It is typified in the
following sentence:

> At the university he was class historian, a member of Blue Key,
> Skull and Bones, and Kappa Sigma fraternity.

The sentence makes two statements: he was class historian and he
was a member of the three organizations listed. The word "and"
belongs after "historian." Some other examples of illegitimate listing are:

> The board of trustees approved three student assessments,
> several faculty promotions, leaves, and retirements.
> The basement of the new building will contain bowling alleys,
> storage and utility rooms.

Another common writing fault discussed in detail by Fowler is
what he calls "elegant variation." Its use sometimes contributes to
obscurity because things which are the same are given different
names. The following sentence from a press association dispatch is
a typical example found in news writing:

> The northeastern meet will be at Wilkes-Barre, the north-
> western competition at Clearfield, and the southwestern finals at
> Washington.

As worded, the sentence would seem to imply that "meet," "competition," and "finals" are different types of events. Another example containing two such unintentional and disturbing contrasts is
the following:

> Writers favoring the resolution numbered 53, and authors
> opposing it totaled 22.

Words and Meanings

As a young man, Somerset Maugham devoted himself, as have
thousands of other people with the itch to write, to building his vo-

cabulary. One of the tasks he assigned himself was to go through the London Museum noting the curious names of stones and minerals, the feel of textiles, and the colors of jewels, with the aim of enriching his prose. He may not have wasted his time doing this, but the fact was, as he has confessed, he fortunately never made use of the words and epithets he so painstakingly garnered. Many other people who have set out consciously to learn new words and expressions— gems with which to stud their writing—have decided, as did Maugham, that they were using the wrong approach.

Word study, of course, is necessary for anyone who writes and who wants to improve his writing. But studying words merely to accumulate a big vocabulary is like shooting at a squirrel in a tree and bringing down a bunch of leaves: the aim is not right. The importance of the writer's vocabulary study is not as much in learning new words as it is in appreciating the quality of words.

The thesaurus-hound—a person who goes through a book of synonyms looking for words to substitute for others he has written— most often worsens rather than improves his work. The word "say," he thinks, is overused. The thesaurus provides him with many possibilities: assert, asseverate, declare, opine, state, vouchsafe. Almost invariably he chooses an unfamiliar synonym, although it may not express his meaning as well as the word originally written.

In training himself to write, the young person should not neglect the task of increasing his stock of words. He can write better if his vocabulary is big enough for him to choose, without conscious thought, the exact word to express his meaning. But the size of the vocabulary has less to do with readable and clear writing than some other factors.

Use of Familiar Words. Readers find it hard to understand writing which contains words whose meanings they do not know. Hence, the first advisory rule given by nearly everyone for simple, clear writing: Prefer the familiar word.

The advice, of course, is especially appropriate for the news writer: his articles are meant to be read by large numbers of persons, differing in age, education, and experience. Most of them are not educated beyond high school, most of them are not widely read— in fact, read little—and most of them lack precise knowledge about many of the topics with which the news deals. The news writer faces a problem of using words within the small vocabulary range of his poorer readers, at the same time making his work interesting to his superior readers.

Nobody knows exactly how many words there are in the English language; estimates vary, but those appearing in comprehensive dictionaries exceed a half million. Despite this huge vocabulary, the number of words in everyday use is small. Counts made by E. L. Thorndike and Irving Lorge of words appearing in books and magazines indicate 80 percent of all words in print are contained in a list of 1,000 words, and 98 percent in a list of 10,000 words.

A person can be fairly sure, then, that he will use few words not known to his readers if he checks his writing by the lists of those most commonly used. Such a course, however, is hardly practicable for the news writer; an easier way of avoiding unfamiliar words is sugggested by Flesch and Gunning. Since they both rate the difficulty of words by the number of syllables they contain, a useful general guide for simple writing is, therefore, to stay clear of words with many syllables.

Fowler, in urging writers "to be direct, simple, brief, vigorous, and lucid," included among his recommendations the following: "Prefer the Saxon word to the Romance." The basis for this advice is that many of the words most used in everyday living are those of Anglo-Saxon origin: most of us would prefer "home" to "domicile," "start" to "inaugurate," "try" to "endeavor," "many" to "numerous," and "think" to "cogitate." Unless we have studied philology, however, most of us will find Fowler's advice hard to follow. Another drawback to Fowler's advice is that Latin, and Greek also, is the source of many of our most common words—words that did not exist in the time of King Alfred. They include such familiar terms as radioactivity, refrigerator, automobile, telephone, and television.

Measuring the difficulty of words by origin and number of syllables must seem artificial and arbitrary to any discerning person. Better results probably can be obtained by developing proper mental attitudes. The writer who reminds himself that he must not be pretentious or affected will seldom be guilty of using words above the vocabulary level of his readers. When he writes something that he considers dubious, he should ask himself: "Would I put it this way in talking?" If the answer is "no," he should change his wording to something he might use in everyday speech.

Levels of Abstraction. Useful contributions to more easily understood writing have been made by the new science of semantics—the study of meanings—which deals with words as symbols or signs. It emphasizes that words have different meanings to different people because of their individual experience and that a word should not be confused with the event or object for which it stands.

Of the semantic principles, one of the most important for the newswriter is the level of abstraction. On the level of experience, we may have, for example, a cow—a tangible object of flesh and bone. There may be a specific cow to which a name has been given, say "Elsie." The word "cow" itself stands for all animals that have cowlike characteristics. And so, getting further away from the object of tangible experience, we may refer to cows as livestock, as farm assets, as wealth.

The words that lead to misunderstanding and confusion are those on the higher levels of abstraction—democracy, liberty, socialism, communism, beauty, ethics. An interviewer who asked ten persons what they meant by the word "democracy" would probably get ten different answers. Hence, the advice to writers who want to be clear: Prefer the concrete word to the abstract. Or, as the semanticist would put it: Find the referent, that is, the object for which the word is a sign or a symbol.

The sentence, "The present administration in Washington has been more democratic than the previous one," is semantically meaningless. To be sure, politicians might argue for hours over the statement, but in the end no one could prove it was true or not true. A meaningful discussion could ensue only if specific things were cited —protection of civil rights, support for desegregation, adoption of fair employment practices acts, fairer treatment of minority groups, resistance to pressure groups.

The reporter, in his straight news reports of accidents, crimes, fires, and disasters, is not likely to write on a high level of abstraction. He runs into this danger in covering speeches by politicians and reports by government agencies. Often he cannot tell just what a speech or report says precisely, and it seems better to quote than to attempt to translate into plain English.

Too Many Words. Padding is a good thing in proper places— mattresses and chair cushions. It does not belong in prose. When we consider that people spend only a few minutes a day reading the news, we can see the importance of keeping stories short. People do not want to read or listen to 1000 words when they can get the same information—more clearly—in 500 words.

Unnecessary words in news stories are often attributed to the speed with which the reporter writes. He does not have time, it is said, to be brief, to organize his material so that it goes directly to the point, to prune out the verbiage. This is an excuse, not a reason, for the reporter can train himself to write concisely.

One of the most common types of padding in journalistic prose is the verbal phrase made up of a noun or adjective attached to a general-purpose verb:

make contact with	furnish grounds for
be subjected to	have the effect of
give rise to	make itself felt
render inoperative	take effect
play a leading part in	serve the purpose of
exhibit a tendency to	get under way

If the reporter tries, he can find simple verbs for such attenuated expressions.

Similar defacement of writing occurs when the reporter replaces simple prepositions and conjunctions with phrases like the following:

with respect to	for the reason that
in view of	in the nature of
along the lines of	in the neighborhood of
in order to	for the purpose of
with reference to	with a view to
in the event that	on the grounds that

Sometimes these wordy expressions give a better rhythm to a sentence, but generally it is best to avoid them. Using such conjunctions and prepositions as *like, for, because, if,* and *so* instead of the cumbersome phrases speeds reading and saves time.

Professional Jargon. One of the most infectious word diseases which may weaken prose is the specialized terminology of the professions and sciences. It is as stealthy as a virus and as habit-forming as dope. The writer often does not know he has caught the disease, so accustomed is he to repeating phrases and terms he has picked up in court opinions, scientific papers, and governmental reports.

The jargon is sometimes traditional, as in law, which has continued to employ the Latin terms in use in medieval courts: *amicus curiae, capias, caveat, certiorari, corpus delicti, habeas corpus, mandamus, mittimus, nolle prosequi, nolo contendere, praecipe, quo warranto, remittur, subpoena.*

In the exact sciences and medicine the specialized terminology is needed so that all who engage in them will know precisely the meanings of the words used. When scientsts need a term not already in use, they prefer to create an entirely new word from Greek and Latin stems rather than use an English word or word combination. Hence, we have telephone instead of "far-speaker," geology instead of "earth-study," ophthalmology instead of "the study of eye diseases."

Unfortunately, the social sciences have imitated the exact sciences in developing their own specialized language. Much of it seems to be due not so much to the need for being precise—none of the social sciences is an exact science—as to the desire to appear profound. Many an abstruse article in the scholarly journals, after the meaning has been wrung out, is found to consist of nothing but commonplaces.

Of the specialized jargons, the one that causes most trouble for newsmen is the variety known as "federalese" or "governmentese." Maury Maverick, when he was a member of the House of Representatives, coined the word "gobbledygook" to describe the muddy prose of government reports, but perhaps the best word for it is "bafflegab," the creation of an unknown genius.

The aim of the bafflegabber is to make plain English incomprehensible; the job of the reporter is to translate bafflegab into plain English. The bafflegab artist never uses a short word when a longer one is available: he writes "directive" rather than "order," "category" rather than "class," "units of currency" rather than "money," "integrate" rather than "combine." He prefers the passive voice to the active and circumlocutions to direct statements. He would find the sentence, "Hens lay eggs," too simple. The novice in bafflegab would phrase it: "Egg-laying characterizes hens." The true expert would write: "Gallinaceous ovulation is effected by hens."

Freshness in Writing. Perhaps the chief factor that makes journalistic writing hard to read is staleness and uniformity. The reporter, working under pressure, does not have time to choose words for their meaning or invent phrases that will make his information vivid and clear. His stories are built by tacking together prefabricated phrases.

No one, of course, can write without using clichés. Even in discussing them and warning against them, a person is likely to use the hackneyed terms himself: bromides, rubberstamps, stereotypes, secondhand expressions, prefabricated phrases. If they must be used, they should be used sparingly.

One type of cliché—the overworn figure of speech—has been attacked so much in English composition courses that only the most unperceptive would use them. These include such well-known metaphors, similes, and word combinations as the following:

babbling brook	cool as a cucumber
murmuring stream	busy as a bee
bolt from the blue	nipped in the bud
grim reaper	blushing bride
Jupiter Pluvius	bated breath
sea of upturned faces	hale and hearty
cloak of secrecy	bright and shining
watery grave	green-eyed monster

Actually, some figures of speech can be employed without loss of vividness when they have become so familiar that they have the effect of an ordinary word. They include what are known technically as dying metaphors: iron resolution, stepping stone, in the spotlight, sifting of evidence. Many of our common words are dead metaphors: whiskey, which means "water of life"; language, which means "tongue"; mystery, which means "close mouthed."

In journalistic writing the reporter is not so apt to bore with trite figures of speech as he is with secondhand phrases conventionalized by other news writers. They are so familiar that the reporter is almost as unaware of using them as he is of breathing. Some examples are:

one of the most outstanding	play host to
took the witness stand	made his appearance
rushed to the hospital	fire which broke out
prospects were bright	completely destroyed
plans will be made	refused to comment
took action to	at a late hour
launch a drive	authority on the subject
conduct a probe	one of the most successful
explore every avenue	well-known civic leader

Frequently, reporters are so accustomed to such expressions that they seem to be unconscious of their meaning. For instance, newspapers in small cities with only one police station often carry a statement that an arrested man was taken to "headquarters." Police may be falsely described as "grilling a suspect," a building damaged by fire as being "gutted," a saloon after a brawl as being "a shambles." The only cure for this is for reporters to pay more attention to the words they use.

ASSIGNMENTS

1. Using either the Flesch or Gunning formula, score some of your news stories for readability. Are they easy to read, fairly easy to read, or hard to read? Rewrite the story of greatest difficulty to make it easier to read.

2. Rewrite the sentences below to correct faults discussed in the text.

a. Six accidents have occurred since yesterday, four of them the result of automobiles skidding on ice-covered streets and two from falls on slippery sidewalks.

b. Roberts pulled one of the greatest upsets of the day as he raced the supposedly unbeatable Masters to win by ten yards.

c. The total includes 8,000 pounds for entertaining royal and overseas guests, hiring cars, and railway expenses.

d. The opening of the new building also opens the permanent U. N. headquarters for the first time to full-scale tourist visits.

e. A procedure is now being formulated which is expected to be more concentrated than the system used last fall.

f. Cutting China's population in percentage figures, 40 percent opposed the Communists, 20 percent were indifferent, and 40 percent interested, the speaker said.

g. In the hope that a larger audience will be able to hear the lecture, attempts are being made to schedule it in the fieldhouse instead of the university auditorium.

h. Middletown ranks ninth among the cities in the state in traffic safety, with Smithville having the best record.

i. The president appointed a committee of three persons to study the problem. The three members are Arthur A. Peters, chairman, Theodore Walsh, and A. M. Powers.

j. Moscow's action was regarded as being tantamount to de jure recognition of the new state.

k. A defense witness in the trial of Arthur Parker for the murder of James O. Adams testified today that he had made threats against the Middletown farmer the day before the body was found.

l. Plans are being made by the Chamber of Commerce to hold a celebration in connection with the opening of the new bridge across the Red River to traffic.

m. He is the author of three novels, numerous magazine articles, and has written radio and television shows.

n. The workshop, conducted by Dr. Allan B. Cain, associate professor of dramatics, Stewart Jones, Martha Cook, and William Dunn, graduate students, will be held Thursday.

o. Born in Springfield, Mo., he was married February 13, 1954, to Miss Janet Arbuckle in Philadelphia.

3. Readability tests show that the stories below are difficult to read. Rewrite them to make them easy to read.

WASHINGTON—The house foreign affairs committee today capitulated to administration pressure and eliminated a provision written into the foreign aid bill yesterday which would have denied further assistance to countries exporting to the Soviet bloc items on the American embargo list.

The committee, which yesterday subjected the administration's $4,860,000,000 authorization measure to several other crippling amendments, came close today to making a nearly $1,000,000,000 reduction in the $3,000,000,000 which the White House has requested for military aid in the 1957 fiscal year.

Rep. Richards (D.-S.C.), chairman of the committee, who said he himself favors a "substantial cut" in military assistance, said it was likely there will be another attempt to push a heavy slash through when the committee resumes action on the measure Tuesday.

WASHINGTON—The Defense Department, increasingly perturbed by persistent loss of highly skilled personnel in the armed services, has proposed to Congress that special financial bait be offered to the men whose retention in the service is most wanted. The money required would come from the existing re-enlistment compensation fund—but only because men in service who do not have the critically needed skills would not get any such reward for re-enlistment.

The proposal, advanced by Carter L. Burgess, assistant secretary of defense for manpower, marks a considerable departure from tradition in that it would provide different compensation for servicemen within the same rank group, and thereby would establish a premium on something other than faithful performance of assigned duty. Burgess defends his proposal stoutly.

"Right now we pay the same re-enlistment compensation to all men of the same grade and length of service, regardless of the demand for them," he explained today. "As demands inside the service change, we generate excesses of certain talents.

"But unless the individual has capacity for retraining, it may be that he should no longer remain in the service. This would break with the traditional view that a man who has merely kept out of trouble has a place in the service as long as he elects to stay. It is time to break with such tradition.

"We have no place for the half-lazy, the half-talented. I visualize a system with flexibility. It would pay a higher re-enlistment compensation to the individuals in short-supply, and a lower amount to those in over-supply."

The manpower chief pointed out that Congress already has approved distinctions in favor of special talents whereby doctors and dentists get extra pay.

He wants to go further to meet a situation in which the combat arms today are 25 percent short in men qualified for the three top-pay grades, and 25 percent long in purely administrative specialists.

4. As a class project, choose from a newspaper twenty words that might be considered difficult for readers. Use each in a sentence and list beneath four choices of words that might explain the unfamiliar word in the sentence; only one of the choices, however, should be suitable. Each class member should submit the test to ten persons and have them check what they think is the correct word under each sentence. What do your findings indicate about the newspaper's estimate of the level of knowledge of its readers? A sample test question is given below:

He described the riot as one of the most *sanguinary* in the history of the state.

The word in italics means:

a. horrible
b. bloody
c. indefensible
d. serious

CHAPTER 12

NEWS IN TERMS OF PEOPLE

The Rise of Human Interest

LINCOLN STEFFENS, summing up his experiences as a financial reporter, wrote: "The human side of Wall Street was only gossip which made good stories to tell in the city room after the paper went to press or to entertain people at dinner."

Like Steffens, most reporters have a repertoire of good stories to tell that do not find a place in their newspaper. They do not consider as news the personal details they know about the people who make the news.

This does not mean that newspapermen do not appreciate the value and appeal of stories about people. Newspapers for many years have printed reports, in the form of the human-interest story, which emphasize the people involved in an event. The New York *Sun* is one of the famous American newspapers because it originated this type of journalism in the 1830's and developed it into an art during the editorship of Charles A. Dana in the 1890's.

But human-interest news has primarily been looked upon as something apart from straight news. Thus, Frank Luther Mott in *The News in America* defines it as "a report which is interesting not because of the importance of the specific event or situation reported, but because it is amusing or pathetic or striking or significant as a bit of the texture of our human life." He cites as examples a blind man, selling pencils on a street corner, who has a word of philosophical advice for those who drop a nickel into his tin cup; a girl who, discovering after boarding a bus that in her hurry to make it she had put her dress on backwards, draws her arms out of the sleeves and with a wiggle and a twist reverses it; and a three-year-old on a hot afternoon who has removed her clothes to play in a street puddle and is the victim of a mock arrest by a policeman.

Such events are obviously not important news. They could be omitted from the newspaper and their absence would make no difference to anyone. Their purpose, unlike the regular run of the news, is to entertain, not to inform.

Another conception of human-interest news is expressed by Helen MacGill Hughes in *News and the Human Interest Story*. She extends the term to include the reports about crime and scandal exploited in the yellow press of the 1890's and the tabloids of a later era. In these the concern is not with the trivial happenings of life, but with the tragic and the violent. In her opinion such reports constitute a form of popular literature, or, as Silas Bent termed them, "the printed folklore of the factory age."

It remained for *Time* magazine, when it was established March 3, 1923, consciously to make human interest an integral part of the reporting of important news. In its twenty-fifth anniversary issue the magazine, referring to its founders' original prospectus, described the role of people in events:

> News is made not by "forces" or governments or classes, but by individual people. The world's movers and shakers, said the prospectus, are "something more than stage figures with a name. It is important to know what they drink. It is more important to know to what gods they pray and what kind of fights they love." Stories told in flesh and blood terms would get into the readers' minds when stories told in journalistic banalities would not.

In recent years there has been an increasing demand for newspapers to report the news in flesh and blood terms. A group of Nieman Fellows at Harvard University, for example, urged in the book, *Your Newspaper:*

> The news should be told, whenever feasible, in terms of people— those who make the news and those who read it. As to the former, the paper will try to sketch in each important news-making individual's character, motives and orientation. A statesman who forms a foreign policy, or a scientist who makes some new discovery, is in a sense more interesting, and significant, than his policy or his discovery. The statesman, for instance, representing a geographical section, a system of education, a class, an environment, a point of view, sums up in his own dramatic person the conflicts and influences that led to the policy. Explaining the man helps to explain the policy in human terms.

This is undeniably true, but there is a question of the extent to which the newspaper reporter can follow this advice. He writes by the clock, and ordinarily has only a few minutes to do his story. He has no time to produce the article—a careful blend of description, character portrayal, background and exposition—that his compeer on the weekly magazine can write. Moreover, since his information must be gathered hastily, he can obtain oftentimes only the surface facts, and he frequently must rely on secondhand sources for his information, thereby missing many of the particularizing details that would make his story more interesting.

There is a question, too, as to whether the reporter should attempt to interpret a person's actions by his psychological motivations. To try to do so opens a broad, indefinite area of speculation that may result in gross error and misunderstanding.

Another danger in this approach to news is that it might reduce all news to mere gossip about people. The Nieman Fellows cite science news as a field that can be made more meaningful by writing about the scientist as a person. Scientists themselves say that is just what is wrong about science reporting: instead of writing an enlightening account of an experiment or a discovery, reporters do a human-interest story about the scientist—that he sometimes is so intent on his researches he forgets to eat, that his favorite dog is a spaniel, that he prefers a pipe to a cigaret. Nothing could be more irrelevant. What the reader wants to know is how the discovery or experiment affects him.

Finally, to tell all the news in terms of people would be an impossible and pointless task. Most people who make news do so every day. It would be redundant to describe or psychoanalyze them in every story.

Although the human side of the news must often be relegated to the fringes of daily journalism—to the "human-interest story," the interview, the sidebar or follow-up biographical story, and eyewitness reports—the reporter can sometimes inject the "human" details into a straight news report simply by his writing technique. Then, too, the inverted-pyramid, impersonal news formula can be abandoned more often than it is for feature treatment. Such story telling can help solve a problem that has perplexed editors—how to get people to read the important, but often dull news of the day: developments in foreign policy, fiscal programs of government, and problems of labor and management.

Readability and Human Interest

Both Rudolf Flesch and Robert Gunning, in developing their tests for readability, included as a mark of readable style the number of references to people—the more personal references in an article the easier it is to read. Flesch, in addition, provided for a count of the number of sentences with human interest.

Flesch's category of human-interest words includes names, personal pronouns, the word "people" itself and all words that have masculine or feminine gender. He considered as human-interest sentences those addressed to the reader (questions, commands, requests) and sentences addressed to one or more listeners quoted in the text.

The journalistic canon of objectivity, which requires the reporter to keep himself out of his story, has been one of the chief influences in the development of a journalistic style that discourages the use of human-interest words and sentences. To give an appearance of objectivity, the news writer tends to overuse the passive voice and to write in generalities and abstractions. He sees the event, not the people; the organization or the group, not its members. He writes: "The 30th annual district meeting of Kiwanis clubs will open here Friday with an attendance of 500 expected," instead of: "Five hundred people will attend the 30th annual district meeting of Kiwanis clubs opening here Friday." He writes: "Thirty polio cases were reported in the county today," instead of: "Thirty children in the county are ill with polio today." He writes: "Two hundred arrests for traffic violations were made in the city during July," instead of: "Police arrested 200 drivers for traffic violations during July."

That the writer can create a little human interest, even in a routine story, by keeping his eye on the people and mentioning them can be seen in a comparison of the two stories below:

The police drive aimed at cracking down on speeders and drunken drivers continued Sunday with the arrest of 32 persons and the issuing of 200 tickets for moving violations.

These arrests were made and tickets were issued late Saturday and early Sunday following the arrest of 29 persons and the issuing of approximately 200 tickets late Friday and early Saturday.

Police continued their drive against speeders and drunken drivers Sunday when they arrested 32 persons and issued tickets to almost 200 other persons.

Their latest crackdown came late Saturday and early Sunday. They arrested 29 persons and issued about 200 tickets late Friday and early Saturday.

Members of the traffic bureau

Members of the traffic bureau used two cars and 20 motorcycles in various parts of the city, mainly in the City Park section and around Chef Menteur highway.

Officers said teen-agers and young college students were among those arrested and some of them were caught racing in two cars traveling as fast as 80 or 90 miles an hour.

The drive will continue with special emphasis being placed on the week ends when most of the speeding and other dangerous driving practices are noted on the city's streets, police said.

used two cars and 20 motorcycles in various parts of the city, mainly in the City Park section and on Chef Menteur highway.

Officers said their arrests included teen-agers and college students, some of whom were racing in cars going as fast as 80 or 90 miles an hour.

Police said they will continue their drive, placing special emphasis on week ends when they have found that most speeding and other dangerous driving practices occur.

The "You" Approach in Writing

Flesch's second method for measuring human-interest elements—the percentage of sentences addressed directly to the reader—is more difficult to achieve in the news story than is the frequent mention of people. Since it is the function of the news story to impart information, the "you" approach of direct address and command cannot often be used. But there is no question as to its desirability: it is an easy method of obtaining immediate rapport with the reader, of involving him in the story.

The report of scientists, for example, on the dangers of an atomic bomb may be of compelling interest merely as figures and statistics; the number of probable casualties from a bomb dropped on a metropolitan area may even appall the reader. But he still may be reluctant or unable to include himself among the statistics. He cannot avoid doing so if the "you" approach is used, as in the following opening of a story in the Chicago *Daily News:*

> Two and a third million Chicagoans would still be able to breathe and crawl if an H-bomb walloped Chicago.
> Your chances of being among them are two out of three.
> You may even be among the 45 percent who escape to points 15 miles from the Loop.
> Not that lucky, you could still be among 245,000 surviving casualties—with injuries ranging from splinter cuts to severe burns.
> If you're among some 97,000 requiring hospitalization, you stand

a 70 percent chance of being evacuated to suburban area hospital units.

If not, then you'll hope that emergency first aid stations are still operative. . . .

Though the "you" approach is effective and easy to employ, it is not, of course, the only way to make the reader feel involved in the news. Paul R. Mickelson, general news editor of the Associated Press, warned against overuse of it in a comment on one of Flesch's readability reports, remarking that it applies best to feature writing or to columns. "The point is," he added, "we do not want to break out in a rash of first and second person stories about things that call merely for simple, straightforward news writing."

Instead of addressing the reader familiarly, the reporter can bring him into the story by showing how the event may affect his daily life. For example, an electric utility may ask for a rate increase. The hearing before the regulating board or commission is likely to bring out that the increase of 5 percent, say, will mean an extra income of $1,000,000 a year for the corporation. The story will come home to the reader if the news is translated into terms of his own living—that the increase will add 50 cents to his monthly bill.

The hottest political issue in Pennsylvania one year was whether the state, to obtain $500,000,000 in new revenue, should adopt an income tax or increase the sales tax. The public was assaulted with figures aimed to show that the tax would or would not bring in the needed revenue, that it would harm business, or that it was unfair to special segments of the populace. The standard argument against the sales tax was that it placed a bigger burden on the small wage earner than on the man who had a big income. The stories that really brought the issue home to the reader were those that purported to show how each tax would hit persons of various income levels.

The Story-Telling Technique

Newspapers could well adapt, more often than they do, the treatment of problems in human terms which magazines have developed in recent years. If a farm magazine wants to show how supplemental irrigation may increase crop yields and income, it publishes not an article that generalizes about the topic, but one that *tells a story* about one farmer and how he profited by adopting the new practice. A popular magazine article, in presenting the problem of over-coming physical handicaps or illness, does not devote many words to national statistics on how many people have been rehabilitated and to descriptions of rehabilitation programs in general; rather, it *tells a story* about one person who has overcome his difficulties.

The story-telling technique can be used in newspaper writing. Below is a conventional newspaper report on medical research lead-ing to a new and successful treatment for a disease. It is undramatic and uninteresting.

> A new application of antibiotics which may reduce the dangers of colon resection and which is expected to change ideas on how and why some complications occur in large bowel surgery is re-ported in the Annals of Surgery this month as the discovery of researchers at the Louisiana State University school of medicine.
>
> This technique, which may have application in all types of large bowel surgery, is one of the means to prevent postsurgical leaks from the colon.
>
> "It is one additional safety factor to those undergoing surgery of the large bowel and will have great benefit in battlefield surgery and in the surgery of those who have received an injury to the bowel as the result of an accident," said Dr. Isidore Cohn Jr., who conducted the research with Dr. James D. Rives, head of the department of surgery, and medical student Charles D. Langford, of Gibsland.
>
> The new practice has already been used at Charity Hospital, and in one case has been definitely credited with the saving of a life, he said. . . .

There is no point in continuing the quotation, for by this time the reporter has probably lost his reader, in spite of the fact that medicine is one of the most enthralling of scientific topics.

Dealing with almost exactly the same sort of scientific report, the Associated Press story below departs from the news-writing formula. Human-interest appeal is assured because the story focuses on one person and tells how a new treatment cured him.

> BALTIMORE—A nine-year-old boy lay critically ill in Syden-ham Hospital here. He suffered from a skin eruption with a secondary infection that would ordinarily lead to death.
>
> Doctors administered huge doses of wonder drugs streptomycin and penicillin. They did not help.
>
> Then they called Johns Hopkins physicians who have been experimenting with a new, powerful germ-killer, polymyxin.
>
> The Hopkins scientists injected the drug, in the form of a white

powder, underneath his skin. Three days later, the eruption began to clear. He was well after eight days.

The unnamed boy was the first human to be treated with polymyxin. In the last several months, similar speedy cures have been effected by the drug in cases of undulant fever, whooping cough, certain types of blood poisoning and meningitis.

The Hopkins doctors—Perrin H. Long, professor of preventive medicine, and Morton S. Bryer, Eleanor A. Bliss and Emanuel Schoenbach—told of the first cure last night in giving their preliminary conclusions as to the usefulness of polymyxin in a series of papers before the Hopkins Medical Society.

They reported the drug may lead to a final triumph over bubonic plague. It will be sent to India soon to find how it works against that ancient curse of mankind.

Typhoid fever, various urinary tract infections, tularemia (rabbit fever) and certain deadly infections are among the ailments caused by the germs against which the doctors said they found the new drug "uniquely effective."

One big advantage polymyxin has over other recent "wonder drugs" is that the germs it attacks do not develop a resistance to it, the doctors reported.

The trite, the tawdry, the dull can be made interesting if described in terms of people. This is also true of stories about a holiday or celebration, events which are especially difficult to make interesting and readable. How can anyone say anything fresh about Christmas, Thanksgiving, the Fourth of July? The answer—tell a story about people—is illustrated by Miller Davis' Memorial Day story written for the Chicago *Daily News:*

Why do we have Memorial Day?

Mr. and Mrs. John A. Ingram never explain why.

Monday they will climb into their little car and drive 157 miles from Hammond, Ind., to Danville, Ill.

Mrs. Ingram will wear a new hat for the trip, and she will carry a small bouquet.

About noon, just off State Route 1, they will walk through the gate of a small cemetery A few yards across the neatly clipped grass is the grave of their son, John Howard Ingram.

For a moment, Ingram will just stand there; perhaps he will twist a few weeds from around the small, marble gravestone.

Mrs. Ingram will place the flowers near the headstone, and then she will kneel and whisper a prayer.

A few moments later they will climb back into their car and drive home to 1313 Harrison, Hammond.

This is Memorial Day for a small, gray-haired woman and her husband, a mechanic at Inland Steel. There is no bitterness; they have come to understand the reasons.

Eleven years ago Saturday Johnny Ingram was blown out of the sky. He was pilot of the lead plane in the largest B-17 raid of World War II.

Eight other men were in the plane when German fighters reeled out of the sun and literally sliced the bomber in half with 20-mm. shells.

"We heard about it over the radio," relates his mother. "They said that 2,000 American bombers had just destroyed the oil refineries near Madgeburg, Germany.

"They didn't say, of course, that Johnny was dead.

"We learned that 48 hours later. The War Department sent us a long telegram."

Three crew members survived; they jumped just before the B-17 exploded.

"I remember seeing Johnny for the last time," recalls Eddie Czyz, of 60 W. 15th St., Chicago Heights.

"He saved our lives, you know; he put the plane on automatic pilot. This kept it right side up so we could clear the ship with our chutes.

"I don't remember much after that," Czyz says. "My chute became entangled and I fell pretty fast.

"But Johnny stuck with the plane; he was in the nose when it blew up."

Czyz, 34, remembers Johnny Ingram as a kid who loved life and lived it full force.

"He never did anything half way. He made certain we smacked those oil refineries. He was the best pilot I ever knew."

I remember a younger Johnny Ingram, his roommate in college.

A grinning cyclone who burned up Indiana basketball floors, he was all-state at Hammond High in 1939 and later starred on the Wabash College teams of 1940-1941.

Johnny wanted to be a coach and an English instructor.

But most of all he wanted to live in Hammond and rear a family.

He never got the chance; he was married to pretty Aleta Hoeppner for only 14 months before the fatal mission.

The shock of Johnny's death hurt his father most.

"I thought my husband might never get over it," says Johnny's mother. "Then one day I told him how Johnny would have felt about it.

"Johnny would have said, 'Dad, don't be unhappy. You know how I hate unhappiness.' "

Then smiling and clear-eyed, she adds thoughtfully:

"You know, it isn't Memorial Day that causes that deep-down, inside ache.

"It is the ordinary days—and the quiet house. You never quite escape that.

"But you pray, and it helps. It really helps."

ASSIGNMENTS

1. Clip several examples of stories that you think are successful in conveying the news in terms of the people involved, and describe the techniques and methods used by the writers.

2. (a) Using the Flesch formula, rate three news stories according to their use of personal words. Count first the number of words in the articles and then the number of personal words. If there are 6 personal words per 100 words, an article can be read with ease and interest; if there are fewer, the article lacks human interest.

(b) Rewrite the article with the lowest human-interest score, putting in more personal words. What is the percentage of personal words in your rewritten article?

3. Clip a straight news story which you think can be improved through the use of the human-interest approach, and rewrite it.

4. Write a feature article about an anniversary or celebration in which the event's universal significance is expressed through the telling of a story about individuals and their observance of the day.

CHAPTER 13

AS NEWS EVENTS DEVELOP

Timing in News Stories

EVENTS ARE NO RESPECTERS of newspaper deadlines and editions. They happen, or are in the process of happening, all the time, and the reporter is faced with numerous problems in handling stories which are still developing at the time his newspaper goes to press. His problems are complicated by the fact that his account of an event may reach his readers several hours after he has written it.

Two types of stories, from the standpoint of time element, are fairly easy to write: the advance story, or announcement of an event scheduled to take place, and the report of an event that has taken place. If the reporter is assigned to write, for the Monday issue of his newspaper, an advance story about a convention to be held on Thursday, he faces no difficulty: he merely uses the future tense to tell when and where the sessions will be held, who will speak, and what business will be taken up. In writing an account of the convention for the issue appearing on Friday, he merely uses the past tense to tell what happened.

But if he covers the convention for a Thursday afternoon newspaper, while the sessions are still in progress, he has a much more difficult job. If, writing for a noon deadline, he confines himself to what happened at the morning session, he may have very little of interest to report. Since his newspaper will not reach readers for several hours, he cannot use the future tense to tell what is to happen in the afternoon. By the time the subscribers get the paper, the events will already have happened. Nor can he safely use the past tense to say that scheduled events took place. Something might happen to prevent their occurrence, and his report would be false. In

this situation he writes an anticipatory story which, though written in advance of an event, conveys the impression it is an actual report of something that has happened.

Newspapers frequently have occasion to publish accounts of events that have previously been fully reported in another newspaper. Since many readers will have read the earlier stories, the newspaper late with the news must print stories that give the appearance, at least, of containing fresh information. Techniques have been developed for doing this in a type of story known as the rewrite or second-day story.

Another important technical problem in writing is handling the follow-up story. Many events are of such a nature that there are new developments every day or perhaps several times a day, and the newspaper attempts to keep abreast of them by printing accounts of these new developments as they occur. The principal writing problems here are to present the new developments and relate them to previous happenings in such a way as to be quickly comprehended by the reader.

Metropolitan newspapers, which publish several editions during the day, and press associations, which serve newspapers across the country with different deadlines, have an especially difficult problem in keeping abreast of rapidly developing events. They have worked out special techniques for handling these in what are called continuous action or running stories.

Anticipatory Stories

Anticipatory stories, and other types of stories which involve keeping abreast of happenings, are more often found in afternoon newspapers than in morning newspapers. Since most of the nation's activity goes on during the daytime hours, the writers on the morning paper can give a complete report of the previous day's events. The reporter for the afternoon newspaper, however, must frequently gather information and write his stories while they are still happening. The morning newspaper reporter most often faces similar problems in writing accounts of night meetings, speeches, and sports for editions which, though they carry the next morning's date, appear before midnight.

The reporter must watch his tenses carefully in writing an advance account of an event which will have ended by the time the

newspaper reaches the reader. Suppose, for instance, he is writing a
report of a convention held during that day for the home-delivery
edition of a newspaper. The reporter writes his story for a 1:30 p. m.
deadline, but most of his readers will not see it until after 5 p. m.

One writing device which resolves this problem is to use the present tense, a practice more common in newspapers now than formerly because of the influence of radio newscasts. The following
lead, making use of the progressive form of the verb in the present
tense, was used by an afternoon newspaper:

> The Eagles are climaxing their 48th international convention
> here today in a gala spirit with a parade, boat race, dancing, and
> fireworks.

But the present tense cannot be used throughout such a story, and
so the news writer overcomes the time problem for the afternoon
events by the use of such expressions as "was scheduled," "is expected," "was to be," and "was planned." For example, the second
paragraph after the above lead was:

> The paraders were to begin their march at 1 p. m. Among the
> 116 units are 32 musical groups, 16 floats, and a host of uniformed
> aerie and auxiliary drill teams and degree teams, drum corps,
> and variety units.

For events scheduled that night, however, by which time it can be
assumed that readers have received their newspaper, the news writer
uses the future tense, as in the following:

> A free outdoor show, "Salute to Pittsburgh," will be presented
> at 7:30 p. m. in Point Park. An illuminated barge at the wharf
> steps will serve as the stage. On the program will be Ray Eberle
> and his orchestra and the Fontaine Sisters, vocalists.

Reports of speeches are still another frequent occasion for stories
which jump the gun. Most speakers provide the press with advance
copies of their speech, and the report can be written and printed
before delivery, if it is properly qualified early in the story. The
conventional qualification is a statement that the speaker made the
remarks in a speech prepared for delivery.

> WASHINGTON—Secretary of Labor Mitchell said today that
> two-thirds of the nearly two million job accidents recorded last
> year could have been prevented through greater safety efforts.
> The accidents resulted in 14,200 deaths, he said.
> Mitchell's remarks were prepared for the opening session of

President Eisenhower's three-day conference on occupational safety. Eisenhower also was due to address the more than 2,000 business, labor and farm leaders. . . .

In writing any story in which the situation is likely to change before the newspaper reaches the readers, the reporter must employ a phraseology that will not create the impression of completed action. For example, the following wording would not do for a newspaper account:

State Police are searching the Susquehanna River below the Shamokin dam for the body of a man thrown into the stream when his automobile struck the side of a bridge about 10 a. m. today.

This phraseology is dangerous because police may locate the body and end their search before the news report gets into print. To anticipate this contingency, the reporter should write the lead as follows:

State Police began a search of the Susquehanna River below the Shamokin dam shortly after 10 a. m. today for the body of a man thrown into the stream when his automobile struck the side of a bridge.

The story written for an early edition of a newspaper before any developments have occurred must consist for the most part of background information. The handling of such a story is illustrated in the following press dispatch which cleared the wire at 9:28 a. m. for use in early editions of afternoon newspapers.

PITTSBURGH—The powerful wage policy committee of the United Steelworkers meets again today to work out demands the USW will present to the basic steel industry in coming contract negotiations.

After a session yesterday of the 170-man committee, David J. McDonald, USW president, said he was hopeful that an agreement could be worked out with the steel industry "well in advance" of the June 30 contract expiration date.

The union's 39-member executive board unanimously approved contract proposals yesterday and recommended adoption.

Provisions of the proposals were not disclosed, but it is generally believed that a substantial wage increase, a supplemental unemployment benefit program, improved insurance benefits and premium pay for weekend work are included.

McDonald said the policy committee is "taking very seriously" a plan for Saturday and Sunday premium pay. He added that union demands will be based on the industry's current boom and reports of record profits.

If agreements are not reached with 172 basic steel firms by midnight June 30, the USW is free to call a strike of some 650,000 union members. . . .

Second-Day Stories and Rewrites

The journalistic emphasis on recency as an element of news has resulted in the practice of attempting to give day-old happenings a "today" angle in newspapers late with the news. This is especially true in cities which have morning and afternoon newspapers. An event occurring during the night is first reported in the morning newspaper; if it is of sufficient importance, the afternoon newspaper of the same day will also carry a story about it.

If there are new developments not covered in the morning newspaper's account, the afternoon newspaper of course emphasizes these in its follow-up story of the event. In cases where there is nothing new to report, the afternoon newspaper will seek to maintain interest in the event by giving it a different treatment. Such an account will also provide information for those persons who do not read the morning newspaper or for those who may have missed it.

Most rewrites and second-day stories are written from clippings from another newspaper. The city editor hands these out to rewritemen or reporters covering the runs which were the source of the stories, with the notation that they should be rewritten or followed up. The reporter should seldom do a rewrite without checking the indicated source of information by telephone, for there may be new developments that justify a follow-up story rather than a rehash of old information. Frequently, too, he may obtain different particulars or fuller information that will make for an improved story. Moreover, by checking the facts himself, he does not run the risk of repeating errors committed by the reporter on the other newspaper.

To make the rewrite sound like a fresh story, the writer should first see if the original story missed the feature. If so, the rewriteman's task is simple: all he has to do is recast the story, playing up what is in his opinion the most important or most interesting element. Even if the writer agrees with the emphasis in the first story, he may nevertheless discover still another angle. How a new approach can be used in a rewrite is shown in the righthand story below:

ORIGINAL STORY

The Masters Super Mart was robbed of about $150 last night by an armed man who forced Henry R. Masters, the owner, to give him money from two cash registers.

Masters told police he was getting ready to close the store about 9 p. m. when the bandit entered.

Pointing a gun at the store owner and T. R. Adams, clerk, the bandit ordered Masters to open the cash registers. He then took Adams' apron, put it on, and ordered him to the basement.

After the bandit got the money, he told Masters to go to the basement and have the clerk return to the store. About that time Fred R. Smith, 2201 E. First Street, a customer, entered and asked for Masters.

"He's downstairs, but he'll be back in a minute," the bandit replied.

As Smith decided to wait, the bandit told him: "I'm going off duty now." He removed the apron, placed it on a pile of oranges, said "good night" and walked out.

REWRITTEN STORY

A bandit who donned a store clerk's white apron and waited on a customer made off with $150 in a robbery at the Masters Super Mart last night.

The bandit entered the store just before closing time at 9 p. m. Pointing a gun, he told Henry R. Masters, the owner, to take the day's receipts from the cash registers. A clerk, T. R. Adams, was ordered to the store's basement after being told to hand over his apron.

Wearing the apron, the bandit stood by while Masters emptied the cash registers. Then he ordered Masters to the basement and told him to have the clerk return to the store.

Just then Fred R. Smith, 2201 E. First Street, entered the store and asked for Masters. The bandit told him the owner was downstairs and asked him to wait.

Then, taking off the apron, the bandit said it was time for him to go off duty. He said "good night" and left the store.

When there is no new angle in a second-day story, the time element may be omitted from the lead and the present or present perfect tense used:

WASHINGTON—A $125,203 grant to help 30 municipalities in Pennsylvania develop master plans and undertake general urban studies has been approved by the Urban Renewal Administration.

The agency said yesterday in a statement that the grant was awarded the Pennsylvania Department of Commerce, which will supplement the money with $128,000 from its own budget to extend the planning assistance to communities.

This method is perhaps better than attempting to give the story a spurious "today" angle in such beginnings as "James R. Pierce, president of the First National Bank, was dead today following . . ." or "A suit by Arthur A. Perkins asking damages of $10,000 from the

Intercity Transit Co. for injuries received in an accident last month was on file today in District Court."

Very often it is possible for the reporter to give the appearance of newness to a rewrite by indicating the next probable development. The reporter knows, for instance, that an arrest is followed by a hearing in court, an accident by an investigation, a crime by a search for the criminal, a death by a funeral. The following leads illustrate how the latest developments mentioned in the earlier story can be played up in the rewrite:

> Peter A. Warner, 23, arrested last night when he was captured inside a grocery store after breaking a rear window to gain entry, was to be given a hearing today in magistrate court.
>
> Fire department officials today continued their investigation of a blast, believed caused by escaping gas, which wrecked a five-room house last night at Fairview and Oakmont.
>
> A statewide search was under way today for two bandits who held up the branch bank of the First National Bank at Fairview and Lawrence yesterday afternoon and were last spotted on Highway 22 near Springdale.
>
> Funeral services will be arranged today for Robert J. Brown, president of the First National Bank and Middletown civic leader, who died yesterday morning after a long illness.

In striving for new approaches or searching for possible new developments for rewrites, the reporter should not depart from the truth. The following rewrite contains obvious fabrications that the writer put in his story to make it read as though there were new developments:

> A gasoline tank-truck driver today drew the grateful thanks of Allentown residents for courageously averting an explosion-fire.
>
> He is Robert A. Donovan, 220 N. First Street, whose big rig got out of control while ascending steep Lincoln Avenue yesterday afternoon.
>
> While Donovan desperately wrestled with his foot and emergency brakes, the tanker rolled backward down the busy street for 200 feet.
>
> Rather than abandon the rig and its lethal cargo, the driver swerved it into a fire hydrant where it came to a halt.

The story appears to be false on two counts: it is unlikely that the residents took any overt action at all to express their "grateful thanks," and the driver's feat, if it can be called that, hardly seems to be particularly courageous.

When publication of an account of an event has lowered its news value, it still may be of interest if rewritten in the form of a feature story. A morning newspaper carried a straight news report about an 18-month-old girl killed when she pulled away from her mother and ran into the path of a truck. Several paragraphs down in the story the information was given that the mother had taken the child downtown for her first visit to stores during the Christmas season. Rewritten as a short feature, the story was still front-page news for the afternoon newspaper:

> Yesterday had been a big day for 18-month-old Nancy Ann Springer of 400 S. First Street, College Heights.
> That was the day her mother, Mrs. Arthur A. Springer, had promised to take Nancy Ann on her first real Christmas shopping trip. And the occasion was fully up to expectations.
> But when it came time to go home about 2 p. m., Nancy Ann wanted just a few glimpses more. She pulled away as they waited for a street car at Second and Main and ran into the street.
> Mrs. Springer tried to catch her, but it was too late. Nancy Ann was crushed by a truck driven by Theodore A. Neill, 200 Westerly Drive, and was dead when taken to a doctor.

The most common method of rewriting is to condense the original story into a paragraph or two. The news interest has declined because of previous publication, and a boiled down story meets the newspaper's standard of completeness of coverage for subscribers who may not read the rival newspaper.

Another occasion for rewriting occurs when stories from out-of-town publications, wire service reports, and publicity releases contain a local angle. Take the case, for instance, of a wire service story on an organization's state convention: the telegraph editor, on discovering in the body of the story that a local resident has been elected to the office of vice president, gives the story to the city editor, who in turn directs a reporter or rewriteman to give it a local angle by placing in the lead the election of the home-town man to office.

Follow-Up Stories

The follow-up story differs from the rewrite or second-day story in that there are new developments to be included. It is both a reporting and a writing assignment: the reporter must obtain information about what happened after the first account of the event, then write it into a story.

Most stories describe not single-incident events but incidents which are part of a related series and which occur over a period of time ranging from a few hours, to months, and even years. The reporter has occasion to write follow-up stories more often than not.

For example, a robbery, because of new developments, may appear in the news for several months: the first story gives the details of the robbery as reported to police, and may be followed by stories reporting on the police investigation; the investigation may result in the arrest of two suspects; the suspects are given a hearing in a justice of the peace court and held for action by the grand jury; the grand jury indicts, and the accused men are given a trial; the trial lasts for several days, and the newspaper reports on what happens in the court; the accused are found guilty by the jury and sentenced by the judge; they ask for a new trial, which the judge denies; they appeal to the state supreme court, which upholds the conviction; finally, the two men begin serving their sentence in the penitentiary. Only then do they and the robbery cease to be news. But the story may be revived sometime in the future when the convicted men receive a parole, attempt to escape, or do something else that brings them into the news again.

New developments, however, may not be the only basis for a follow-up story. One may be warranted in cases when the reporter obtains information not available to the newsman who first covered the event, when he can correct errors in previously published articles, when he can find causes and motives not previously revealed, and when he can interpret the consequences or obtain opinions about the event from other persons.

The lead of the follow-up story should emphasize the most recent important development, and be written in such a way that the reader can understand immediately how it ties in with earlier developments. A person who enters a movie theater after the picture has started needs a few minutes to orient himself before the actions on the screen take on any meaning. The lead of a follow-up story orients the reader at once. This is usually accomplished by a brief tie-back:

> John H. Parker, 18, and Russell Anderson, 21, *arrested yesterday on a charge of robbing the Adams Jewelry Co. at gun point last week,* will be arraigned in justice of the peace court today.

If the tie-back is not enough to give the reader all the information needed for understanding the new development, the reporter should give additional background in the second paragraph:

> The two suspects were identified in a police line-up last night by Arthur B. Adams, owner of the store. Adams was alone in the store just before closing time last Thursday when the two men entered, pulled out guns, and ordered him to empty the cash register. They knocked him unconscious and fled with about $300 in money and miscellaneous jewelry valued at $3,000.

In all follow-ups the reporter faces a problem of determining how much background information is needed and where to put it in the story. If there has been a lapse of time between the publication of the earlier accounts and the current account, he must include enough background for those who may not have read the earlier stories and enough to recall previous developments to his readers' minds. This is a matter of judgment which can only be decided by individual cases; no general formula will fit all situations. It is probably better to give too much information than too little. Newspapers and press associations are careful to include an explanatory background statement early in the follow-up, even for events which have been given major news display day after day. The following example is from the New York Times:

> PARRIS ISLAND, S. C.—The commandant of the Marine Corps declared today that S/Sgt. Matthew C. McKeon deserved to lose a stripe and be transferred for stupidity.
> This was the punishment that Gen. Randolph McC. Pate declared he would mete out to the sergeant, were he to decide. McKeon is accused of manslaughter in the death of six recruits during a disciplinary march of 74 into Ribbon Creek April 8.

Once the reporter has identified the event for the reader by his tie-back in the lead and a background sentence or paragraph early in the story, he should continue with a follow-up account of the new developments. He may conclude his story with additional background details reported in earlier stories.

The Running Story

Keeping abreast of events as they occur poses difficult problems for metropolitan newspapers with several editions a day and press associations serving clients with different deadlines. Their accounts must be revised at intervals to include new developments, since readers should have the fullest report possible in their edition of the newspaper.

The handling of a running story by an afternoon newspaper with several editions may best be explained by example. The newspaper publishes four editions: one that goes to press at 9:30 a. m. for early street sales and distribution to other state towns and cities; one that goes to press at 11 a. m. for the noontime crowds on the street and for distribution to communities within the immediate trade area; one that goes to press at 2 p. m. for home delivery in the city; and one that goes to press at 3 p. m. for the homeward bound people at the end of their day's work.

At 9 a. m. the city editor receives a report that an abandoned manufacturing plant, a landmark in the city, is afire and likely to burn to the ground. There is no time for a detailed story, but the city editor can get a short account in the first edition, published under the heading, "Bulletin":

> One of the principal landmarks of the Southside, the huge former plant of Rogers, Inc., was threatened by a five-alarm fire which started shortly after 8 a. m. today. The blaze, started by a wrecker's acetylene torch, rapidly gained headway and within 30 minutes the whole west end of the block-long structure was in flames.

A bulletin, as used by newspapers and press associations, is a short, complete report of an event, comparable to an omnibus lead that answers the Five W's. Ordinarily, it is only one paragraph long.

By the time of the 11 a. m. edition deadline, the rewriteman receives enough information from reporters at the scene for a story:

> A fire which quickly engulfed the huge former plant of Rogers, Inc., one of the principal landmarks of the Southside, threatened this morning to spread to the business district west of the block-long structure.
>
> All city fire-fighting equipment and equipment from three suburban communities were concentrated in the area to keep the blaze from jumping across Wilson Avenue to a row of business establishments.
>
> The blaze was started by a workman employed by the Armstrong Wrecking Co., who was cutting out pipe at the southwest corner of the main building shortly after 8 a. m.
>
> His acetylene torch burned into an oil line containing residual oil. The pipeline became an incendiary tube which quickly set fire to the oil-soaked floors, walls, and beams of the structure.

Within minutes a roaring fire had mushroomed upward through the old five-story brick building and spread westward, first through a three-story brick addition, then to a separate one-story galvanized-metal warehouse, and finally to a three-story frame structure once used as an administration building.

So intense was the heat that firemen were driven back to fight the blaze from the middle of an open lot a half block away.

The fronts of the business structures across Wilson Avenue were scorched and their occupants forced to vacate. Some 20 families also fled apartments on the second and third floors above the stores.

A pillar of dense smoke from the fire rose nearly 1,000 feet in the air and could be seen from miles around. Flames could be seen from midcity buildings.

A crowd of more than 5,000 persons was attracted by the smoke and leaping flames and the constant shriek of sirens on newly arriving fire trucks.

People strained at police barricades to get a closer look, and the 50 foot-traffic patrolmen assigned to keep order could hardly hold them in check. Police sealed off from the public an area of two blocks on each side of the region in which the fire was concentrated.

For the 2 p. m. edition the newspaper carries a revised version which brings readers up to date on developments. Instead of throwing away the story in the 11 a. m. edition and writing a completely new story, the rewriteman uses the early account as the basis for his new version. By a new lead, inserts within the body of the story, and additions to the end of the story, he works in the new developments and details not available earlier. He preserves as much of the early story as possible to save time in writing and in setting material into type.

In bringing the fire story up to the minute, the rewriteman clips the story from the 11 a. m. edition and pastes it on a sheet of copy paper. Since there have been important developments after 11 a. m., he decides that the lead of the original story must be replaced. Using "New Lead—Fire" as the guideline, he turns out the following:

New Lead—Fire

The huge former plant of Rogers, Inc., one of the principal landmarks of the Southside, was destroyed by a roaring fire this morning.

Firemen, who fought the blaze for four hours before bringing it under control, succeeded in their efforts to keep the fire from jumping across Wilson Avenue to a row of stores, offices, and apartments.

All city fire-fighting equipment and equipment from three suburban communities were used to combat the blaze, which quickly engulfed the block-long building after being started by a wrecker's acetylene torch.

Four firemen were injured, none seriously, by falling debris when the west wall of the five-story structure fell outward into Wilson Avenue. Six other firemen were overcome by smoke but rejoined their companies after being treated by the fire department ambulance unit.

End New Lead Fire

Turn Rule

It will be noticed that "lead" as used above is not a paragraph summary of the story. All new material written as a precede for a revised story, even if it runs to several pages, is called the "lead." The designation, "Turn Rule," at the end is an instruction to the typesetter to turn a slug or line of type upside down at the end of the type matter. Printers, observing this, will know that other type matter must be placed at this point.

The rewriteman notices that the additional descriptive details he has received from reporters at the fire can be fitted in smoothly after paragraph five of the original story. He therefore writes an insert, as follows:

Insert A—Fire

The frame building burned to the ground, and the west wall of the five-story main building fell with a roar into Wilson Avenue at 11 a. m., leaving a huge pile of brick lying three quarters of the way across the street.

The main structure, an affair of many windows with metal casements, became an enormous open box of flames, its heavy steel girders white-hot and writhing in the midst after the roof collapsed at 11:15 a. m.

End Insert A—Fire

Turn Rule

If, at subsequent places in the story, the rewriteman should want to use other inserts, he would label them "Insert B—Fire," "Insert C—Fire," and so on.

The rewriteman decides to put the information about the injured firemen at the end of the first story. Labeling this material "Add All—Fire," he writes the following:

Add All—Fire

Firemen injured when the west wall of the building fell into Wilson Avenue were Oscar Barnes, 200 N. First Street; Alexander Casey, 1205 W. Maple; Charles A. Gunther, 3330 Lancaster Drive; and Peter O. Elkins, 923 N. Tenth Street. They were taken to Mercy Hospital.

On his pasted-up clipping of the story as it appeared in the 11 a. m. edition of the newspaper, the rewriteman crosses out the first two paragraphs and writes at the side: "Kill for new lead. Turn rule." Between paragraphs five and six he draws an arrow and writes the words: "Turn rule for insert A." This sheet, called a "markup," goes to the composing room to be used as a guide by printers in putting the new type matter at the proper places in the story and in killing parts of the earlier story no longer usable.

The newspaper emphasis on recency, which has resulted in revising stories from edition to edition, has one major danger: the real news is often buried in the body beneath a string of later and minor developments. This was a criticism made by the Associated Press Managing Editors Association in an analysis of the wire report. One editor commented: "My greatest complaint is against the A. P.'s desire to subordinate in the new leads the real news in order to play up the latest development." The criticism is well taken, since most people read only one edition of a newspaper a day. For them, stories should stress the most significant facts about an event and not the latest developments, if they are of only minor importance.

ASSIGNMENTS

1. From morning and afternoon newspapers published in the same city, clip three local rewrites and the original stories on which they were based. Indicate which stories are originals and which are rewrites, and give the name of the newspaper and the date. Describe the method used in disguising the rewrites, point out any discrepancies in facts, and criticize the rewrite job.

2. Clip from a newspaper three local stories that would appear as rewrites in another newspaper published in the same city. The events reported should not be ones likely to have new developments. Rewrite the stories, using methods described in the text to obtain freshness.

3. Clip a series of local stories illustrating the treatment of new

developments in follow-up stories. In marginal comments note the
new developments, the handling of background information, and
any discrepancies in facts between earlier and later stories.

4. Clip from successive editions of a newspaper (mail, early home,
final home, etc.) stories illustrating the handling of a continuous-
action story. On the early edition stories cross out the material killed
for the later editions and indicate the places where inserts and adds
have been used. Note particularly how the new material has been
written to dovetail with material in earlier stories.

5. The following story appeared in a morning newspaper:

> Top-level leaders in civic, industrial, labor, educational, and
> religious affairs will be asked today to come out in support of the
> city's $10,000,000 bond issue.
>
> Invitations to attend a luncheon at the Chamber of Commerce
> for a report on what the proposed five-year program of capital
> improvements will mean to the city have been issued to 50 com-
> munity leaders.
>
> Mayor Jerome Poole announced he will give a "pep talk" to
> get all organizations behind the bond issue to be voted on at a
> special election September 11.
>
> The city council approved the bond issue last week.
>
> Included in the projects that would be carried out if the bond
> issue passes are $2,000,000 for the municipal airport, $3,000,000
> for construction of a bridge across the White River at 36th Street,
> $1,500,000 for erection of a new junior high school and three
> grade schools, $1,500,000 for enlargement of the sewage disposal
> plant, and $2,000,000 for a municipal auditorium.
>
> "I want everyone in the city to have a chance to become ac-
> quainted with the details of the improvements program and to
> know what its completion will mean to the city's future," Mayor
> Poole said yesterday in announcing the meeting.
>
> "If the leaders in our community work actively for the program
> and if the citizens are adequately informed, I am sure that the
> bond issue will carry at the polls."
>
> Besides the mayor, speakers at the luncheon will include Preston
> A. Sawyer, president of the Chamber of Commerce, and Donald
> Flannagan, Ward Three councilman.
>
> Among the organizations invited to send representatives to the
> luncheon are the following:
>
> Central Labor Union, Building Trades Council, Retail Credit
> Association, Chamber of Commerce, Board of Realtors, Ministerial
> Alliance, Junior Chamber of Commerce, Kiwanis Club, Rotary
> Club, Lions Club, League of Women's Voters, Business and Pro-
> fessional Women's Club.
>
> Parent-Teacher Association, American Legion, Veterans of For-

eign Wars, Recreation Council, Hospitality Club, Community Forum, Economy League, Allied Arts Council, Flower and Garden Club Council, Federation of Women's Clubs.

Using only the facts contained in the story, do a rewrite for the early editions of the afternoon newspaper appearing the same day.

6. Using the new information given below, bring your story in the early editions up to date for the 2 p. m. edition with a new lead and whatever inserts will be needed. Indicate on your original story which paragraphs will be killed and the places where inserts will go.

In his talk to the approximately 50 persons attending the luncheon, Mayor Poole said that the five-year improvements program will require no boost in city taxes unless the voters fail to approve the $10,000,000 bond issue.

The mayor said: "If the bond issue fails at the polls, a tax increase will be needed in all probability because of the city's commitment to the bridge across the White River and the airport."

He also told the group: "I want each one of you to get acquainted with provisions of the improvements program, to tell your friends about it, and to do whatever you can as individuals and organizations to get out a big vote in favor of the bond issue."

Announcement that their organizations had gone on record in favor of the bond issue was made by John A. Freeman, Central Labor Union; Walter Acorn, Building Trades Council; and Preston A. Sawyer, Chamber of Commerce.

PART III

The Major News Assignments

CHAPTER 14

SPEECH REPORTS AND MEETINGS

Coverage of Speeches

LIKE DEATH AND TAXES, speeches are something that cannot be escaped. At any gathering a person attends—from a group of a half dozen to several thousand—he is likely to hear a speech. Even if he stays home, he can hardly turn on his radio or television set without tuning in on one. And should he miss hearing a speech, he usually can find a report of it in his newspaper.

Speeches are news, and frequently important news. They give us information about our government—in addresses by officials, in debates in legislative assemblies, in hearings by commissions, and, in a modified form, at the public forum we call a press conference. Our first reports of developments in science, medicine, economics, and other fields often come from speeches made at conventions and conferences.

Consequently, facility and accuracy in handling public utterances, whether by speech, interview, press conference, court trial, or legislative committee hearing, are a requisite for any news writer.

A speech may be given at a special gathering arranged for the sole purpose of hearing the speaker, or it may be but a part of a program with the speaker of secondary importance. If the former, the reporter may write a straight speech report, describing the occasion only briefly. If the latter, he may subordinate the speech or speeches to other details of the occasion.

Getting accurate reports of what speakers have to say is made easy for the reporter when he is provided an advance copy of the speech. A speaker may do this for two reasons: to insure accuracy of quotation and summary, and to obtain a fuller report—and therefore better play—than he might get if the reporter based his story on his own incomplete notes.

Since advance copies of speeches are often available, many speech reports are written before delivery. Press associations file advances on the wire for release at a fixed time or with a hold-for-release note. On newspapers, the speech report may be written, copyread, headlined, and set in type before the speech is made.

When the newspaper goes to press before the speech is delivered, the story must contain in the lead some sort of qualification as a part of the attribution, such as: "Senator John T. Adams said in a speech prepared for delivery today."

An omission of this qualification may place the newspaper in an embarrassing position if the speaker is unable to make his speech, if he suddenly changes his mind and does not give the prepared speech, or if he makes changes or additions that are more newsworthy than the prepared text.

Typical of such embarrassment was that of the Associated Press in an advance story on a speech given by President Truman at the Jefferson-Jackson dinner in 1952. There was speculation as to whether he would be a candidate for a third term, and the A. P. said he made no disclosure of his intentions in the speech. Unhappily for the A. P., the President, in an addition to his prepared text, announced his decision not to run again.

When copies of a speech are not available, the reporter should attempt to get the speaker's own copy or notes, either before or after delivery, in order not to have to rely entirely on his own necessarily abbreviated transcript. This is not necessary, however, if the reporter knows shorthand and is sure that he has a verbatim record of statements he intends to put in quotation marks.

The need for accuracy in reporting oral statements has become greater in recent years than formerly because many speeches are now recorded on tape. With no recording available of what was actually said, the reporter had an out when a speaker declared, "I was misquoted." Many people never believed the speaker's claim because it was often a convenient excuse when reaction to his statements was not what he expected. But today, with tape recordings frequently available, claims and counter-claims can be checked, and there can be no reply except a correction and apology when a reporter misquotes.

An example of this is an Associated Press dispatch in March,

1954, setting the record straight on a speech given by Senator Joseph McCarthy. The reporter's version was substantially correct, and few people would doubt that the meaning read into the speech was what McCarthy intended. But the tape recording showed that McCarthy's statement differed from the reporter's version.

WASHINGTON (AP)—Senator McCarthy (R.-Wis.) has telegraphed the Associated Press, with a copy to the White House, that he did not specifically name President Eisenhower in referring to critics of his investigative methods in a Chicago speech March 17. He termed an AP lead "completely untrue" and asked for "appropriate corrections."

The story in question, dated Chicago, March 18, was written by John Chadwick, an AP staff reporter who accompanied McCarthy from Washington.

Chadwick's story said in part:

"Senator McCarthy (R.-Wis.) today challenged critics of his Red-hunting methods—from President Eisenhower down—to name any Communists they have exposed.

"In the face of indirect criticism from Eisenhower and other top leaders of his party, McCarthy bluntly said he didn't give 'a tinker's dam' if people in either the Republican or Democratic party—no matter how high or how low were 'unhappy' about his methods."

McCarthy's telegram said: "President Eisenhower's name was not referred to even remotely in this section of the speech."

A transcript of McCarthy's speech, as taken by the AP, quotes the senator as saying:

"May I say to you, my good friends, tonight, to the American people, that I don't care, I don't give a tinker's dam how high or how low—how high or how low people in either the Republican or Democratic party—either party—are unhappy about our method. This fight is going to go on as long as I am in the United States Senate."

An ethical problem arises in speech coverage when a speaker, even knowing that reporters are present, declares that some of his remarks are "off the record" or "not for publication." How anything said before a large group can be so considered is beyond reason, of course, since the oral utterance constitutes publication. If the speech is at a public meeting, as when the sponsors state it is open to the public or when they charge admission, the reporter need not omit such so-called off-the-record statements. Some meetings, however, are private gatherings which the reporter attends in the role of a guest. Any convention open only to members of an organization constitutes such a private gathering. Without prior agreement regarding coverage of whatever occurs on the floor of the convention, a reporter could not in good conscience print the remarks which the speaker labeled "not for publication."

A related problem of such speech coverage was raised by the late Dr. Alfred C. Kinsey, a scientist who made a study of sexual practices of American men and women. Kinsey contended that scientists have a right to check, before publication, news stories based on speeches to technical groups, declaring: "We have an obligation to protect the public from inaccuracies which might be published unless the scientist helps the reporter in this fashion."

He insisted that reporters sign a forty-word statement in which they would agree to submit to him their stories on his speeches before scientific groups. No such requirement was made for speeches before public groups. While many newspaper people criticized him, he no doubt was well within his rights. A scientific group can bar reporters from its sessions if it so desires, and similarly it can insist upon certain ground rules for coverage.

Writing Speech Reports

Writing a story about a speech requires condensing several thousand words into a half dozen or so paragraphs. Since only the most important points can be reported in the story, they are usually arranged in the inverted-pyramid order of importance and not in the order set forth by the speaker.

Because of the need for extreme telescoping of a speaker's remarks, and because the writer rearranges the speaker's material, the story is harder to write than it might at first seem. The requirements for a good speech report are well set forth in a letter sent by the Baltimore Sunpapers to a speaker to check on the accuracy of a published account of his speech. He was asked to answer these questions:

(1) In those passages in which statements are attributed to you in quotation marks, were your statements correctly quoted?

(2) In those passages in which the article purports to paraphrase your remarks, are the paraphrases an accurate and objective summary of what you said?

(3) Does the article as a whole fairly and objectively present the essence of your views as you expressed them in your address?

(4) Were your views as expressed in your address presented fully,

or was any portion omitted? If so, did the omission have the effect of distorting or misrepresenting your views?

Before starting his speech report, the writer should make a list of the main points to be covered. Then he should decide what would be the best type of lead. The lead should be more informative than the mere statement that a speaker talked on a certain topic before a certain group at a certain time. The following, for example, is inadequate:

> Mortimer T. Rover, noted newspaper correspondent and author of several books on European affairs, discussed "The Crisis in the Kremlin" at the third Community Forum program last night in the Municipal Auditorium.

This lead contains no more information than what appeared in the preliminary stories about the address.

Instead, the lead should be based on something that the speaker said. It may be a summary statement giving the gist of his ideas or revealing his attitude toward the topic discussed, or it may be devoted to a single important point made.

The problem may be illustrated by a speech given by William P. Rogers, United States deputy attorney general, to policemen at graduation exercises of the Federal Bureau of Identification National Academy.

Some of Rogers' remarks, directed to the graduates and of no interest to the general public, must be ignored by the news writer. This is a frequent situation. Because many speeches are made to specialized groups, the reporter's account does not always emphasize the parts that specialists consider the most important; the reporter is concerned mainly with the sections of interest to outside people.

In his speech Rogers made two main points:

(1) Law enforcement is especially important today because "the country is faced with an efficient, well-organized criminal army whose leaders pose, and are frequently accepted, as reputable citizens," and because in the struggle between the free nations and the Communist nations every failure of law enforcement is exploited by the Communists throughout the world.

(2) Public opinion should be mobilized against the glorification of criminals in radio and television programs, comic books, and movies.

Both the major points, or even a secondary point under the main

headings, are of great concern to the public. The type of lead written might vary with the individual judgment of the news writer.
A summary-type lead would be:

> William P. Rogers, U. S. deputy attorney general, declared last night that law enforcement is complicated by the encroachment of criminals in legitimate business, by the cold war between the East and West and by the glorification of criminals in the entertainment media.

But more than likely the reporter would choose a single feature to play up. Some possibilities follow:

> The country is faced with a well-organized criminal army whose leaders pose as respectable citizens, William P. Rogers, U. S. deputy attorney general, declared last night.
>
> A call for an aroused public opinion to stamp out the glorification of criminals and the presentation of "lurid details of criminal escapades" in radio, television, movies and comic books was sounded last night by William P. Rogers, U. S. deputy attorney general.
>
> Public apathy to the encroachment of criminals in politics and business was assailed last night by William P. Rogers, U. S. deputy attorney general.
>
> A boycott of corporations run or financially controlled by criminal elements was urged last night by William P. Rogers, U. S. deputy attorney general.

In these sample leads, the occasion for the speech has not been given. Normally, details about the occasion should come in the second paragraph.

In writing the lead, the reporter will seldom have occasion to use a complete direct quotation. This is because it is usually difficult to find a direct quotation that performs the functions of a lead—one that adequately summarizes the speech, reflects the speaker's attitude toward his subject, or gives the keynote of his address.

The type of lead chosen determines the arrangement of material in the body of the story. To maintain coherence, all details relating to a particular point should be in one block of information in the body. There should be no skipping back and forth from one point to another.

In condensing the speech, the reporter makes use of direct quotation, paraphrase, and summary. Parts chosen for direct quotation should be key paragraphs. If a passage is wordy, consists of long,.

involved sentences, contains jargon or technical expressions, or uses big words the reader might not know, the reporter should not quote it but rather should give the thought in his own words.

Quotation marks enclosing material are an indication of a verbatim statement. Reporters, therefore, should not use quotation marks around any utterance that is not in the exact words of the speaker. If, in taking notes, the reporter does not get the complete quotation, he should not construct one from the few phrases and expressions in his notes. Such a passage can be written partly as paraphrase and partly as direct quotation.

Newspaper practice is to alternate passages of direct quotation with indirect quotation or paraphrase. This is done to indicate that the material in quotation marks is not a continuous passage in the speech.

Handling Speech Tags

An attribution or speech tag is required repeatedly throughout a news story based on speeches, interviews, reports, surveys, and documents whether the material be direct quotation, indirect quotation, or paraphrase. The repeated use of the attribution is shown in the following story:

> Public apathy to the encroachment of criminals in politics and business *was assailed* last night by William P. Rogers, U. S. deputy attorney general.
>
> Speaking at the graduation exercises of the Federal Bureau of Investigation National Academy, Rogers *warned* that the country is faced with "an efficient, well-organized criminal army whose leaders pose, and are frequently accepted, as reputable citizens."
>
> These criminals, *he charged,* have made inroads into politics by supporting and financing crooked politicians and into business by investing money in legitimate enterprises.
>
> "These two facts have been treated with apathy by far too many Americans," *Rogers said.*
>
> *He declared* that politicians known to be backed by crooks should be thrown out of office and that corporations known to be financially controlled by criminal elements should be boycotted.

Tags for Direct Quotations. Attributions for direct quotations may come at the first of the sentence, at a natural pause within the sentence (at the end of a phrase or a clause), or at the end of the sentence, as in the following:

Touching upon new demands by labor unions for wage increases, *Senator Smith said:* "I don't see how we can raise wages and at the same time hold the line on prices."

"Is it a fair description," *the senator asked*, "to call this new American foreign policy a 'get tough with Russia' policy?"

"Russia does not want war," *the senator said*. "America does not want war. We both are in the United Nations to prevent war. I hear much more war talk here than I did in Paris."

A comma is used to separate the speech tag from the quotation. When the tag precedes the quotation, however, as in the first example above, the colon is preferable, especially if the quotation is a long one. When a quotation extends over several paragraphs, quotation marks are used at the beginning of each paragraph and at the end of the last paragraph. In a long quotation extending over several sentences or paragraphs, the tag should be given near the beginning. The single quote mark is used for quotations within quoted material.

Tags for Indirect Quotations. In indirect quotations no comma is required if the attribution precedes the speaker's statement:

He said that good reporting of local government is a sacred assignment.

When the attribution comes in the middle of the statement or follows the statement, the attribution is set off by commas:

Good reporting of local government, he said, is a sacred assignment.

Good reporting of local government is a sacred assignment, he said.

The word "that" either stated or understood introduces an indirect quotation. It can be omitted if the sentence reads smoothly:

He said good reporting of local government is a sacred assignment.

Certain verbs, however, require the "that." The sentence, "He advocated city hall news be placed on page one," is incorrect without the "that."

When the statement of the speaker consists of two or more clauses, "that" may either be omitted before the clauses, be used before all the clauses, or be used before the first clause and omitted before the following clauses. But it should not be omitted before the first clause and used before the second or following clauses.

Correct:

He said good reporting of local government is a sacred assignment and such news deserves page one display.

He said that good reporting of local government is a sacred
assignment and that such news deserves page one display.

He said that good reporting of local government is a sacred
assignment and such news deserves page one display.

Incorrect:

He said good reporting of local government is a sacred assignment and that such news deserves page one display.

Tense in Attributed Statements. In an indirect quotation the
tense of the verb in the subordinate clause, ordinarily, is in the past
tense if the verb in the main clause is in the past tense:

He said that the rise in prices *was* due to higher labor costs.

If, however, the statement in the subordinate clause can be considered as being permanently true, the present tense is used:

He said that the world *is* round.

Newspapers, however, tend increasingly to use the present tense
even for statements that might not be permanently true. If the
statement is true at the time of writing, the present tense is acceptable:

He said that there *is* no cure for the common cold.

He said that there *are* many people in the country who *oppose*
the president's program.

The tense of the speaker's statement is preserved when the attribution is used parenthetically within the statement:

He will not sign the measure, the governor said, because he does
not think that it will be held constitutional by the Supreme
Court.

Avoiding Monotony. The requirement that practically all statements of a speaker be attributed to him may result in monotonous
repetition of tags, or in their becoming distracting if not handled
deftly.

One way *not* to avoid monotony is copying from a thesaurus all
the synonyms for "said" and sprinkling them throughout the news
story. The reporter need not strain himself to find synonyms for

"said." The word is unobtrusive and usually is the right verb to describe the way most remarks are uttered. Many substitutions for "said" found in news stories are inappropriate synonyms. "Stated" and "declared" should be reserved for formal utterances. "Claimed" may be used as meaning an assertion of something as a fact; it is often improperly used as a synonym for "said" or "asserted," or "maintained." "Added" should not be used unless the statement is actually an addition to a previous statement. "Concluded" as the tag for statements given in the last paragraph of the story should be avoided unless the statements actually are the termination of the speech.

The reporter need not, however, confine himself to the innocuous verb "said" if stronger verbs are needed. If the speaker *really* rants, roars, shouts, screams, bellows, jibes, jeers, derides, or swears, the reporter should not hesitate to use the descriptive verb.

Use of the following expressions as speech tags should be avoided: he felt, he thinks, he believes, he regards. They should be preceded by the verb "said": He said he felt, he said he thinks, and so on.

To avoid monotony and overuse of speech tags the following practices can be followed:

(1) The placement of the tags can be varied: before a quotation, within a quotation, or at the end of a quotation.

(2) One tag at the beginning can be used to introduce two or three paragraphs of direct quotation.

(3) One attribution can be used to introduce several points, recommendations, suggestions, etc., of the speaker:

> To reduce the tax burden, he made the following proposals:
> 1. A reassessment program should be carried out.
> 2. Home owners should be allowed a $1,000 homestead tax exemption.
> 3. A greater effort should be made to tax intangible property.

(4) Various constructions may be employed to link together related ideas, to shift from one topic to another, and to introduce new topics:

> While seeking to include adherence to basic moral principles of Islam, Mr. Mohammed Ali laid more stress on the secular recommendations. . . .
>
> As examples of the standards of his appointments, he cited the renaming of Irving Ben Cooper as. . . .

Discussing his adversaries one by one, he began by characterizing Jerome T. Smith as. . . .

Taking up the charges and claims made by his rivals, he said: "Is there anything wilder than the promises being made by the candidates. . . .

He assailed American policies in the orient sharply, saying: "It is absolutely ridiculous not to recognize. . . .

He then turned from immediate prospects for an improvement in business and went into detail in explaining the theory of the business cycle.

(5) Instead of verbs of assertion (he said, he declared, he stated) other appropriate verbs and expressions can be used:

His appraisal of the situation was. . . .
He condemned the practice of. . . .
He emphasized his opposition to the plan, declaring. . . .
The president disclosed that. . . .
The president reiterated his belief that. . . .
The premier cited the improving stability of the franc as. . . .
He charged the present administration with. . . .
He accused the present administration of. . . .
He demanded that. . . .
He urged that. . . .
He expressed confidence that. . . .
He argued that . . .
He depicted his opponent as being. . . .
He described as fantastic the charges that. . . .

Mixing Direct and Indirect Quotations. The mixing of direct and indirect quotation in the same sentence should generally be avoided, although words or phrases may be quoted if they are striking or controversial, or if for any other reason the reporter feels that it is important to attribute them definitely to the speaker. Thus: The speaker condemned "appeasers" and "missionaries of confusion here at home."

The mixing of a direct and indirect quotation that involves a change in person should be avoided. For example: Wadsworth said that American support of the Canadian proposal took him by surprise; *not* Wadsworth said American support of the Canadian proposal "took me by surprise." The long-established grammatical rule is that any statement preceded by *said that, remarked that,* etc., is indirect and no part of it need be enclosed by quotation marks.

In combining an indirect quotation with a direct quotation, it is better not to begin with a partial direct quotation that extends over into a new sentence, as: The senator said that he advocates a "live and let live policy. I think it possible to work out an accommodation between Russia's communism and our western democracy." This should be recast in one of the following ways:

> The senator said that he advocates a "live and let live policy" and that he thinks it possible "to work out an accommodation" between Russia's communism and western democracy.
>
> The senator said that he advocates a "live and let live policy." "I think it possible," he explained, "to work out an accommodation between Russia's communism and our western democracy."

Omissions and Interpolations. Reporters should also avoid both the use of three periods, x's, or asterisks to indicate omission of parts of a direct quotation and the interpolation of bracketed words to indicate an explanation or a change in the quotation. Most readers do not know what they signify, and material usually reads more smoothly if handled as a simple paraphrase or indirect quotation.

The following, for example, is unnecessarily complicated:

> Another said that "they (employers) are asking for men who will be definitely drafted."

How much better to make the whole statement indirect:

> Another said that employers are asking for men who will be definitely drafted.

The following monstrosity appeared in a press association report:

> It was a fighting speech all the way. And the general, in his 12-minute talk, declared "that although my public life is now closed," X X X he would continue "to advocate a positive and realistic policy for Korea, designed to bring the war to an early and honorable end."

A clear, smooth reading of this would be:

> It was a fighting speech all the way. The general, in his 12-minute talk, declared that although his public life was now closed he would continue "to advocate a positive and realistic policy for Korea, designed to bring the war to an early and honorable end."

Routine Meeting Reports

It is a rare American who does not belong to at least one club, society, or organization. He bands together in groups for entertainment, for carrying out good deeds, for propagandizing his beliefs, for promoting his professional and business interests. And his meetings are news.

Stories about organizations are a good illustration of the cafeteria nature of news carried by the press. Although the activities of most organizations are seldom of interest to the general public, that apathy is counterbalanced by the enthusiasm of the members. Thus, though the general interest may be slight, the news is published for the few who care.

Publishing news of organizations is a way of building good will. Since almost everyone in a community belongs to some club, the newspaper has a wide field in which to publish news of personal concern to many people—people who might not otherwise have any notice taken of their interests.

A metropolitan newspaper, of course, cannot publish stories about all the thousands of clubs and societies in its area. It has to be very selective, printing only news of broad public interest created by organizations. The newspaper in the small city, however, is less discriminating. Almost any organization can have its affairs reported, especially if it takes the trouble to provide the newspaper with the information. The small city paper prints such news in line with its policy of being a complete record of community affairs.

In judging the relative news value of organizations, the reporter must consider whether the group is of general or restricted interest. A philately club ordinarily would not have great news value, since few persons are interested in stamp collecting; a camera club might have greater news value, because more persons are interested in photography than are interested in philately. Some organizations take an important part in community affairs, and thus their activities may have considerable public interest. The stand on issues taken by the League of Women Voters in an election, the child welfare program of the Parent-Teacher Association, the scholarship fund of the Lions or Kiwanis Club—all such political, civic, or welfare activities are newsworthy, and the more an organization engages in them the more it will figure in the news. The size of the membership is another factor in the news importance of organizations.

News reports of routine meetings require only perfunctory reporting and writing. Information for both advance stories and follow-ups is generally obtained from an officer or the publicity chairman; since such material seldom lends itself to very original or colorful treatment, the writing should be straightforward and usually in the inverted-pyramid pattern.

The advance story's lead should emphasize anything of general interest about the meeting. Usually this is to be found in the purpose of the meeting or in the program, which might include the nomination or election of officers, a report of a committee, the name of a speaker and his subject, the celebration of an anniversary, the initiation of new members, or a visit by national or state officials of an organization.

Two essentials in all advance stories, usually placed in the lead, are an exact statement of the time and place of the meeting. Neither, however, should be emphasized at the very start of the sentence. The following are undesirable openings:

> At 7:30 p. m. today the Kiwanis Club will hold its weekly meeting in the Rainbow Room of the Hotel Middletown.
>
> There will be a meeting of the Kiwanis Club at 7:30 p. m. today in the Rainbow Room of the Hotel Middletown.
>
> The Rainbow Room of the Hotel Middletown will be the scene of a banquet for Kiwanis Club members and their wives at 7:30 p. m. today.

Other facts which may be included in an advance story are: the type of meeting (regular, special, business, or social, open or closed to the public); details of the program or entertainment, and who will take part; names of the committee members in charge of the program; name of the chairman or toastmaster; special guests; and the decorations, if unusual.

While routine meeting reports do not offer much opportunity for freshness in writing, certain stale expressions should be avoided. These include "the highlight of the meeting will be," "the principal business to be taken up," "the purpose of the meeting will be," "an interesting program has been planned," "the speaker for the meeting will be," "all members are urged to attend," "the public is cordially invited," and "all interested persons are urged to attend." Some of these are wordy, others editorialize, and most are superfluous.

A follow-up story of a meeting, even if nothing of particular interest occurred, is usually expected. One of the worst faults of lazy reporters is to make the follow-up consist merely of a rehash of the advance story, with the future tense changed to the past tense. If the reporter did not attend a meeting, he should interview someone who did to find out what happened and what was said, and make this the feature of his lead.

If there was a speaker, his remarks may be the basis for the news report, with the length of the story determined by the extent of public interest expected in his statements. Any business transacted by the organization may be emphasized or, if members merely discussed a topic without reaching a decision, what they had to say should be brought out.

As in writing his advance story, the reporter should avoid such stereotyped expressions as "the principal topic of discussion was," "featured at the meeting," "one of the most interesting meetings," and so forth. After a meeting, the time and place are no longer important. The time may be reduced to "last night" or "yesterday" and the place may be omitted.

Coverage of Conventions

The most important and most newsworthy meetings that the reporter has to cover are district, state, and national conventions. Complete coverage of such gatherings is given by newspapers in the host city and abbreviated reports are carried by the press associations. If for no other reason, the meetings are newsworthy because of the number of people who attend.

Some organizations—fraternal orders and extremely specialized groups—may be difficult to report because their affairs are of little interest outside the membership. A good reporter, however, who possesses acute perception for the interesting and literary skill above the ordinary can turn out readable copy about even these. Information for such stories is more likely to come from talks with individual members attending than from session proceedings.

Other organizations are highly newsworthy because they represent or are the spokesmen for important segments of society, and therefore may be an influence in public affairs. It is important that the nation know what policies labor unions adopt at their meetings, or what attitudes are expressed by such groups as the National Association of Manufacturers or the United States Chamber of Commerce at their meetings. Scientific gatherings are important because they are often the occasion for announcement of discoveries and new developments.

Almost every national convention adopts a set of resolutions stating opinions on issues not directly related to the organization's primary interests. Such resolutions may be significant as representing a large body of opinion, even though the organization has no official status.

In covering conventions, the reporter has a considerable problem: much of the program is of concern only to the members, yet he must make it interesting to outsiders. If he writes a story that adequately reports proceedings to the satisfaction of the members, it may be so dry and so filled with technical or professional jargon as to repel nonmember readers. On the other hand, if he picks out only the most sensational or most unusual matters for treatment in an effort to write down to the public, he may not do justice to the organization. A meeting of scientists, for example, might be stirred by a new discovery about the particles in an atom, while the public might be more easily interested in a report on possibilities of flying to the moon. The reporter should not ignore the significant scientific development simply because it is hard to understand and write about, nor should he play up the one that has popular appeal simply because it is easy to make interesting. He must employ his ingenuity and skill to translate the significant, if esoteric, topic into terms understandable to the layman.

Any gathering that brings several thousand visitors to a city has great news interest. City officials and civic leaders want the municipality to put its best foot forward so that the outsiders may receive a good impression. Operators of hotels, restaurants, amusement spots, and other places where visitors may be expected to gather will want to know full details. A large convention is a stimulus to business, and the newspaper is expected to help make it a success.

Consequently, local coverage of a convention may begin weeks or even months before the sessions start. The newspaper works with local arrangements committees in preparing articles to serve as a publicity buildup. Early stories may include brief notices of convention plans with such information as the number of persons to attend, the number of chapters and states to be represented, important speeches scheduled, business to be taken up, arrangements to house delegates, entertainment to be given, names of local people to serve on arrangements committees, and so forth.

The reporter assigned to cover convention sessions can make his work easier if he plans for it far in advance. He should arrange with the local committee in charge to have convention officers and speakers send photographs, biographical information, and advance copies of speeches. The photographs and biographical data can be used for preliminary stories so that advance notices will not be just a rehash of the same general material. Advance copies of speeches will simplify the coverage of the convention when it is in session.

The first-day convention story usually should be a roundup of information which may have been previously published piecemeal, giving the public an over-all picture of the meeting, its purpose, the prominent persons attending, the program to be given, the business to be discussed, the arrival of early delegates, and so forth. At this time it should be possible to get fresh information by interviews with officers. If any notables are present, the reporter may want to obtain personality or opinion interviews from them. The reporter, however, should not ignore lesser-known delegates: short interviews with a dozen or half-dozen delegates may be consolidated in a single story.

After the convention opens, the reporter's job is mainly one of covering speeches and business discussions. Some speeches may be worth a separate story; others may be incorporated into the general convention story. Where there are a number of speeches of only limited interest, the reporter may summarize them in a paragraph or two, possibly picking up a few sentences of direct quotation.

Routine matters which must also be covered during the convention include the appointment of committees, the election of officers, the selection of the next convention city, the resolutions, the reports of officials and committees, and so forth. In addition to information about what happened during the day's sessions, the story should include details about the sessions coming up the next day. Since most of this material has probably been reported in advance stories, it usually can be buried at the end of the current account.

A large convention with several different sessions going on at the same time may offer a difficult task for one-man coverage. The reporter who had the foresight to obtain advance copies of speeches and papers is at an advantage. He often can write parts of his story ahead of time, and he can skip some of the sessions to obtain side features or to get information on controversies brewing within the membership or on issues planned for the business sessions.

When a convention seems to offer little of general interest, the newspaper may not assign a reporter to full-time coverage. This is no excuse, though, for a convention story which is merely a rewrite of the printed program. The reporter may have time to drop in at convention headquarters to talk with officers for a secondhand version of what went on and to pick up copies of speeches delivered or resolutions adopted. When time does not permit even this limited coverage, a few minutes at the telephone will usually provide the reporter with a topic.

Because of the numerous subjects to be included in a report of a convention—speeches, business transacted, factual matter on the number of delegates and states represented, entertainment, and so forth—the reporter faces a difficult problem in news evaluation and story organization. Fundamentally, however, his problem is the same as in any multiple-incident story. He may write a summary lead or a main-feature type lead and arrange the material in the body of the story according to one of several logical plans. For instance, if he selects a speech as the most important convention event, he may summarize it in his first paragraph and devote several paragraphs to amplifying details. He may then write a secondary lead or catchall paragraph summarizing other convention events, then give additional material on the speech, and continue with details of other events. Or he may write a summary first paragraph, give the convention highlights in several paragraphs, and follow these with fuller details about each topic already mentioned, ending his story with miscellaneous minor information.

ASSIGNMENTS

1. Compare the published text of a speech with newspaper and press association reports. Do the several reports agree on the material played up in the lead? Does the order of presentation of details in the reports differ? Do the paragraphs selected for direct quotation coincide? Do you consider any of the reports unfair or incomplete?

2. (a) Clip five speech reports from newspapers and underline the speech tags and attributions. Does the writing conform to instructions given in this chapter?

(b) Compile from newspaper speech reports a list of devices used to link or to contrast ideas, to shift from one topic to another, or to introduce a statement. Compile a list of substitutions for the verbs of assertion such as "said," "stated," and "declared."

3. Write a speech report based on a published text in a newspaper or other publication such as *Vital Speeches*.

4. (a) Attend a speech or lecture and write a story based on it.

(b) Compare your story with those appearing in local newspapers. How does your evaluation of the speaker's remarks compare with the published reports in respect to material chosen to play up in the lead, to the order of presentation of ideas, and to passages selected for direct quotation?

5. (a) Take notes on a radio broadcast of a speech by a national figure and write a news story based on it.

(b) Compare your story with newspaper and press association reports.

6. Write a news story based on the following program for a convention to be held on your campus:

STATE HIGH SCHOOL PRESS ASSOCIATION

20TH ANNUAL CONVENTION

Saturday, May 15

9:00-10:30 a. m.
Registration, main floor of Journalism Building. Registration fee is 50 cents and luncheon tickets are $1.00.
Campus tours conducted by members of Sigma Delta Chi, men's journalism fraternity; Theta Sigma Phi, women's journalism fraternity; and Alpha Delta Sigma, advertising fraternity.

10:30 a. m. Convocation, University Auditorium.
Chairman, Arthur A. Porter, president, State High School Press Association, Parkville High School.
Welcoming Address: Joseph T. Spencer, director, School of Journalism.
Address: "Your Future in Journalism," Thomas Denoyer, publisher, Edgerton Gazette.
Address: "The News in Perspective," Marquis W. Childs, Washington correspondent for the St. Louis Post-Dispatch.

12 Noon
Luncheon, ballroom, Student Union Building.
Chairman: Alice Henderson, vice president, State High School Press Association, Benjamin Franklin High School, Centertown.
Address: "Adventures Here and There," Inez Robb, columnist, United Features.
Presentation of awards in the annual newspaper, writing and advertising contests, Mr. Spencer.

1:30-3:00 p. m.
ADVISERS' ROUND TABLE, 200 Journalism Building.
Chairman, Miss Hazel Carter, Hopeville High School.

Discussion leaders: Thomas A. Rodgers, Columbus High School; Miss Thelma August, Springdale High School; Miss Harriet Slocum, Mountain View High School; Miss Hazel Wentworth, Jefferson High School, Barnesville.

EDITORIAL WORKSHOP, 100 Journalism Building.
Chairman, Angus McPherson, Edgerton High School.
Discussion leaders: Jack Sampson, Scott Township High School, Woodsville; Thomas Ryan, Durward High School; Margaret Lovelace, Waterton High School; Laverne Euclid, Bellville High School.

ADVERTISING WORKSHOP, 210 Holloway Hall.
Chairman, Roberta Beidler, Parkville High School.
Discussion leaders: Laura Schwartz, Phoenixville High School; Donald Argus, Moore High School; Milo Watkins, Stewart High School; Betsy Lawson, Center City High School.

YEARBOOK WORKSHOP, 110 Holloway Hall.
Chairman, Scott Adams, Springdale High School.
Discussion leaders: Maurine Nobel, Springfield High School; Jerome Atterbury, Warren High School; Rosamond Tilbury, Central High School, Waterbury; George Schonberg, Lowell High School.

CHAPTER 15

DEATH STORIES AND OBITUARIES

Life or Vital Statistics

"THE TROUBLE with most obituaries is that they show signs of rigor mortis before the copy comes out of the typewriter," wrote Carl Lindstrom, managing editor of the Hartford *Times*. "You seldom read one that brings home the realization that the body under discussion has just stopped being a warm, breathing person."

Lindstrom's complaint points to the need for better reporting and writing about death. Because of the tendency to rely on information filled out on obituary blanks left with funeral homes, the news story too often consists merely of the vital statistics in a person's life—date of birth, schools attended, positions held, membership in organizations, and survivors. The result is an account that omits the human-interest factor.

Though death is the occasion for all the stories, the obituary page should be devoted to life. On it, in the words of Richard G. West of the New York *Herald Tribune* writing in *Late City Edition*,

may be found the summing up of the glories, the achievements, the mediocrities, and the failures of life which the rest of the paper chronicled day by day. A few columns on one morning may tell the last of a physician whose researches saved the lives of thousands, of a woman who fought to end the sweatshops, a statesman who sold the Spanish Loyalists down the river, a banker whose one step outside the law was remembered when his years of honor were forgotten, a vaudeville juggler, a missionary in China, an anticigarette crusader, a writer of immortal tales for children, a grower of prize pumpkins, and a conductor who traveled two million miles on the Erie Railroad. In the democracy of the obituary page they lie side by side; the disparate headline sizes do not alter the lead paragraphs of each story. They all died.

Unlike most of the newspaper's stories, the obituaries are not for the day only. They are clipped for preservation among the family archives and copies go to relatives and friends in distant places. In writing the obituary, the reporter should look for material that reveals character and personality. Such material has a place even in the short obituary. For example, in a 175-word story about the death of a lawyer, the New York *Herald Tribune* found room for this paragraph:

> For one term, 1917-1918, he was village president and attracted attention by his refusal to sign the annual tax assessment rolls, in which the village trustees and president, as assessors, vouched that they had assessed all property at full value. The practice then as now was to assess at partial value, and Mr. Smith refused to sign the affidavits. The rest of the board did, and made them legal.

This incident, though it happened years before the man's death, revealed his fundamental character. Many longer obituaries with scores of facts are not nearly so informative as this one paragraph.

Lindstrom, in his appeal for better written obituaries, cited a press association dispatch reporting the death of Constant Lambert, London critic and composer, which "gave all the vital statistics and other routine data which might have fitted a college professor or a railroad-crossing tender." Looking for personalizing details, Lindstrom discovered that Lambert was deaf in one ear but was fond of saying, "I hear music easily. It is only as far as conversation is concerned that deafness affects me." The composer had also been described as a "big man physically, with broad shoulders, a fleshy body and a brow-profile of Churchillian expanse." "That quotation from Lambert himself," Lindstrom wrote, "and these other little details were brush strokes toward the making of a portrait. In the obit department we need more portraits and fewer cadavers."

Leads for Obituaries

The first-day story of a death should start usually with a simple statement of the facts—the name, identification, a statement that the person died, the time of death, the cause of death, and the age. The pattern does not allow for much variation; most obituaries begin with the name followed immediately by the identification.

Since the person's age is one of our first questions on hearing of someone's death, this information belongs in the lead. It may be given as a part of the identification:

> Dr. John T. Smith, 76, a physician here for 50 years, died of a heart attack last night at his home, 2001 N. Lake Drive.

Another possibility is to omit the age in the identification and to give it in a separate sentence after the statement of death: "He was 76 years old," or "His age was 76." Or the age may be made a part of the statement about the death:

> Dr. John T. Smith, a physician here for 50 years, died of a heart attack last night at the age of 76 at his home, 2001 N. Lake Drive.

Because the person's age is important, newspapers should be accurate in computing it. A common error is in not taking into account the birth month and day. For example, a man born November 1, 1910, who dies May 1, 1957, is not 47 years old at the time of death but 46. He does not become 47 until his birthday.

In choosing the identification, the writer should attempt to find one that best summarizes or highlights his subject's life and career. The identification, therefore, more often is by reputation and achievement than by address or position. Frequently it is based on an achievement of the person's early years. Examples follow of identifications that succeed in assessing the person's place and importance in life:

> William Linn Westermann, professor emeritus of ancient history at Columbia University and a world authority on ancient economy and papyrus writings, died today in White Plains Hospital. His age was 81.
>
> Rabbi Meyer Mordecai Silverman, who is said to have been the oldest Orthodox rabbi in New York, died Sunday at his home, 329 South Fifth Street, Brooklyn, after a long illness. He was 96 years old.
>
> Alan Devoe, who from childhood wrote about wild animals, died Wednesday night at New York Hospital after a brief illness. The author-naturalist, who was 45 years old, maintained as a wild life sanctuary his 100-acre farm, Phudd Hill, Hilsdale, N. Y., where he had resided since 1934.
>
> Lemuel Ayers, theatrical scene designer and play producer, who strikingly showed his talent in the settings for the musical success, "Oklahoma!" in 1943, died Sunday in the New York Hospital at the age of 40.

Russell Owen, famous New York Times reporter who covered
Admiral Richard E. Byrd's first Antarctic expedition, died of a
heart attack here at 6:20 p. m. today in the home of his daughter,
Mrs. Jean Gibson.

Euphemisms or figurative language—passed away, called to his
Maker—should not be used in obituaries. Except for accidents or
crimes in which a person is killed, burned to death, shot, stabbed, or
fatally injured, people "die" in news stories. The word "succumb"
should not ordinarily be used as a synonym for "die," although it
may be used when a disease or long illness was the cause of death.

The expression "died suddenly" is frowned upon in some newspaper offices on the theory that all deaths are sudden—a person is
alive one second and dead the next and nothing could be more
sudden. The proper expression, these theorists hold, is "died un-
expectedly." In giving the cause of death the preferred expression
is that a person died "of" a disease and not "from." Newspapers bar
the expressions "died of an operation" or "died from an operation,"
since doctors maintain that the death is due to conditions existing
before the operation and not to the operation itself. The newspaper
wording is "died *after* an operation" or "died *following* an operation."

The cause of death is an important element in the obituary and
should be given, except for persons who die of old age or senility. If
the scientific term is likely to be unfamiliar it may need to be explained. Often it is not necessary to use the scientific term; to say
that a person died of heart disease or a heart attack serves just as
well as to say that he died of coronary thrombosis or coronary oc-
clusion. The unscientific expression, "heart failure," probably
should be avoided, since it is asserted that all deaths are due to
heart failure. If death follows an illness, it is proper to state the
duration.

The question of whether cancer should be given as the cause of
death is a debatable one, although in recent years newspapers have
increasingly tended to do so. The viewpoint of those who advocate
listing cancer as the cause was stated in an editorial in the Yonkers
(New York) *Herald Statesman* quoted in *The Bulletin of the American Society of Newspaper Editors*. It argued that writing about the
disease helps in the effort to find a cure for it, stating:

There is no "shame" therein; there is, on the contrary, a tremendous value for those who survive—for the whole community

and the nation. We look forward to the time when we can print the name of a valuable citizen and say of him, "He was *cured* of cancer."

The opposing viewpoint was given by Jonathan Daniels of the Raleigh (North Carolina) *News and Observer,* who said:

> I can't remember our ever saying that a person died of cancer and I doubt that in the foreseeable future, barring a strange exception, we will do it. I am not impressed by the social significance aspect of the business. We try to run our obituary column in such a way as to please, as far as possible, the relatives of the deceased, and I think we will stick to that policy.

There seems to be no valid reason for newspapers to maintain the taboo against mention of cancer or to regard it as different from any other disease. Newspapers which have decided to give it as a cause of death have found that the public accepts it after a time. When survivors request that it not be mentioned, the newspaper should of course follow their wishes; but it should do that for any cause of death.

Writing the Story

The length of the obituary depends upon the subject's newsworthiness—his prominence and importance. In addition to the lead information (name, identification, age, cause of death, time and place of death) most obituaries, regardless of length, should include the following information: biographical facts, survivors, and funeral and burial arrangements. A long obituary of a prominent person differs from a short one only in the amount of detail.

A routine obituary customarily follows a standardized pattern:

John T. Adams, 53, custodian at Middletown High School for the past five years, died of heart disease last night at City Hospital. He suffered a heart attack Sunday at his home, 238 W. Elm Avenue.	Lead: Name, age, identification, time of death, place of death, cause of death.
Adams was born in Middletown Sept. 15, 1902. He attended the public schools and worked as a carpenter until he was employed as custodian at the high school in 1950. He was a member of the First Baptist Church.	Biographical facts.

Surviving are his wife, Mrs. Alice Duncan Adams; a son, Joseph A. Adams, 221 E. First Street; and two daughters, Mrs. Peter A. Smith, Prairie Grove, and Mrs. Thomas O. Rogers, Reedburg.	Survivors.
Services will be held at 2 p. m. tomorrow at the Atkins Funeral Home. Burial will be in Fairlawn Cemetery.	Funeral and burial arrangements.

The death of a prominent person calls for a longer and more detailed account, but the pattern of the short obituary, with modifications depending on circumstances, may generally be followed in respect to the order of presentation of material.

The lead for a long obituary may be followed by a paragraph or paragraphs devoted to the circumstances of death—full details about the cause, the bedside scene or those present at the time of death, and last words or messages. This information may be very detailed for a world famous personage, as in the International News Service prize-winning account of the death of Pope Pius XI:

> VATICAN CITY (INS)—Pope Pius XI, supreme spiritual sovereign over 350,000,000 Roman Catholics, died early today with a blessing for the world on his lips.
>
> The "Pope of Peace" breathed his last at 5:31 o'clock this morning (11:31 p. m. EST, Thursday) after suffering his second heart attack in twelve hours.
>
> He died as he had lived—peacefully—only two days before the 17th anniversary of his coronation on the Throne of St. Peter's as the Vicar of Christ.
>
> The Holy Father was 81 years old when death overtook him in the still early morning hours.
>
> Until the very last, the 261st ruler of the Catholic Church remembered the dominating motive of his long and active life. Just before he died, the Pontiff recovered consciousness for a moment or two sufficiently to half-raise his hand in benediction and mumble the words:
>
> "Jesus. Mary. Peace to the world. Peace."
>
> Suddenly his frail hand fell on his chest and Pius, the warrior for peace and righteousness and universal brotherhood, died.
>
> Twenty-seven minutes later the official word went out to the world that His Holiness had lost in the valiant battle to survive and carry on his work. . . .

Ordinarily, however, the circumstances of death are described more perfunctorily:

Mr. Smith had recently had one or two minor heart seizures but appeared to recover completely from them. He was stricken early this morning and a physician was summoned immediately. He appeared to be resting comfortably throughout the day. He was dead when his daughter went into his bedroom this evening.

PHOENIXVILLE, Pa.—Owen J. Roberts, retired associate justice of the United States Supreme Court, died today at his home. He was 80 years old last May 2. He retired from the bench in 1945.

The former justice suffered a heart attack and died at 10:25 a. m. His wife and their only child, Mrs. Elizabeth Hamilton, were at his bedside.

After the account of the circumstances of death, the obituary ordinarily continues with biographical details. If the subject has had an important public career or is noted for accomplishments in any field, the article very likely will not be just a chronological story of his birth, schooling, and career. Instead, it should give the highlights of his life, an assessment of his influence, or a description of his character before the chronological narrative is taken up.

Thus the Associated Press in reporting the death of a noted scientist summarizes a career:

MIDLAND, Mich. (AP)—Dr. William J. Hale, a research consultant with the Dow Chemical Co. and one of the nation's leading organic chemists, died today after a brief illness. He was 79 years old.

Known as the "father of chemurgy," a word he coined to describe farm chemistry, Dr. Hale developed processes to increase production of indigo, chloracetic acid and phenyl ethyl alcohol.

Dr. Hale was born. . . .

The New York *Herald Tribune* in its obituary of a famous poet portrays him as a man and a writer:

HARTFORD, Conn.—Wallace Stevens, 75, one of the most distinguished of contemporary American poets and vice president of the Hartford Accident and Indemnity Co., died today at St. Francis Hospital.

Mr. Stevens had undergone an operation in April and re-entered the hospital on July 21 for further treatment. His home was at 18 Westerly Terrace in Hartford.

When Mr. Stevens was awarded an honorary degree by Yale University last June, he was cited as one in whom "the two worlds of practical affairs and art have found a perfect marriage." He led his double life far from the limelight of publicity, his name coming to the fore only when he received one of the many honors heaped upon him in recent years. He was, in fact, as one critic put it, "the country's best least-known poet."

"Poetry," Mr. Stevens once explained, "is my way of making the world palatable. It's the way of making one's experience, almost wholly inexplicable, acceptable."

To one critic, Mr. Stevens was "the most finished poet of his age." To another, his poetry was "a strangely fastidious and hermetic art." To a third, "his perspective was that of the man of art, the museum-and-concert-goer, the student of French poetry . . . the esthete in the best sense of the word."

To Mr. Stevens—who composed his poetry as the urge seized him, often on scraps of paper brought to his office for his secretary to transcribe—his "unromantic" life was important.

"It gives a man character as a poet to have this daily contact with a job," Mr. Stevens himself said. "I doubt whether I've lost a thing by leading an exceedingly regular and disciplined life."

He was born. . . .

Even after the reporter has given the place and date of birth and would ordinarily continue with education and later events, he may not find it feasible to stick to chronology. Later life may need to be handled in related blocs of information if the person has had a varied career overlapping several fields. Thus, it may be desirable to keep separate a person's business or professional career, his record as a civic leader, his endeavors in other fields, honors conferred upon him, and so forth.

Survivors should be listed after the biographical facts are given, in the order of closeness of relationship. This order is: wife or husband, children, parents, and brothers and sisters. When there are grandchildren the number but not the names may be given.

There are only a few methods of introducing the list of survivors. Acceptable ones include:

> Surviving are. . . .
> He (she) is survived by. . . .
> Survivors are. . . .
> He (she) leaves. . . .

When there are only one or two survivors, the form may be changed:

> A sister, Mrs. John W. Smith, Pittsburgh, survives.

The names of survivors given early in the story should not be repeated in listing other survivors. The omission may be indicated in several ways:

> Besides his wife, he is survived by. . . .
> He leaves besides his wife two sons. . . .
> He also leaves. . . .
> He is also survived by. . . .
> Also surviving are. . . .

Although opinion differs as to whether the term "widow" or "wife" should be used in listing survivors, argument seems pointless, and either term may be found in well-edited newspapers.

Newspaper practice also varies concerning the use of Christian names and maiden names for wives. Here again there seems to be no reason for setting a positive rule. One argument in favor of using the maiden name is that it may recall to readers that the widow is a member of a certain family, an important point if the family is a prominent one.

In listing survivors the separate categories of relations should be set off by semicolons, with commas used between the names of individuals within each category, as in the following:

> He leaves his wife, Mrs. Josephine Smith Adams; three sons, John J. Adams, 200 E. First Street, Arthur A. Adams, 800 N. Maple Avenue, and Luther T. Adams, Pittsburgh; two daughters, Mrs. Robert Ryan, Pittsburgh, and Mrs. Peter A. Foster, 220 W. Second Street; and his parents, Mr. and Mrs. Joseph O. Adams, Altoona.

Ordinarily, in naming the sons and unmarried daughters as well as brothers and unmarried sisters, it would seem better to repeat the last name for each and to give addresses for identification. To save space, however, many newspapers prefer not to do this.

For the first-day story the funeral arrangements more often than not are incomplete. This part of the obituary may then consist of only a sentence to the effect that funeral arrangements will be made at a certain funeral home. The name of the funeral home is generally not given in metropolitan newspapers—it goes in the paid obituary notices—but it is usually considered an essential part of the story in small-city newspapers.

Since it takes time to collect all the details needed for a long obituary, newspapers prepare for the death of prominent persons by keeping advance obituary biographies on file. Such biographies are also sent out by the press services. They may be rewritten and incorporated into the current death story or, as is the practice on some newspapers, appended as dash matter.

The reporter handling the death story should check the prepared obituary to see that it includes up-to-date information and that the passage of time has not changed the subject's reputation and renown. The person who was worth columns—when the obituary was written at the height of his fame—may be worth only a brief report if death comes after many years.

When a person has been a leader in his community and noted for his good deeds, there may be an unfortunate tendency for the reporter to go overboard in praising him. A straightforward recital of his activities is more impressive than fulsome adjectives and gush. A person's death comes as a shock to those who knew him, and many are grieved, but the occasions are few when "the whole city was bowed in grief" or "the entire community mourned the passing" of anyone.

The obituary should be an honest one, but telling the truth does not necessarily mean that ancient scandals should be raked over. When a person has figured prominently in the news at one time in adverse or sensational circumstances, the obituary can hardly overlook the facts. But these early scandals should not be overemphasized and they should be viewed in the perspective of the person's entire career.

Follow-Ups and Funerals

The follow-up or second-day story about a death ordinarily begins with a statement of the funeral arrangements in the lead. As with the opening paragraph announcing a death, the lead generally conforms to a pattern when the person is not prominent:

> Funeral services for John T. Adams, 53, custodian at Middletown High School, will be held at 2 p. m. tomorrow at the Atkins Funeral Home. Burial will be in Fairlawn Cemetery.

The lead may be followed by additional details about the services —the minister in charge, the names of honorary and active pallbearers, the type of ceremony (if a special one, such as a military funeral, is planned), and clubs or lodges having a part. The story may end with a résumé of the circumstances of death and biographical details.

If the person is prominent, the follow-up story may include additional information—statements from other prominent people about him, messages of condolence received by members of the family, resolutions adopted by clubs and other organizations, proclamations by public officials calling for flags to be flown at half staff or for business to cease during the time of the funeral, memorial services held or planned, and arrangements for the body to lie in state for public view.

Only for prominent or otherwise newsworthy persons do newspapers print accounts of funeral and burial services. Such a story would include statements and summaries from the eulogy, a description of the scene, and the reactions of the mourners and others in attendance.

ASSIGNMENTS

1. Clip five obituaries from a newspaper which in your opinion have poorly chosen identifications. Rewrite the leads to improve upon the identifications.

2. Below is a typical obituary report blank with information filled in. Write a news story based on the information.

OBITUARY REPORT

Name in full: James Arnold Hester.
Address: 1400 E. Tenth Street.
Place of death: City Hospital.   *Time:* 12:30 a. m.
Cause of death: Cancer.   *Length of illness:* 6 months.
Circumstances of death: Became ill six months ago and was taken to hospital two weeks ago.
Date of birth: Oct. 15, 1910.   *Place:* Middletown.
Survivors: Wife or husband: Mary Cramer Hester.
    Parents .... *Address* ....
    Brothers: Robert O. Hester *Address:* 230 N. Elm Ave.
              Peter R. Hester *Address:* 340 W. Tenth
    Sisters: Mrs. A. T. Adams *Address:* Reedville
            .... *Address* ....
    Sons: James A. Jr. *Address:* Home
            .... *Address* ....
    Daughters: Janet *Address:* Home
            .... *Address* ....
Date of marriage: 1935   *Place:* Middletown
Residence here since: All his life.
Previous residences and dates. ....
....
Last occupation: Lawyer.
Previous occupations: County attorney, two terms—1936-38, 1938-40.

Schools attended: Middletown public schools.
College and degrees: State university, B. A. 1932, LL. B. 1933.
Church affiliation: First Methodist.
Military service: Captain in 32nd Division, World War II.
Time of funeral . . . .*Place* . . . .
Person in charge . . . .
Pallbearers . . . .
Music . . . .
. . . .
Burial place . . . .
Additional information: Chairman of county Democratic central committee
    at time of death. Taught Young Men's Bible Class at First Methodist
    Church. Named Citizen of the Year by the Chamber of Commerce in
    1953—that year he served as president of the Rotary Club and as
    chairman of the Community Fund drive.

3. Select a well known personage—writer, musician, politician—
supply details about his presumed death and obtain biographical
information. Write a full length death story and obituary.

4. Obtain biographical material about a well known public figure
and write an assessment of his career and a personal portrait to be
used as a "wait" obituary for the newspaper's morgue.

⑤ Write a news story based upon the following information:

> As police reporter for an afternoon paper in a small city, you
> check with Chief John Chambers for news. He tells you that
> police are investigating a suicide—the death of Homer L. Brady.
> "He was found dead about 10 o'clock last night in the garage
> by his daughter when she returned from a movie with a friend,"
> Chambers tells you. "He had rigged up a hose to the exhaust
> pipe of his car and had run it through one of the car's windows.
> He was in the front seat and the motor was still running when
> his daughter discovered him."
> "I guess there's no doubt it was a suicide," you say. "Did he
> leave a note or anything?"
> "No," Chambers says, "but his daughter said he had been in
> bad health. He suffered a stroke last year. His daughter says he
> was always complaining he was no good to anybody any more
> and was a burden to her."
> The daughter is Miss Elinor Brady, 30, a third-grade teacher at
> Emerson School. She lived with her father at 1020 N. Tenth Street.
> She had left home about 7 p. m. with another teacher at the
> school, Miss Alice Coburn, 800 N. Ninth Street, to attend a
> movie, going in Miss Coburn's car.
> After being dropped off by Miss Coburn on her return home,
> Miss Brady was unable to find her father in the house. She looked

for him outside and found him in the garage. Her neighbors, Mr. and Mrs. James A. Forest, 1024 N. Tenth Street, helped her get him out of the garage into the open air. Mr. Forest tried artificial respiration until a doctor arrived.

Chambers tells you that Coroner Peter A. Foltz will conduct an inquest at 2 p. m. tomorrow at the Larson Funeral Home, where the body was taken.

Checking with Miss Brady, you find that her father had been despondent since being partly incapacitated by a paralytic stroke last year. "He often said he might as well be dead as to be unable to work any more," she says. "He said he was nothing but a burden to me."

Mr. Brady was a native of the city, being born October 23, 1897, the son of Mr. and Mrs. Arthur O. Brady. He was educated in the public schools of the city and served in the army in World War I. He married Miss Wanda Meyers of Meadville in 1924. She died five years ago.

Mr. Brady's first employment was as a carpenter. He established the Brady and Lawrence Construction Co. with Abel L. Lawrence in 1926 and was active in the concern until two years ago when ill health forced his retirement.

He was a member of the Chamber of Commerce, of which he was president in 1934, the Rotary Club, and the First Baptist Church. He was a member of the Board of Education from 1934 to 1938.

Survivors include two sons, John A. Brady, Meadville, Oscar L. Brady, Columbus, Ohio, and six grandchildren.

CHAPTER 16

STORIES ABOUT PEOPLE

Human-Interest Stories

HUMAN-INTEREST STORIES in the real tradition of the form are found most frequently today in the short items called "brighteners" in many newspaper offices. Often they receive emphasis by being enclosed in a box. They are distributed by press associations, and some newspapers print them under such headings as "Oddities in the News," "Flashes of Life," and "The Human Side of the News."

The subjects for human-interest stories of this type are as varied as life itself. Because they are usually encountered by the reporter, rather than sought out, he must be able both to see the potentialities of a happening as a human-interest feature and to write about it effectively.

In writing the human-interest story, the reporter may abandon the rules set up for the straight news account. He may present it in narrative sequence, saving the climax for the last; he may resort to dialogue and dialect; and he may improve upon the real event by a little imaginative embroidery.

One of the perennially popular subjects for human-interest stories is children. The incident described below happens perhaps several times a day somewhere in the United States, but this particular one was news all over the country because a reporter was able to tell it in a different way.

> OKLAHOMA CITY (AP)—For all his judicial power State Supreme Court Justice Nelson Corn couldn't even spring his baby grandson from imprisonment.
> Like uncounted thousands of other tots, 15-month-old Robert

Baxter Case wandered into the family bathroom and accidentally shot the bolt.

Justice Corn delivered several opinions through the door with no results whatever.

The habeas corpus action was finally carried out by Fireman Delbert Gee, who did a second-story job while the law smiled.

From the earliest days of the human-interest story, the courts have provided excellent examples of the genre. Here is a typical one:

CHICAGO (AP)—A 31-year-old brunette said Thursday in superior court that when she asked her husband what time it was he threw the clock at her.

And, Mrs. Eleanor Espe added, he said:

"What do you care? You have a face that would stop a clock."

Divorce granted.

The human-interest story runs the gamut of emotional appeals. Frequent examples of the pathetic can be found:

KANSAS CITY (AP)—For 24 years now the "hot dog king" of the American Association baseball park here has played Santa Claus to the old people of the county home.

Herman Erlanger gathered fruits, candies and small gifts from likely donors each Christmas time.

Herman found Thursday that old age had caught up with him.

At 71, unmarried and without immediate relatives, Herman said he found it necessary to transfer to the old people's home himself.

The appeal of the curious or the unusual accounts for many of the shorter human-interest stories. *Time* each week prints a column of them, condensed from newspaper stories, under the heading, "Miscellany." Typical of its curiosa are:

In Cincinnati, workmen erecting a fire escape on the Wanda Lee apartments accidentally set the building on fire.

In Melbourne, John Desmond Withers explained why he had stolen $11 from his fiancee: he needed the money for her engagement ring.

In San Pedro, Calif., Carl Krueger, 58, was acquitted of charges of shoplifting and eating a chewy candy bar after he bared his five teeth to the jury, revealed no two of them met.

Brevity to this degree is not usual in newspaper reports of such happenings, although the daily press keeps items to the point:

ATLANTIC CITY—A wallet containing a sizable sum of money, lost on the street here, made its way back to the owner in Brooklyn through the U. S. mails unwrapped, unaddressed and unstamped.

Mrs. Ruth Dickson of Brooklyn reported that the wallet was presented her by the postman. Money and papers were intact.

Another fruitful source of the short "interesque," the term used by the International News Service for these items, is in "life's little ironies." Typical of such anecdotes is the following:

SHREVEPORT, La. (AP)—A $2,000 bank roll that Travis McCreary hid in a cook stove at his home appeared perfectly safe from hold-up men.

Who would go to a cook stove looking for money?

But McCreary, a grocer at nearby Rodessa, forgot to tell his wife about his cache when he put the money in the oven last Saturday afternoon while the banks were closed.

Came suppertime preparation. Soon after lighting the stove, his wife smelled smoke.

Investigation revealed a pile of parched folding money, by that time little more than ashes.

The only consolation for McCreary today was an opinion of Postmaster S. O. Wilson that the ashes may bear sufficient parched serial numbers to be identified and replaced.

Just as popular as stories about people are stories about animals, especially if animals can be given human attributes. Dogs which die shortly after their masters, apparently the victim of grief; the talking dog; the horse that can count; the pet that finds its way back home after being carried off hundreds of miles—these and many others have been subjects for "human" interest stories and will continue to attract readers. Stories similar to the following can be found almost every year:

CHICAGO (UP)—A horse dropped into a bar here yesterday for a beer.

When the sun got too warm, Old Admiral, a plow horse, deserted the fields and went to the nearest tavern where he clattered a hoof against the bar.

"What'll you have?" asked the bartender, who had seen everything.

Old Admiral neighed. The bartender drew a beer and set it on the bar. At that point, the horse's owner, Marshall Polo, arrived and sized up the situation. He paid the dime and started to lead Old Admiral out, but then he had another thought. He ordered a beer for himself and he and the horse stayed around for quite a while.

One of the dangers in the composition of human-interest stories is overwriting. Nowadays the story is usually kept short, the style simple. While the story need not be kept to the dimensions of a joke, the writer should not let himself go in framing overwrought appeals to the sensibilities or in squeezing out the last drop of humor in a funny situation.

The Interview Article

In one sense the term "interview" refers to the technique by which most news is gathered. The reporter who calls on his news source for facts about a situation or happening is conducting an interview. In another sense, it means a special literary form or type of article that emphasizes the personality or ideas of the person interviewed.

As a journalistic article, the interview provides a means for the reader to "meet" people whom he would ordinarily never have a chance to encounter. People whom the public is likely to want to meet vicariously through this medium include:

The Celebrity. Since the public seems never to tire of reading about prominent people, their every appearance in a new situation may warrant an interview. Thus, when a noted person visits a town, even for only a few minutes during a plane stopover or a change in trains, local reporters may seek an interview. The actor who makes a hit in a new play, a public official who retires from office, a business leader who goes to a new job—these changes in situation may and usually do provide occasions for interviews.

People who come suddenly into the limelight are also good subjects for interviews. The new sports champion, the newly appointed cabinet member, the girl who wins a beauty contest, the 4-H Club member who wins a national trophy, the 10-year-old who saves a companion from drowning, the unknown author whose book becomes a best-seller, and others previously uncelebrated are almost invariably interviewed when fame touches them. The public is eager to know what kind of people they are, how they look, how they act, and what their ideas are on various topics.

The Colorful Personality. People do not have to be famous to be interesting. Some of the best interviews are with the comparatively unknown. The teacher who has spent a half century in the classroom, the handyman who is hired as much for his sage philosophy as for his repairman ability, the wheelchair-bound person who carries on a successful business—many who are unhonored and unsung are "unforgettable" characters well worth interviewing.

The Person with Interesting Experiences. What people do or have done is as interesting as what they are. The explorer back from the Amazon jungles, the man rescued from a mine explosion which brought death to his fellow workers, the woman who served as a missionary in Africa—these are some of the people who have done things or have had experiences that the public will want to know about.

The experiences need not even be breath-taking or extraordinary. Interviews with people about their work on their jobs have resulted in good stories—what the complaint clerk in a department store thinks about customers, how the night watchman passes the lonely hours, what the ticket-seller in the theater lobby thinks about, how a waitress feels at the end of a day of serving plates of roast beef, mashed potatoes, and buttered peas.

People's hobbies are perennial sources of interviews. The banker may spend his nonworking hours painting landscapes, the haberdasher may don dirty overalls to dig in his garden raising cabbage and okra, the football coach may be a collector of books about Chinese art—if so, each can be interviewed.

The Expert in Certain Fields of Knowledge. If Congress passes a new tax law, the newspaper interviews an economist to get his opinion on how it will affect business. There is a wave of juvenile delinquency, and the newspaper asks ministers, social workers, or school teachers for explanations of the causes and suggestions for cure. The transit company announces a change in bus routes, and the riders are asked if they think service has been improved. The newspaper not only covers events that happen daily but it also uses the interview to find out what the knowledgeable expert and the plain citizen think about them.

Most newspaper interviews are timely, based on something in the daily grist of items which furnishes a "news peg." Sometimes the interview is in the nature of a follow-up story on an incident already covered as a straight news report. The morning newspaper may carry an article about a farm boy whose purebred steer won first place in a livestock show and was auctioned off for $4,000. The afternoon paper may interview the boy and do a personality sketch of him telling how he went about winning the contest. Or the story may suggest an interview with the county agricultural agent on what other young farmers are doing.

Dozens of stories that come over the news desk daily can be followed up by interviews with the persons involved or with others who might comment on or explain or interpret an event for the public. Sometimes the occasion for the interview may be slight—the great man is interviewed on his birthday or the military leader on a patriotic anniversary.

Planning the Interview

The basic requirement for conducting a successful interview is that the reporter find out in advance all that he can about the life, character, ideas, and achievements of the persons he plans to interview. Thus armed, he will be prepared to ask intelligent questions and to adopt an approach that will elicit information of interest to his readers.

Too often newspapermen approach a person blithely ignorant of his personality, his background, or even his claim to fame. The famous journalist and author Oswald Garrison Villard, describing his experiences with interviewers, said he had encountered reporters who admitted they did not know if he was an editor or a hardware merchant or a politician and others who "could not understand the simplest developments in international affairs and showed their ignorance of outstanding men in American political life."

Obtaining basic biographical facts about the person to be interviewed is the minimum advance preparation that the reporter should take. If he has time and the information is available, he should also find out something of the personality and character of his interviewee. Finally, if the interviewee is an expert in a particular field—an atomic scientist, an authority on Mayan civilization, a noted collector of medieval tapestries—the reporter must prepare himself to converse intelligently on topics relating to that field.

Ideally, the reporter should make an appointment for an interview, letting the person know what type of information he seeks and how much time will be required. If the two can sit down and chat at leisure, the reporter has an opportunity to sound out the ideas of his interviewee and to obtain the personal details and impressions that will contribute to a rounded character portrayal.

But often the circumstances for the interview cannot be so ar-

ranged. The interview may have to take place while the notable
shaves and dresses for the banquet that starts in thirty minutes, or
while the movie star dodges autograph hunters. The reporter may
be able to ask only three or four questions between the time the
visitor lands from his plane and is whisked away in a taxi. In such
situations, the reporter must reduce his questions to the half dozen
vital ones which will produce the salient information.

Writing the Interview

If the reporter's interview is productive, he should have more
material than he can use when he sits down at his typewriter to
start writing. Consequently, one of his first steps is to eliminate
extraneous information. His interview article should have unity—
unity of tone as well as unity of material. An interview that gets
nowhere, that is a mere assembly of unrelated quotations and paraphrases of the speaker's remarks, will not be good reading. No matter how rambling the talk with the interviewee, the article that
unrolls itself from the typewriter should have a dominant theme,
and the quotations and other material should be marshaled in the
proper order to amplify and illustrate the theme.

If the interview deals primarily with the ideas or opinions of the
interviewee, the material may be handled much the same way as in
reporting a speech. The opening may be a summary of the idea,
expressed by a striking or startling statement, a pungent quotation,
or just a simple sentence that gives the gist of the information. Such
a treatment was used in an interview in the Minneapolis *Star* that
began:

> Vannevar Bush, one of the world's top scientists and former
> head of the United States wartime science team, took an optimistic
> view of the chances for peace as he stepped off the train in
> Minneapolis today.
> "We can avoid war with Russia," he declared. "There is a
> military stalemate now and I think the balance which exists today
> can be maintained."

The remainder of the article, in which was interpolated one paragraph of biographical facts and a statement of the occasion for
Bush's appearance in Minneapolis, consisted of quotations and
paraphrases of his ideas on relationships with Russia.

Or the dominant theme of the article may be found in the personality of the person interviewed, as in the following, also from the Minneapolis *Star:*

> The things Mrs. Mary McLeod Bethune wants for herself are what she wants for all Negro people.
> "I want to be myself and nothing else," said the noted Negro educator in Minneapolis today, "but I want to be my best self. And that's what education and opportunity will do."

The theme was developed not only by means of quotation but also by an account of the achievements of the woman who founded Bethune-Cookman College at Daytona Beach, Fla.

The statement of the theme, however, is only one of the countless beginnings available to the writer of interview articles. His methods will depend upon his purpose and upon the nature of his material. He may want to describe the person interviewed:

> A slight, bespectacled lawyer who confides "I'm a good listener" hears Chicago's gripes about alleged police misconduct in traffic incidents.
> Albert H. La Plante, 51, chainsmokes cigarets and cocks his head intently to hear such words as these, made by an elderly, well-dressed man:
> "I wasn't speeding, but the policeman thought I looked like a soft touch. . . ."
> Or he hears a serious Gary steelworker telling that a park policeman helped himself to one of three $20 bills from the steel-worker's wallet, commenting, "One will be enough. . . ."—Chicago *Daily News.*

or to picture him in his home background or his business or professional setting:

> "Ooooh—a lady bus driver!"
> That's how people greeted Mrs. Annie Ruth Lee when she started wheeling one of the big yellow busses of the Aurora City Lines.
> "Hop aboard and take a chance," she answered.—Chicago *Daily News.*

or to characterize him:

> NEW YORK (AP)—Anybody who thinks a woman can't keep a secret should meet the wife of the next secretary of state.
> A chat with Mrs. John Foster Dulles reveals that in the 39 years of their marriage she has accompanied her husband on many of his trips as a representative of Uncle Sam, as adviser at councils

of foreign ministers in Europe, as special representative to nego-
tiate the Japanese peace treaty.

or to show the unusual nature of his achievement:

> It's just like selling ice boxes to the Eskimos.
> Anna Bell Brunner plans to sell fashions to the French.
> Come June, the vivacious West View girl will set up shop on
> the Riviera and sell her own models and designs in beachwear.—
> Pittsburgh *Press*.

or give the news peg on which the interview is hung:

> On Thursday Wilhelm Thorleif Munthe Morgenstierne, Nor-
> wegian ambassador to the United States, will begin his forty-
> sixth year in the diplomatic service of his country.
> And, it may be revealed without breaching the protocol that
> governs international relations, the ambassador will enter his
> forty-sixth year as a diplomat without a single pair of striped
> trousers in his wardrobe.
> The absence of the striped pants is symbolic of some of the
> changes in the ways of the world and diplomacy since Ambassador
> Morgenstierne decided on the foreign service as a life's career.—
> Washington *Post and Times Herald*.

The interview obtained primarily for information may be devoted mostly to what the person has to say, but at the same time he
should not be just a disembodied voice oracularly expounding upon
topics suggested by the reporter. The best interview stories permit
the reader to see the subject as he appears, as well as to read what
he has to say. Thus, physical descriptions, characterizations, the
interviewee's mannerisms, the sound of his voice, and other details
that help the reader to envisage him should be given. Although, in
regular news, writing the person's speech is not copied to indicate
accent or unusual pronunciations of words, the newspaper rule that
everybody must be made to speak correctly does not apply to the
interview, and the writer can by misspellings and other devices
attempt to indicate the flavor and sound of a person's talk.

The Biographical Article

In accordance with the growing acceptance of the notion that
more knowledge about the people in the news contributes to the
understanding of the news, there is an increasing demand for biographical accounts and assessments of careers. Like the interview,

the biography can be an important supplement to the spot news of the day.

The biography—even where it is included in straight news reports, such as the obituary—should be more than just a stodgy account of place of birth, schools attended, jobs held, membership in organizations, and achievements. It should try to portray the subject as a human being.

Because one of the best sources of information for a biographical sketch is the subject himself, an interview with him should be obtained. The reporter should check his impressions of the person's character by additional interviews with members of the subject's family, his friends, and his associates. Published sources of material should also be consulted—the newspaper's morgue clippings, standard reference works like *Who's Who* and *Current Biography,* and articles in magazines.

All individuals have many facets to their personality, yet from an intimate knowledge of a person a dominant trait is likely to emerge. If the reporter can determine such a dominant trait, he should make this the focus of his article.

For example, *Time* found what it considered such an outstanding trait characterizing Franklin D. Roosevelt in a remark by his mother. It summed up, in the magazine's opinion, two viewpoints on the quality in Roosevelt which his friends called decisiveness and his enemies called arbitrariness. Mrs. Roosevelt once said of her son: "Franklin had a great habit of ordering his playmates around and was generally permitted to have his way. Once I said to him: 'My son, don't give the orders all of the time. Let the other boys give them sometimes.' 'Mummie,' he said, lifting a soil-streaked face, 'if I didn't give the orders nothing would happen!'" This was used as the keynote for a long personality sketch.

In general, the biographical article should give, besides the main facts in a subject's life, his philosophy or guiding motives, a portrait of his appearance, and quotations that reveal his character and his thinking.

The newspaper biographical article must be kept brief. It therefore cannot give the numerous personal details and the illuminating anecdotes found in the famous profiles of the *New Yorker* and the cover articles in *Time.* But these accounts, as well as the biographical articles in other magazines, can well be studied as guides to what the newspaper should attempt in its shorter pieces.

ASSIGNMENTS

1. Write a short human-interest story based on some current happening that you have observed or heard about, or on some past incident that you recall.

2. From today's newspaper choose three spot news reports that you think would justify follow-up interviews. Indicate what type of interview would be suitable and what additional information is needed. List the questions you would ask the person to be interviewed.

3. Choose a question or issue currently in the news and ask fifteen or twenty representative persons their opinion about it. Write a group interview story based on your findings.

4. Using the verbatim report of a press conference of a public official or the question-and-answer interview in the *U. S. News and World Report*, write an interview article, supplying personal and background details that you think will make your article more readable.

5. Carefully making advance plans by obtaining background information and framing questions to be asked, hold an interview with some person whom you think has something interesting to offer and write an interview article.

CHAPTER 17

ACCIDENTS AND DISASTERS

News Interest in Catastrophe

NEWSPAPERS HAVE BEEN CONDEMNED for having "a vested interest in catastrophe" because of the large number of articles carried concerning sudden death and violence—people killed and maimed in automobile wrecks, airplane crashes, fires, explosions, industrial mishaps, and storms.

In an appeal for a better-balanced view of the world, Harry A. Overstreet wrote in an article, "Daily Disaster Diet" (*Saturday Review*, February 19, 1949), of the use of calamity as a yardstick for news:

> It means that day by day, year in and year out, all of us, young and old, are being moved to accept a one sided, distorted view of life. We get life in its hostile and catastrophic patterns more often than in its friendly and constructive patterns. Ours is a culture in which newspapers have influenced most people, from their childhood on, to suppose that "eventfulness" is mostly conflict and catastrophe.

Most editors also probably regret the necessity for considering disaster as a determinant of news. Much as they might like to concentrate on the smiling aspects of life, they realize that danger is always with us in our mechanized and mobile society. Ignoring this fact will not reduce the huge toll of casualties in accidents—in excess of 90,000 killed and almost 10,000,000 injured annually. Editors hope that if the public is made cognizant of the danger by reports of accidents, opinion will support remedies. Perhaps the death and injury totals would be even greater if the public did not have its "daily disaster diet."

213

Accident stories, though they differ in scope and in the way they happen, have certain factors in common. By keeping these in mind, the reporter assigned to cover an accident can make sure that he obtains all the information he needs. Getting the facts is sometimes difficult, because the people involved may not be interested or able to provide information—they may be hurt or excited if they figured in an accident, or may have more important things to do if they are charged with relief work or investigation.

In all accidents the factor of greatest importance is the human element—what our statistics list as casualties. A disaster, defined by the National Safety Council as any accident causing the death of five or more persons, is more newsworthy than a mishap which causes no deaths. An important precaution to keep in mind in covering major disasters is to avoid exaggerating the casualty totals. First reports are likely to have many more persons killed and injured than actually were. Thus, the 500 reported killed and injured in the first-day stories may dwindle to half that number in subsequent reports.

Conservatism in reporting the first casualty estimates is desirable because (1) scare stories of scores or hundreds killed and injured may arouse needless fear in people with relatives and friends in the disaster area; (2) rescue and rehabilitation work may be hampered by telephone calls and the appearance of sensation-mongers at the scene; and (3) the newspaper's reputation for accuracy suffers when final casualty totals are much lower than the original reports.

The first and perhaps most difficult task in covering a disaster is to obtain an accurate casualty list. The information should include the name, age, address, and identification. Correct information may be hard to get, as bodies may not be identifiable, incomplete and inaccurate data may go on morgue and hospital records, and facts have to be assembled hurriedly from a variety of sources.

In a major disaster with a big casualty list, information may be kept to a minimum of name and identification. When the number is small, the reporter may include details about the exact cause of death and the nature of injuries.

In addition to casualties, the human factor in disasters and accidents may include information about survivors other than those injured—who they are, how they escaped, and their versions of the event.

Next to injury and loss of life, property destruction is perhaps the most important news element in disaster stories, especially in fires, explosions, floods, and storms. The reporter, from his own observation and the accounts of witnesses, should obtain an exact and detailed description of what was damaged and the nature of the damage, together with estimates of the monetary loss. His story, based on careful accumulation of details, may combine narration and description in an account which places the reader on the spot when the event began and which allows him to see the havoc and destruction as it develops.

A part of the descriptive detail should include rescue and relief work and efforts to prevent further destruction in the case of storm, flood, and fire. This information should include the care given the injured, the aid provided for those left homeless, and estimates as to what additional assistance will be required.

Some accidents may involve legal action immediately or later. In automobile accidents there may be arrests, and in other types of mishaps there may be official investigations to discover the cause and to fix responsibility. In many states a coroner's inquest may be required to determine the cause of an accidental death and to discover if the accident was due to criminal culpability or negligence.

In addition to searching out the factual information for straight news reports—the casualties, property damage, cause, and details of what happened—the reporter should look for human-interest material and side angles. Eyewitness accounts, told in the words of the victims while the drama and danger are still vividly impressed upon their minds, are one type of article possibility. Any acts of heroism should provide material for personality articles. There may also be unusual aspects that will make good features—miraculous escapes, freak occurrences, astounding coincidences. Some of these, however, should be taken with a grain of salt. No major disaster occurs, for example, without someone recalling after the event that he had had a premonition of danger, and other stranger-than-fiction anecdotes similarly seem to repeat themselves year after year.

Automobile Accidents

According to *Accident Facts,* annual report of the National Safety Council, someone is killed in a motor vehicle accident every 15 minutes, and someone is injured every 25 seconds. Automobile fatalities, numbering in excess of 36,000 annually, account for 40 percent of the accidental deaths in the United States; the number injured annually exceeds 1,250,000. The property loss amounts to more than $4,400,000,000. There is good reason, then, for the belief that the automobile death toll is the nation's No. 1 news story.

In consequence, though every automobile accident is an isolated event and can be reported as such, many newspapers handle each one as a part of a running or continuing story. This may be done by incorporating in the lead a statement giving the new total of traffic deaths reached when the current fatality is added, as: "His death was the fifth in the city in June due to an automobile accident and the 38th this year." Or it may be done in a separate box score giving such statistics as the number of fatalities in the city, county, and state for the month and for the year, and the comparative figures for the previous year.

Police reports of accidents are ordinarily given in detail, and the reporter can rely to a great extent upon official information for his news. His sources will be city police for accidents within the city, and the sheriff's office, state police, or highway patrol for accidents outside the city. Official reports include the names, ages, and addresses of those involved; the location of the accident; the names of those killed and the cause of death; the names of those injured and the hospital to which they were taken; the names and statements of witnesses; a description of how the accident occurred, frequently with a rough diagram; a description of the damage to the car or cars and an estimate of the monetary loss; a statement of arrests made or other legal action taken; and the names of investigating officers.

Because of deadline pressure, however, the reporter may not have time to wait until the official investigation is completed. His information may have to be obtained personally from investigating officers and from witnesses. Information about injuries and the condition of the injured should come from the hospital.

In writing his story the reporter must be careful not to fix blame for an automobile accident, even when there has been an arrest. It is safer, from the standpoint of preventing libel, to say that two automobiles collided than to say that one automobile crashed into another. Similarly, the reporter should avoid stating, except when the evidence is overwhelming, that a driver was speeding, that he was driving recklessly, or that he was intoxicated. If there has been an arrest, the reporter can print that fact and the charges, but statements made by police as to how the accident occurred and who was to blame are printed at the newspaper's risk.

In reporting a death due to a vehicular accident, the reporter should make it clear whether the person died at the time of the accident or later. The news writing convention for doing this briefly in the lead is to say that a person was "fatally injured" if he died after the event and to write that he was "killed" if he died at the time. Since "fatally injured" smacks of journalese, it should be used sparingly. The meaning can be conveyed in other ways:

> Two University of Buffalo students died early this morning after their car went out of control in the south drive of Delaware Avenue near Nottingham Terrace and struck a tree.

> A 21-year-old Lackawanna man died shortly before 11 o'clock this morning of injuries suffered Wednesday night when the car in which he was riding overturned on Newton Road.

> His throat badly cut from flying glass, a Middletown man died while being taken to Mercy Hospital last night after his automobile collided with another automobile at the intersection of E. First Street and Kenyon Boulevard.

Automobile accidents in which there are no injuries or deaths are reported briefly and routinely in small-city newspapers, but are ignored by metropolitan newspapers unless there is an unusual circumstance:

> A policeman answering an emergency call escaped injury today when his cruiser hit a utility pole with such force that his pistol discharged a bullet into the car seat.

> Ten minutes after he was a witness of one automobile accident, James J. Atkins, 28, of 200 N. First Street was himself involved in one when his car collided with another at N. First Street and College Avenue yesterday afternoon.

Roundup stories containing reports on several minor traffic accidents are frequently used in newspapers. These may be written with a summary lead followed by details of each accident, or they may have a lead which plays up the most serious accident. A summary lead example follows:

> Four persons were injured, none seriously, in three separate automobile mishaps over the weekend.
> Arthur Smith, 14, of 2300 E. First Street, was run over Sunday afternoon after he had crawled under a truck near his home to keep out of the rain.

The truck driver, Peter Adams, 800 N. Beaver Avenue, decided to move the truck and, not knowing the boy was underneath, drove off. Young Smith suffered a fractured hip.

Two persons were injured in a two-car collision in the 1300 block of Elm Avenue Sunday. They are. . . .

To give the story a main-feature angle, it might be written as follows:

A 14-year-old boy discovered Sunday afternoon that crawling beneath a truck isn't the safest thing to do to get out of the rain.

Arthur Smith, 2300 E. First Street, was run over when the driver of the truck under which Smith had sought shelter decided to move it. Smith suffered a fractured hip. The truck driver was Peter Adams, 800 N. Beaver Avenue.

Three other persons were injured, none seriously, in other automobile accidents over the weekend.

Two persons were injured in a two-car collision in the 1300 block of Elm Avenue Sunday. They are. . . .

Other occasions for roundup stories about traffic accidents are holidays and bad weather conditions. In fact, the news of national observance as well as local observance of a holiday is likely to be featured by the death and injury toll. Here, for example, is part of an Associated Press dispatch on a Memorial Day toll:

Highway deaths throughout the nation mounted—but at a somewhat slower rate than expected—as the Memorial Day holiday neared an end.

The National Safety Council said in a guarded statement there might be a "good chance" the toll for the one-day holiday would fall below the 110 traffic fatalities it had predicted.

The normal figure for a non-holiday Wednesday at this time of year is 70.

By 7 p. m. EST Wednesday 56 lives had been lost in automobile accidents. There were 7 drownings and 11 deaths from miscellaneous causes for an over-all accident total of 74.

Last year the Memorial Day holiday fell on a week end and 369 persons were killed in traffic accidents over the three-day period. Total accidental deaths that holiday numbered 596.

A typical local handling of the same Memorial Day is the following from Des Moines *Register*:

Picnicking, hiking, sunbathing, boating, fishing, and swimming lured thousands of Iowans to parks and recreation areas Wednesday.

Highway Patrol Chief David G. Herrick said Wednesday night

that only seven personal injury accidents, none considered serious, and no fatalities had been reported.

Herrick said there usually are "from 12 to 14" such accidents on an average day on Iowa highways. Ten traffic fatalities had been predicted for the holiday.

Only one injury accident was reported to Des Moines police all day and officers said that one was minor. . . .

Coverage of Fires

Although fire is not the killer that the automobile is, it nevertheless is one of the major causes of accidental death in the United States and constitutes one of the important types of news events. In 1955 deaths due to burns totaled 6,300, of which 2,000 were caused by accidental ignition of clothing. The property loss was $885,-000,000. Coverage of a spectacular building fire is a test of a reporter's ability to gather detailed factual information and to write a story that captures the excitement, danger, and color of the event.

A knowledge of fire department organization and operation will assist the reporter in covering fires. The basic unit of the department is the company. In a small community a single company performs all the fire fighting and fire protection duties, but in larger cities a company is organized for operation of each major piece of apparatus. The principal ones are an engine or hose company to take men and hose to the fire, a ladder truck company for rescue and operation of hose lines at a height, and a pumper-ladder company primarily for fires in residential areas where separate ladder companies may not be needed. Other companies may include rescue squads for resuscitation and first aid for persons injured in fires and victims of drowning, asphyxiation, and electric shock; a salvage squad for cleaning up after fires; and a company to operate fire boats.

The fire alarm system is a guide to the seriousness of a fire. A one-alarm fire probably would not be worth firsthand coverage, but if a second alarm is turned in by the lieutenant or captain in charge of operations at the scene the reporter would probably find it advisable to go there. A five-alarm or six-alarm fire, denoting a major conflagration, would cause the city editor to call in other reporters to assist with coverage. The number of the "alarm" indicates the equipment and manpower dispatched to a fire.

The reporter's knowledge of the city and the most dangerous types of fires also serves as a guide as to whether the fire should get on-the-scene coverage. Thus, if a blaze is reported in an area of ramshackle wooden tenements, the reporter knows it will be hard to control and capable of causing death. Types of high hazard fires, according to one fire department manual, are lumber yards; bulk oil storage; chemical plants; enameling or varnish works; feed, flour, and grist mills; imitation leather plants; explosives; and cotton clothing and cotton batting manufacturies.

As with other accident stories, the main element of interest in fires is the casualties. The reporter must obtain the names and identifications of private citizens killed and injured, the names of firemen killed and injured, and details about how the casualties occurred. Other related information includes the number of persons endangered and how they escaped or were rescued. For persons made homeless by a blaze, the reporter should find out what assistance is being given them. The following story, for example, is concerned almost entirely with the rescue of a fire victim:

> Mrs. Mary Adams, 53, was rescued by a fireman early yesterday when flames trapped her in her second-floor apartment above her dry goods store at Eighth Street and Maple Avenue.
>
> Robert Porter, 24, a neighbor at 820 Maple Avenue, suffered a severe cut on the right hand when he scaled a rear shed in an attempt to reach Mrs. Adams.
>
> Porter and Mrs. Adams, who suffered from smoke inhalation and a burn on the left leg, were taken to Mercy Hospital.
>
> Two motorists, James J. Smith, 40, of 200 N. First Street, and Arthur Cain, 23, of 2240 Mason Boulevard, discovered the shop afire about 3:30 a. m. and pounded on a side door until Mrs. Adams awakened. By then her escape was cut off.
>
> A telephone alarm brought Ladder Company 18 from the Tenth Street Fire Station, in the command of Lieut. Curtis Roberts.
>
> Roberts mounted a ladder and brought down Mrs. Adams.
>
> The interior of the building was badly damaged, with the loss estimated at $10,000. Firemen were on the scene about one hour and 30 minutes.

The news story about a major fire should contain information about the building burned. This may include the type of structure—dwelling, apartment house, warehouse; the height; the construction—brick, frame, stone; the floor composition and roof framing; and the names of the owner and occupant. Such details as the following from a fire story help the reader to understand the nature of the blaze: "The inside of the structure was all wood, including the beams. The floors were heavily oiled."

Information about construction details also helps in understanding the origin and spread of a fire. The story should state the room or part of the building where the fire started and the apparent progress throughout the building. The following paragraphs describing the burning of two silos connected by a calf nursery barn are an example:

> Striking one of the huge silos, the lightning ran down it and into some bales of hay and straw in the loading room between the 40-foot structures.
>
> Spreading from the bales, the flames rushed up the twin silos and traveled through the frame portion connecting them.

The cause of a fire is an important element in the news story. In fact, the question, "How did it start?" is one of the first asked when a fire takes place. Since the exact cause may be hard to determine, the reporter usually should give authority for his information about it, as in the following account of an industrial blaze: "A company spokesman said the fire probably started in an oil bath that cools and insulates the transformers." When the cause is undetermined, a statement to this effect with an attribution to firemen should be included in the story.

An important part of most fire stories is a narration and description of the efforts to combat the blaze. While a story need not give details in chronological sequence, somewhere it should report the discovery of the blaze and by whom, the sounding of the alarm, the efforts made to put out the blaze before the arrival of firemen, and the time they arrived. The factual detail should include the number of hose lines, pieces of equipment and ladders used, the time the fire was brought under control, and the time it was completely extinguished or when firemen left.

Such information need not constitute a block in the news story— frequently it can be worked in with the descriptive and narrative content—but it is precise information which a thorough reporter should obtain, as in the following:

> Firemen answered the fire alarm at 1:23 p. m. A general alarm was sounded at 1:30 p. m., and a repeat at 1:38 p. m. By 2:15 p. m., the blaze had been brought under control.
>
> Firemen lined up one aerial truck on Maple Avenue and another on First Street when they found that an excavation on Maple prevented room for two trucks. A gas line is being laid on Maple.

Also answering the three-alarm fire were 12 pumpers and one rescue unit.

Since fires are often spectacular, they immediately attract people to the scene. The size of the crowd and police efforts to control it belong in the news story:

> Motorists, startled by the sudden burst of flames, stopped, clogging up the bridge filled with rush hour traffic. When the flames had died down, choking black smoke, fed by the transformer oil, swirled around the bridge.
> Police finally cleared the bridge, then closed it for half an hour while the fire was being brought under control.

The property loss through fire and explosion is likely to run into considerable money, and estimates as to the value belong in the story. These estimates may be obtained from the owner and from fire department officials. The amount of insurance carried should also be included.

A fire story gives the reporter an opportunity for vivid, descriptive writing, but he will find his account will be more effective if he keeps his mind on collecting factual details rather than on the overpowering adjectives he may have in his vocabulary. Expressions like "holocaust" and "a blazing inferno" cannot match such factual statements as: "The explosion and fire sent a spear of flame 100 feet in the air."

Natural Disasters

Though man has changed the face of the land with his cities, highways, railroads, and power and telephone lines, and has defeated nature in mastering flight and developing heating, cooling, and lighting systems, he nevertheless is as much, if not more, at the mercy of his environment as his primitive forebears. His genius is often powerless when nature strikes in one of her violent moods.

Of all disasters the most devastating, outside of war, are those of natural origin—rain, snow, sleet, and wind. When a tornado, hurricane, or flood strikes, everybody in the vicinity is affected, and therefore natural disasters are of utmost news importance.

The elements of news value—casualties, property damage, and description—are the same as for other accident and disaster stories, but the problems of coverage may be more complex. The sources include not only police, fire departments, hospitals, and morgues, but many other agencies and individuals.

The weather bureau is of major importance as a source of information for stories dealing with natural disaster. The data obtainable include maximum and minimum temperatures; the amount of precipitation, including rain, snow, sleet, and hail; wind velocities; flood stage; predictions; and comparative figures for previous occurrences.

The factor in natural disasters which makes them so newsworthy is their disruption of everyday life. This means that the reporter must cover many areas and check many sources. The most important disruptions are in the basic public utilities—water, heat, and power—all of which are necessary for modern urban living; principal communications disruptions will be telephone and telegraph service and mail deliveries. Commercial transport interruptions will involve railroads, bus lines and street car companies, trucking firms, airports and air lines, as well as streets, highways, and bridges.

Estimates as to damage also must be sought from a variety of sources. They include the transportation, communications, and public utility concerns; owners of property; public agencies such as police and fire departments; the weather bureau; and agricultural officials.

When a community has been devastated by a major disaster, an immediate problem of great magnitude is relief work and restoration of facilities for normal living. These tasks will usually be directed by the mayor or city manager, who organizes municipal agencies and manpower for specific areas of work. In addition to police, firemen, health department employees, and other municipal workers, he also can call upon civil defense, which has personnel trained for disaster relief.

When the havoc is so great that local resources are inadequate to cope with the situation, the state and federal governments may be called upon for help, usually in the form of the national guard or federal troops.

The traditional agency for relief work in a disaster area is the Red Cross with its trained workers and resources devoted to providing food, medical supplies, clothing, and shelter.

As can be seen from the foregoing listing of information to be obtained and sources to be reached, coverage of a major natural disaster is an all-hands operation for the newspaper. The individual reporter, assigned by the city editor to relatively few phases of coverage, will turn over much of his information to rewritemen for incorporation into the general stories. He may, however, write the side stories, eyewitness accounts, and human-interest stories that come across his path.

Coverage of Hospitals

Of all the sources of information about casualties in accidents and disasters, the most important is the hospital. It is not only the most reliable source for facts about injuries, but it also provides the first knowledge that the press may have of many accidents. The fact that someone has been injured in an automobile crash, burned in a fire, or shot by a robber will be turned up in routine coverage of police and fire departments; but there are a great many mishaps that do not require police or official action, and the initial notice of them comes from the check for emergencies admitted to hospitals. Without the cooperation of hospitals and doctors, news coverage, therefore, would be seriously hampered.

The cooperation that the press may expect from hospitals and the medical profession has become standardized since 1947, when representatives of hospitals, the state medical society, newspapers, and radio in Colorado adopted a code of practices. The Colorado code of cooperation has been the model for similar codes adopted in more than 30 states.

In general, hospitals and doctors are bound to protect the right of privacy of patients, but this right, under the codes, may give way to public interest in the case of accident or other emergency, in the case of a personality in whom the public has a legitimate interest, and in the case of unusual injury or illness—when the facts will lead to a better understanding of the progress of medical science. In police cases and others involving official action, hospitals may give information without the patient's consent.

Hospitals will ordinarily provide such personal data as the name, address, sex, age, and, if known, the occupation and firm employing the patient; a statement of his condition, such as "not serious,"

"serious," or "critical"; and information about the nature of the accident, such as automobile collision, explosion, fall, and so forth.

As to specific injuries, the reporter usually can obtain the following information according to representative codes and current practice:

Fractures: the member involved and whether simple or compound. Where X-ray diagnosis is not available, the qualifications "possible" or "probable" are used.

Head injuries: simply a statement that the head is injured. Without X-ray diagnosis, the hospital is unlikely to report on the possibility of a skull fracture.

Internal injuries: the general area of the injury, as chest and abdomen.

Unconsciousness: a statement that the patient was unconscious when brought to the hospital and, usually, the time that he regained consciousness.

Burns: the area of the body burned and the degree.

Skin and flesh: nature of the injury, such as cut, bruise, or scratch. (The medical terms, "laceration," "contusion," and "abrasion," should be avoided in news writing.)

Poisoning: possibility of poisoning and alleged agent.

Intoxication: no information at all.

Shooting and stabbing: only that there is a penetrating wound and the location.

ASSIGNMENTS

1. Write an article on the traffic situation in your community. Phases that might be covered include accident records, efforts of police and city officials to prevent accidents, studies to learn when and where most accidents occur, and policies of the courts in dealing with traffic offenders.

2. Write a news story for a morning newspaper based on the following information:

About 4 p. m. a slight drizzle began, changing to sleet early in the evening. The temperature high during the day was 46 degrees, and the thermometer is expected to drop to 20 degrees during the night. The prediction for the next day is continued cold with more snow and sleet.

The following accidents are on record at the police station: Ed L. Butler, 42, 401 S. Pine, was driving a 1955 Ford sedan north on Lindsay Avenue about 8 p. m. His car skidded completely around when he stopped at the intersection of E. First Street, and crashed into a car coming from the east. The other car, a 1956 Pontiac coach, was driven by Miss Rosalind Jerome, 23, 711 N. Elm. Both drivers said they were traveling about 20 miles an hour. The rear end of Butler's car smashed into the left front fender of Miss Jerome's car. Damage to each car was about $75.

Merton E. Lawrence, 59, and Mrs. Lawrence, 55, 611 Harrison Boulevard, were injured at 10:30 p. m. in an accident in the 400 block N. Fifteenth Street. Lawrence was driving the car. He was half way down the steep hill on Fifteenth Street when his brakes failed to hold. The car gathered speed and Lawrence lost control. At the bottom of the hill, the car crashed into a metal light pole on the northeast corner of Fifteenth Street and Anderson Avenue. Lawrence's car, a 1955 Buick, was badly damaged on the right side where it hit the light pole. Police estimated damage at $500. Both Mr. and Mrs. Lawrence were taken to City Hospital. The police report does not contain details of injuries.

Mrs. Lucy T. Price, 54, 804 N. Adams, driving at 11 p. m. on E. Twentieth Street, skidded into the curb in the 300 block. The right front wheel of her car, a 1957 Chevrolet, was broken. Damage to the car was estimated at $100. A passenger in the car was Mrs. Luther Arthur, 48, of Chicago, a visitor to Mrs. Price's home. She was taken to City Hospital. She was treated for contusions and a fractured right arm.

Discussing the traffic situation with Chief of Police Matthew Ryan, you obtain a warning from him for the public that driving conditions are bad and will get worse. He urges citizens not to drive their cars unless absolutely necessary and to be especially careful if they do.

You check on the condition of Mr. and Mrs. Lawrence at City Hospital. Mr. Lawrence has abrasions and contusions about the face and a scalp laceration that required six stitches. Mrs. Lawrence is still unconscious when you write your story. Her condition is described as "serious." She has a possible skull fracture. A check of the city directory reveals that Lawrence is owner of the Peerless Supply Co., 233 W. Main.

Other emergencies at the hospital are:

Frank Purdue, 60, 805 N. Birch. He has a broken hip. He slipped and fell at 8:30 p. m. on the steps of the City Hall.

Robert A. Swift, 10, son of Mr. and Mrs. Walter L. Swift, 1812 S. Wabash. He was injured at 7:30 p. m. when he slipped on the walk in front of his home. He was treated for a laceration of the scalp.

Checking with Lieut. Albert Preston of the highway patrol, you find that all highways leading into the city are dangerous. There have been numerous automobile mishaps, but no reports of serious injury. He issues a warning that driving on highways tomorrow will be extremely dangerous.

3. Write a story for a morning newspaper based on the following information:

At 4:12 p. m. the fire department receives a telephone call from Charles D. Romberg, 61, that a fire has broken out in a warehouse section of the National Paper Products Co., 1000 Lynwood Avenue. Romberg is watchman at the company's plant. The warehouse is in the center section of a two and three story brick plant that extends from W. Lynwood for about two blocks to S. Warner Street. The warehouse itself is one block long. A red brick, two story building, it was built in 1888 and for many years was a pulp mill. In recent years it has been used as a warehouse for storage of cardboard boxes and other paper products.

A second alarm was sounded at 4:33 p. m. and a third at 4:45 p. m. Altogether, fourteen companies were used in fighting the blaze. Operations at the scene were directed by Fire Chief Ronald Darby.

Because of the highly inflammable contents of the building, the flames spread quickly, shooting high in the air and leaping out the windows. The roof collapsed at 5:10 p. m. and the wall facing Lynwood fell a few minutes later. Smoke could be seen for miles in all directions. By pouring huge quantities of water on adjacent parts of the plant, firemen were able to prevent the blaze from spreading to other buildings. The fire was brought under control about 5:50 p. m., but firemen remained two more hours dousing the rubble in the warehouse.

A crowd of more than 10,000 persons was attracted to the scene. Hundreds massed on nearby Warriors Hill. Traffic was snarled for blocks in all directions, but police traffic officers kept fire lanes open. More than two dozen regular police and auxiliary police were brought in to control the crowd. Sgt. Taylor Prudhon, in charge of police at the scene, commented: "We were lucky that no emergency movement of injured persons was necessary."

Four firemen were injured, suffering cuts, smoke inhalation or eye irritation. They were Don McGregor, 28, 330 S. Elm; Ronald Prato, 33, 1800 E. First; Elmo Darwin, 35, 4322 N. Dartmouth; and Orson Durbin, 1833 N. Wildwood. They were treated at City Hospital and released.

T. B. Miner, plant superintendent, said he estimated damages would run more than $100,000. The contents of the warehouse were a total loss.

Chief Darby said an investigation was under way to determine the cause of the fire. "There is a good possibility the fire was started by two boys, either smoking or playing with matches," he said.

Romberg said he had seen two boys on the grounds near the building about thirty minutes before he discovered the fire near an open window on the first floor. "They ran when I yelled at them," he said. "They may have come back and got in the building through the window."

CHAPTER 18

CRIME AND LAW ENFORCEMENT

Crime as News

SOME TWO MILLION major crimes are committed each year in the United States. In an average day, someone is feloniously assaulted or killed every five minutes and robbed every ten minutes. A theft occurs every thirty seconds and a burglary every minute. At such a rate of occurrence, it is understandable that crime stories appear so frequently in newspapers and that crime is one of the nation's foremost problems. Yet one of the most common criticisms of newspapers is the treatment and space given to crime news.

As to space, the charge that newspapers are filled with stories of murder, rape, robbery, assaults, and other offenses in the criminal catalogue is exaggerated. Actually, the proportion of the news devoted to crime is small, averaging only one or two percent of the total in typical newspapers.

The impression that crime overshadows other news is probably due to the big play given the occasional offense that fulfills the requirements for a "good" crime story: prominence of the people concerned, atrociousness, and elements of mystery and suspense. It is this type of story that evokes often justified criticism, not the everyday coverage of the grist of the police station and criminal courts. When a newspaper decides to play a story with all stops open, it is likely to be guilty of the sins alleged against the press: sensationalism, bad taste, injury to the innocent, and interference with the administration of justice.

In answer to criticism, editors maintain that the continuous scrutiny of law enforcement and the courts protects the people against any improper actions by officials and informs them of the

229

seriousness of the crime problem. Moreover, publicity may be a deterrent to crime and sometimes an aid in the apprehension of criminals. Finally, editors find some justification for their treatment of crime news in the apparent universal interest in crime, pointing out that many of the best-known stories in the Bible are accounts of criminal violence and that the great literature of the world would comprise only a few books if those dealing with crime were eliminated.

The reporting of crime news requires a knowledge of the nature of crime as defined in statutes, of the work of peace officers in law enforcement, and of the procedures followed in the legal prosecution of a person accused of a violation of the law.

What Is a Crime?

Though many human actions may be considered morally, ethically, or religiously wrong, crime concerns only violations of rules of conduct established by law—state and federal statutes and city ordinances. A crime may be, and usually is, an offense committed against an individual, but legally it is considered an offense against society or the state. Thus, we have a distinction between civil and criminal law. Civil law concerns private wrongs for which the injured individual goes to court in his own name to seek redress; criminal law concerns offenses which, though directed against an individual, are prosecuted in the name of the people or the state.

If a person wants damages for personal injuries suffered when his automobile collides with another automobile, he sees a lawyer and files a civil suit for damages. If the driver of the other automobile caused the accident by a law violation, such as driving while drunk, he is prosecuted in a criminal action brought by the state.

Criminal offenses are of different degrees of seriousness. The major offenses—murder, robbery, burglary, arson—are known as felonies, and they are generally punishable by imprisonment in a penitentiary. The minor offenses—disorderly conduct, disturbing the peace, failure to stop at a stopline—are known as misdemeanors, and they are punishable by fine or detainment in a jail. The distinction is important, for the methods of prosecution and the courts having jurisdiction over the case are different.

The reporter, in writing his stories, should use the legal rather than the popular definitions of crimes, since there is sometimes a considerable difference in meaning. The most serious of all crimes is the offense against the person known as homicide, the killing of a human being by another human being. Homicides are considered justifiable when committed in self-defense, when they are the result of an unfortunate accident not due to negligence, or when they are committed by a peace officer in the performance of his duty. Unjustifiable, or felonious homicide, is defined as either murder or manslaughter.

There is an important difference between these two terms: murder is homicide committed with malice aforethought, while manslaughter is homicide committed without malice aforethought. State statutes recognize degrees of seriousness for each offense. First degree murder involves express malice and premeditation—homicides perpetrated by means of poison, lying in wait, or by making advance preparations, such as obtaining a weapon. Any homicide perpetrated during the commission of a felony such as robbery or burglary is also first degree murder. Second degree murder is a homicide committed without premeditation but with the intent to kill or do bodily harm at the time without regard for the consequences. In second degree murder there is no aforethought but there is malice. Manslaughter is either voluntary—committed in a sudden rage of passion or upon extreme provocation—or involuntary—an accidental death resulting from negligence.

Two other crimes against the person where the legal definition differs from the popular definition are assault and battery. Assault is a threat to do bodily harm, and battery is the actual striking of a person. Other crimes against the person are rape, mayhem, abortion, false imprisonment, kidnaping, and abduction.

Society recognizes two serious crimes against the habitation: burglary—breaking and entering with intent to commit a felony—and arson—the malicious burning of another's property or one's own property with intent to defraud an insurance company.

Another classification of crimes includes crimes against property. The most common is larceny—taking and carrying away the goods of another. It is of two degrees—petit (petty) larceny and grand larceny, depending upon the value of the goods taken. Robbery is an aggravated form of larceny when the goods are taken from a person by violence or intimidation. Other crimes against property are embezzlement, obtaining by false pretenses, forgery, and malicious mischief or vandalism.

Society recognizes a number of offenses against morality and decency, crimes often not reported by newspapers unless they can be justified in the public interest. They include adultery, prostitution, pandering, seduction, bigamy, incest, miscegenation, sodomy, indecency, and obscenity.

There are a number of offenses against the public peace: fighting, affray, unlawful assembly, rout, riot, disturbing public assemblies, disturbing the peace, maintaining a disorderly house, criminal libel, carrying concealed weapons, discharging firearms, and setting off explosives.

Offenses against the government include treason, criminal syndicalism, sedition, perjury (lying under oath), subornation of perjury (getting another person to lie under oath), extortion or bribery, embracery (an attempt unlawfully to influence a jury), resisting arrest, compounding a felony (agreeing not to prosecute or give evidence about a felony if the culprit makes reparation), and contempt of court.

There are many criminal offenses against public health, safety, and comfort: violations of traffic regulations (speeding, drunken driving, etc.) ; violations of health regulations (selling contaminated food, failure to maintain sanitary premises in a cafe, etc.); and violations of safety regulations (maintaining a fire hazard, failure to conform to building regulations, etc.).

Law Enforcement and Police

The work of enforcing the law is spread throughout the entire system of government—town and city, township, county, state, and nation. Small villages and towns employ a marshal to enforce the law; larger places maintain a police department. In townships the constable, an official of the justice of the peace court, has police powers. The chief law enforcement officer in the county is the sheriff. State peace officers include the state police or highway patrol and special agents of a state crime bureau. In the federal government, the traditional law enforcement officer is the United States Marshal, though nowadays his chief duties are as a functionary of the United States District Court. Federal police include agents of certain bureaus: the famous G-men of the Federal Bureau of Investigation, the T-men of the Department of the Treasury, post office inspectors, and agents of such divisions as the Department of Agriculture, the Bureau of Internal Revenue, and the Immigration Service.

The city police department, the base for the nation's law enforcement, provides most of the news. Whereas news originating in other agencies of enforcement may be handled by other reporters—those assigned to the county building or courthouse, the federal building, and the state capitol—the police department constitutes a separate run in cities of any size.

The reporter assigned to cover police obtains many tips and much of his information about crimes from departmental records. The principal ones, which he usually can consult, although they are not public records, are:

Complaint or Case Sheet. This record frequently provides the first information received about many crimes. In small departments it is kept by the desk officer, in larger departments by the dispatcher, and in the largest departments by a special officer. Data recorded includes the nature of the crime, the name and address of the victim, the time and place, the person or persons suspected, the officers assigned to investigate, injuries received by victims, property loss, and arrests, if any.

Since premature publication of the details of a complaint might interfere with the apprehension of suspects, some of the reports may be stamped "Not for Publication" or "No Publicity." Police reporters should observe these orders. To violate them might result in the case sheet being closed to the press.

The Radio Log. The Federal Communications Commission requires police departments to keep a log of broadcasts. The log gives the time of the message, the sender, the person to whom it is directed, and the message itself, usually in code. The press room at the police station contains a police short-wave radio, and reporters keep an ear cocked to it for anything of importance.

Reports of Investigating Officers. The fullest recorded details about crimes to be found in the police station are given in the investigation reports that officers are required to write. They include the nature of the crime, full data about the victims and property loss, and the names of persons interviewed and investigated. They are a record of everything the officers did about the case and everything they learned about it.

The Wanted Book. As the name indicates, this book lists persons wanted by the police and gives the names, descriptions, and the reason why the persons are sought.

Auto and Bicycle Theft Records. In larger police departments, theft of automobiles and bicycles is usually recorded on special forms rather than on the complaint or case sheet.

Accident Reports. Special forms for recording investigations of automobile accidents are maintained by larger police departments.

Arrest Records. All persons arrested and locked in jail must be "booked." Information included on the jail register includes the full name of the prisoner; his age, race, sex, and physical description; his occupation; his marital status; the date and hour of the arrest; the place of the arrest; the reason for the arrest—the charge on which the suspect is held; the officer making the arrest; and the manner in which the arrest was made—on sight, on warrant, or by other authority. Information added later includes disposition of the arrested person—released without prosecution, hospitalized, or transferred to some other authority, such as the county or federal district court.

Information recorded at the station frequently gives all the facts needed by a reporter for handling a story about a routine or minor crime. For fuller details about a newsworthy one, however, he may have to interview investigating officers, the victim, witnesses, and sometimes the suspect, if an arrest has been made.

One of the misapprehensions which many people have about police work is that it is solely concerned with crime. Nothing could be further from the truth: police serve as attendants at public functions, parades, and celebrations; they locate missing persons; they direct traffic and guard school children at crossings; they report such hazards as broken sidewalks; they investigate accidents and care for the injured; they assist firemen; and they have other duties that often have little to do with criminal activity. All these—as well as departmental activities such as promotions, statistical reports, citations for heroism, addition of new equipment, reassignments of duty—provide news.

Arrests and Searches

The police reporter covers criminal cases only at their inception—with the arrest of suspects and their incarceration in jail pending the filing of formal charges. The reporter must realize that the charge listed when a suspect is placed in jail does not constitute an accusation upon which the individual can be brought to trial. As will be shown later, no person can be tried for a felony except upon an indictment or presentment by a grand jury, or an information filed in the court of trial jurisdiction by a prosecuting attorney. In most instances such formal accusation has not yet been brought against a person arrested and lodged in the city jail. Such an accusation, if it ensues at all, comes in the course of time in accordance with procedures prescribed in criminal law.[1]

Like the word "charge," the word "arrest" is often loosely used and often misunderstood. An arrest is the taking of a person into custody for the purpose of bringing him into court to be dealt with according to law. A person arrested is entitled to be taken before a magistrate without delay to answer to the charge against him. A reporter will not be around a police station for long, however, before he discovers a great many persons are arrested who are never produced in court. Actually, studies show that from one-third to almost one-half the persons arrested by police are never charged. Bluntly stated, the fact is, in the words of one student of the law, "the great majority of arrests by police officers are illegal in their inception, continuance or termination."

What happens is that many persons are taken into custody as suspects and are "detained" at police headquarters or "held for questioning" while police hunt for evidence to prove their connection with a crime. In such instances the suspects are not booked or charged. If police are unable to find adequate evidence, the prisoners are released:

> The 37-year-old Lorain County man held in Lorain city jail in connection with the disappearance of Beverly Potts was eliminated as a suspect yesterday by Cleveland detectives who questioned him.
> Lorain police arrested him Monday after tipsters informed them they heard him talking about the 10-year-old girl's disappearance and said he apparently knew more about the case than he should.
> Deputy Inspector James E. McArthur, chief of the Cleveland detective bureau, said he was convinced the man had no knowledge of how Beverly disappeared August 24.—Cleveland *Plain Dealer.*

[1] The United States Supreme Court has held that a person is formally charged with crime with the filing of a complaint or affidavit alleging the commission of a crime by him even though some other charge might be required for trial.

Police often avoid the illegality of holding a person while they search for evidence by charging him with a minor offense as a basis for producing him in court:

> Joseph Li Calsi, 39 years old, an unemployed dress manufacturer, was arrested and held on a vagrancy charge here yesterday in connection with the October 4 murder of Willie Moretti in Cliffside Park, N. J.—New York *Times.*

Arrests may be made with or without a warrant, but in the latter case a warrant is usually obtained soon after the person is taken into custody. An arrest warrant is an order issued by a judge, most frequently a justice of the peace or magistrate, ordering a peace officer to take the person described in the warrant into custody, and to produce him in court to be dealt with according to law.

A judge issues a warrant upon a complaint signed by a private citizen or peace officer which alleges the commission of a crime and names the person believed to have committed it. The warrant names the complainant, repeats the substance of the complaint, and directs a peace officer to bring the accused into court.

Police may arrest a person without a warrant when they catch him in the commission of a crime or when they have reasonable grounds for believing he has committed one. The power of arrest, however, is not wholly confined to police, for private citizens may make arrests for crimes committed in their presence.

For some misdemeanors, especially traffic offenses, law violators may be brought into court to answer charges, by means of a summons. The familiar traffic ticket is such a summons. A summons, however, is technically not the same thing as an arrest. If the person served a summons fails to appear in court, a warrant for his arrest will be issued by the judge.

Just as the rights of the person are protected by rules governing arrests, especially the requirement that an accused must be brought into court "forthwith" or "without unreasonable delay," so is the citizen protected against unreasonable searches of his house. In order to enter a habitation, police must obtain a search warrant, defined by the New York Code of Criminal Procedure as "an order in writing, in the name of the people, signed by a magistrate, directed to a peace officer, commanding him to search for personal property, and bring it before the magistrate." The procedure for obtaining a search warrant is the same as that for an arrest warrant.

It cannot be issued except, as the New York code states, "upon probable cause supported by an affidavit naming or describing the person, and particularly describing the property to be searched." Grounds upon which search warrants can be issued generally include the search for stolen or embezzled property, property used as a means of committing a crime, and property held with intent to use it as the means of committing one.

Reporting Police News

Although constitutional and statutory provisions for public trial and court rulings give newspaper reporters legal rights to cover judicial proceedings, these privileges do not extend to police department records. Police records, except for the jail register, are not public records, and reporters therefore cannot demand to see them for news stories. Access to police department news depends not upon legal rights but upon the reporter's relationships with police and the pressure newspapers can bring to bear by the threat of adverse publicity.

Since privilege, in the sense of barring a suit for libel, does not extend to most police records and to statements made by police, the reporter must be scrupulously accurate in his reporting of police news. He must verify names and addresses. When the identity of a person arrested is not positive, he may need to use a qualification such as "a man who gave his name as." The names of persons held as suspects without being booked or charged usually should not be used at all, unless the evidence against them seems to be overwhelming or unless they have previous records of arrests and convictions or are known to be associates of criminals. Because of the difficulty of checking street addresses, especially in case of a gambling raid or other type of raid, many newspapers do not give exact addresses. Instead, they say "the 300 block of N. First Street" or "Maple Avenue near Elwood Drive."

Many police stories are routine and make few demands on reportorial or writing skill. Perhaps the easiest to cover are burglaries, robberies, or thefts in which no arrest has been made. Frequently the complaint or case record gives the reporter all the information he needs—the who, when, where, what, how, and how much—of the incident. If the victim is well known or if he is injured, the story is worth more than if he is not; the more the property is worth, the more important the crime is as news; and an unusual twist makes for a better story.

When police make an arrest or bring in a suspect, the reporting problem becomes more complicated. The reporter must check on what disposition is made of the prisoner, what charges are filed or planned, and when the prisoner will be given a hearing in court. These decisions ordinarily follow the questioning of the prisoner by officers and his appearance in the show-up line for identification by victims or witnesses. If the crime is a serious felony, the district attorney or one of his assistants may be called in to take part in the questioning. In almost all instances police attempt to get a signed statement from the prisoner.

As has been pointed out, many so-called arrests are not actual arrests, in that they are not followed by the filing of charges and producing of the prisoner in court. Consequently, the reporter should be careful in giving names and details before the prisoner is actually booked. A charge can be several things—the statement of the crime alleged on the blotter in booking the prisoner, the statement of the crime alleged in the arrest warrant, or a formal accusation in the form of an information or indictment. A newspaper can safely print the facts about such a charge, but is on unsafe grounds when the allegations have not become a matter of public record. In practice, however, many newspapers print information about an arrest with a statement that charges will be filed, attributing it to a responsible official.

An important legal presumption is that all persons arrested are considered innocent until convicted by a jury. Therefore, in writing about arrests the reporter must be careful not to impute guilt, as in a sentence asserting that a person "was arrested for driving while drunk." A more accurate, and safer, phrasing is "was arrested and charged with driving while drunk" or "was arrested on a charge of driving while drunk." An arrested and accused person should not be referred to as "the robber" or "the burglar." Until found guilty, he is "the suspect" or "the accused" or "the prisoner."

Though in most newspaper stories morbid and distasteful details probably should be avoided, some common newspaper taboos seem unreasonable. For instance, there seems to be no good reason for such euphemisms as "attack" and "assault" in place of the legal term "rape," since no one could be sullied by seeing this word in print. Sometimes the effort to avoid it has strange results, as one newspaper's report of the attempted rape of a 15-year-old girl. The newspaper described the incident: "She was walking on the Wilksboro Avenue footbridge, near her Grittens Street home, shortly after 10 p. m. when the assailant seized her, threw her to the ground and tried to attack her."

The prissy avoidance of the word "rape" may lead to a complete misunderstanding of what actually happened to a victim. This sort of news lead is often seen: "Mrs. Adam Smith, 33, of 220 N. First Street, was attacked about 10 o'clock last night by two men who dragged her into an alley in the 300 block Wheeling Avenue and took her purse containing $10." Readers accustomed to interpreting "attack" and "assault" as "rape" would be wrong in their interpretation of what happened to Mrs. Smith.

The vague term "morals charge" also is subject to misinterpretation. The accused, should he be found innocent, might from the newspaper publicity be thought of afterward as some kind of monster for an act comparatively innocent in itself, and a victim might similarly suffer from being thought the object of outrageous indignities which in fact were never experienced. If the exact crime for which a person is charged is printed, such misconceptions are not likely to arise.

While it is important that newspapers inform the public of the occurrence of crime and the prosecution of criminals, their responsibility should not end there. Their treatment should be sociological rather than sensational. Unscientific reporting, such as attributing an atrocious crime to a "fiend" or "sex maniac," contribute little to the understanding of the causes of crime or to the remedies. Nor does suppression help society. In this respect, J. Edgar Hoover, head of the Federal Bureau of Investigation, has said:

> The press and radio can render invaluable service, not only by disclosing the names of sex offenders and making it plain that sex crimes "do happen," but by campaigning vigorously for more adequate laws and turning the spotlight on delays and failures to adequately handle confirmed and depraved sex offenders. The time has long since passed when any medium of public communications can afford to consider such offenses as "unmentionable."

The reporter covering police should go outside the police station for what help he can get from the studies of criminologists, sociologists, and psychologists in writing constructively about crime.

ASSIGNMENTS

1. Study the crime stories over a week's period in a daily news-paper and write a report covering the following questions:

    a. What is the proportion of crime news to other types of news?
    b. Did any stories show evidence of glorifying or making heroes of criminals?
    c. Did any stories prejudge an accused person or imply guilt to such an extent that he might find it hard to obtain a fair trial?
    d. Did any stories unwarrantedly invade the privacy of relatives or friends of persons accused of crimes?
    e. Were any stories sensationally treated and did any offend good taste by the kind of details given?
    f. Were any stories scientifically or sociologically treated so as to give the public a better understanding of crime problems?
    g. What is the newspaper's apparent policy in the treatment of crime news?

2. From the compiled statutes of your state, list and give brief definitions of crimes in the following categories: crimes against the person, crimes against the habitation, crimes against property, crimes against morality and decency, crimes against the public peace, crimes against the government, and crimes against public health, safety, and comfort.

3. From the compiled statutes of your state write a résumé of laws governing arrests, arrest warrants, and search warrants.

4. Write a news story based on the following chronological report:

    Peter A. Talbott, 44, was awakened at 4:45 a. m. today by a thud and the shuffle of feet in his television and radio shop beneath his apartment at 3300 E. First Street. He picked up the telephone and called police.

    Sgt. Wilbur Dunne received the call at the police station. He radioed scout car officers Timothy Duane and A. J. Kermit to go to the shop and also sent officers William Dodds and Ernest Martino from the police station. Duane and Kermit covered the rear of the shop, while Dodds and Martino investigated at the front and side. Dodds and Martino found a side window forced open. They climbed through it and were met inside by Talbott.

    The thieves were gone. So were Talbott's cash register, containing about $150, a $400 television set, and television testing equipment valued at $500.

    Nearby the police spotted a parked automobile. They examined it and found Talbott's property. They also found a pinchbar. It was obvious the thieves had been surprised and had fled on foot just as they were about to drive off.

Sergeant Dunne was asked for a quick check on the car's license number. A few minutes later he radioed that the car was owned by Angus Sinclair, 19, of 2600 S. Pine. The policemen sped to the address. Light showed through a kitchen window. Duane and Kermit went to the back and from the window saw two young men counting change on a kitchen table. Dodds and Martino hammered at the front door. The young men scooped up the money. Duane and Kermit broke in the back door and arrested them. The change amounted to about $50. One of the young men was Sinclair, and the other was Theodore Patrick, 20, of 2800 W. Fifteenth Street. They were taken to jail and charged with burglary and possession of burglar tools.

Sergeant Dunne said they admitted breaking into Talbott's shop and confessed the change was taken from the Oak Park Grocery, 1403 S. Maple, which they entered about 1:30 a. m. They also said they had attempted to enter a filling station about six blocks from the grocery about 2:30 a. m. but were frightened away when an automobile stopped across the street.

CHAPTER 19

PROCEEDINGS AFTER ARRESTS

The System of Courts

A COPY of any day's issue of a newspaper reveals, to the uninitiated, a bewildering account of court happenings. One story tells of a man being tried in district court for an automobile theft and of another being tried in federal court for the same type of offense. A robbery suspect receives a hearing before a justice of the peace and another a trial in district court. Stories tell of the filing of a suit for damages in justice of the peace court, another in district court, and still another in federal court.

Why all these courts? Why does one person sue in a justice of the peace court and another in a district court? Why is a robbery suspect given a hearing before a justice of the peace and a trial before a district judge?

The answer to these questions is that courts have different functions and powers—summed up in the word "jurisdiction." Jurisdiction is of two types: jurisdiction over the person and jurisdiction over the subject matter. Jurisdiction over the person is partly geographical: a court's authority does not extend beyond its territorial limits. An Ohio court, for example, has no power in Illinois, and a person accused of a crime must be tried in the judicial district in which the crime was committed. Jurisdiction over the subject matter refers to the type of case or to the amount of money involved. Inferior courts, for instance, can hold trials for persons charged with misdemeanors, but trials for felonies must be held in a district court. Violations of federal statutes must be prosecuted in a federal district court. Civil suits involving sums of money of several hundred dollars may be heard in justice of the peace courts, but suits involving larger sums must be heard in district court.

Though state court systems vary somewhat, they follow a general pattern. They include the following courts:

Highest courts of appeals, usually called supreme courts. They ordinarily sit at the state capitol and most of their cases are appeals from lower courts.

Intermediate courts of appeals, usually courts established by statute to relieve the supreme court of the burden of appeals from lower courts.

Local courts of original jurisdiction, called district courts, circuit courts, or superior courts. They are the backbone of the judicial system, having original and exclusive jurisdiction to try persons for felonies and to hear the more important types of civil litigation.

The minor judiciary, or inferior courts, made up of justice of the peace courts, aldermanic and magistrate courts, and such special courts as municipal courts, police courts, and city courts. These courts may try persons accused of misdemeanors, conduct certain preliminary hearings of persons accused of felonies, and hear minor civil suits involving small sums of money.

Unless he works in a large city, the reporter probably will not have occasion to cover a case in one of the federal courts. He should, however, be familiar with the federal system, since he may have to report a local angle of a case, rewrite from press dispatches suits and criminal prosecutions involving home town people, or follow through on cases appealed from district courts to federal courts.

The federal courts consist of the Supreme Court sitting in Washington, ten Circuit Courts of Appeals, and the United States District Courts of which there is at least one district for each state. Federal judicial power extends to all cases arising under the constitution, the laws of the United States, and treaties entered into by the nation; to controversies to which the United States is a party; and to controversies between two or more states, between a state and citizens of another state, and between citizens of different states.

Though the judge is the most important officer of any court, he seldom is the most productive source of news. He may be consulted by a reporter wanting information about general law questions or rules of the court, but it would be improper for him to discuss with reporters trials over which he presides.

The reporter will find the court clerk's office a constant source of news, especially for civil litigation and routine proceedings. Reporters have advance information about criminal prosecutions through arrests, hearings in justice of the peace courts, and action by grand juries, and they also can keep informed of developments through the district attorney's office. But civil suits ordinarily become known to newspapermen only when the first papers are filed with the court clerk.

Consequently, the reporter must keep a close check on the court clerk's records. The most important record is in the large bound volumes called dockets. The current volume is ordinarily kept on a table or desk convenient for listing new cases. When a suit is filed, it is entered in the docket and given a serial number. The docket itself records only basic information—the name of the plaintiff, the name of the defendant, and the nature of the action. From this information the reporter can ordinarily decide if the suit is worth checking for further information. If he decides that it is, he looks up the petition in the case, filed in cabinets according to serial number. For additional information he must consult the parties to the case or their attorneys.

Every stage of the litigation after the filing of the suit—issuance of a summons, filing of an answer, rulings by the judge, and findings by the judge or jury—is recorded in the docket.

The clerk, in collaboration with the judge, prepares the court calendar—a schedule of cases for hearings and trial. Before each day's session of court the clerk prepares a call sheet listing cases to be heard and giving serial numbers and names of the plaintiff and defendant with a blank space left for action by the court. By checking the daily call sheet, the reporter can discover if any action was taken on cases in which he is interested.

The district or county attorney is the most important single news source for developments in criminal prosecutions. He is the official who ordinarily makes the decision as to whether a person will be prosecuted for a crime, and he represents the state at preliminary proceedings in the inferior courts and at the trial. He often is active in the investigation of crimes, working with police and with the sheriff.

Inferior Court Trials

The jurisdiction of the inferior courts—justice of the peace, magistrate, municipal, and aldermanic—is limited in criminal cases to trials for misdemeanors and in civil cases to suits involving small sums of money. The judge also serves as a committing or examining magistrate in felony prosecutions: his duties in this respect are to decide if there is adequate cause to hold an accused person for further action.

Since the power of the inferior courts is limited to such minor offenses as disorderly conduct, drunkenness, traffic violations, and disturbing the peace, the trials seldom are covered by newspapers unless they involve prominent persons, have human-interest appeal, or concern unusual situations. The oddity of the situation in the following case, for example, made it newsworthy:

> Harry Roberts' insistence on police action following an automobile accident October 1 cost him $75 in fines today in the police court of Judge James O. Leader.
>
> Police testified that Roberts, a mechanic living at 1810 Maple Avenue, drove his automobile against the rear of another car at Porter Avenue and Miles Street. The machine was pushed into another, which was stopped preparatory to making a left turn.
>
> The drivers of the other two cars agreed to settle damages without calling in police, the officers testified, but Roberts insisted that arrests be made. He was accommodated, they said, and an intoximeter test proved him to be intoxicated.
>
> "You didn't know when you were well off," remarked Judge Leader, who fined him for careless driving and driving while intoxicated.

Persons are brought to trial in the lower courts upon complaints signed by private citizens or peace officers. The accused is brought before the court and arraigned—that is, the complaint charging him with an offense is read to him and he is asked to plead. If he pleads guilty, the court may sentence him immediately. Penalties are limited by statute to a brief jail term or small fine, but the costs of the prosecution are also assessed against a person who pleads guilty or is found guilty, and frequently they amount to more than the fine.

If the plea is not guilty, the trial may follow the arraignment immediately if witnesses are in court and the accused has an attorney. If not, the trial is set for some future time. The accused can be released from jail pending the trial upon posting of a cash bond or upon his own recognizance, or promise, to appear.

Since the judge can mete out only nominal punishment, jury trials are seldom held in the inferior courts. Quite often, accused persons do not desire to go through the formality of a trial when the punishment is merely a small fine, as it is for many traffic offenses. Persons post bond and forfeit it by failure to appear for trial. So rare are jury trials that the fact a jury is impaneled is newsworthy:

> The first jury trial in Elmwood in 17 years resulted in a verdict of guilty of peace disturbance and a $1 fine for one of two defendants last night. The other defendant received a week's continuance.
>
> Both men were charged with using profane language in a restaurant at 1802 Oak Avenue on August 22. Peter O. Arms, 110 Grand Avenue, received the $1 fine. James O. Jones, 1700 Park Place, got the continuance.
>
> Charles A. Rodgers, attorney for both men, who threw Police Judge Paul A. Taylor's court into an uproar September 11 when he asked for a jury trial for his clients, presented no defense testimony or summation to counter three witnesses for the prosecution.
>
> But he did ask for a mistrial when a waitress in the restaurant declined to repeat the language she asserted the defendants employed. Judge Taylor denied the motion.

Inferior Court Felony Proceedings

Persons accused of felonies can be brought to trial only upon an indictment or presentment by a grand jury, or upon an information filed in the trial court by the district attorney. The procedure before the trial depends upon the mode of accusation and upon whether the arrest is made before or after the accusation.

When arrest precedes the formal accusation by indictment or information, the accused cannot be taken immediately into the court of jurisdiction. To insure that his right of an immediate court hearing is not violated, the inferior courts have been given certain functions pending the securing of an indictment or the filing of an information. These inferior court hearings are for the following purposes:

(1) To inform the accused of the charges against him at a proceeding commonly called an arraignment.

(2) To decide, upon the basis of evidence against the accused, whether there are reasonable grounds for holding him for further action at a proceeding called a preliminary hearing or preliminary examination. The further action is obtaining the indictment or filing the information.

(3) To give the accused an opportunity to effect his release from jail pending further action by obtaining bail. Bail is the posting of

security in the form of money or property, or getting another person to do so, to insure the appearance of the accused in court at a later time.

Suppose police arrest a man and book him on a charge of burglary. As has been pointed out, this charge does not constitute an accusation by which he can be brought to trial, but the prisoner is nevertheless entitled to an immediate hearing in court. The next step after the arrest is a hearing, or arraignment, in a justice of the peace or magistrate court. A follow story on an arrest on a burglary charge might play up this fact in the lead:

> Abner L. Jones, 33, of 200 E. First Street, arrested Tuesday night after a six-block chase by a policeman who saw him crawling out a rear window of the Popular Store, will be arraigned at 3 p. m. today before Magistrate Peter Fortson.

At the arraignment Jones will be informed of the charge against him and will be asked to plead. If he pleads guilty, the magistrate will order him returned to jail for further action—the obtaining of an indictment or filing of an information. The development might be reported as follows:

> A man arrested Tuesday night, after a six-block chase by a policeman who saw him crawling out a rear window of the Popular Store, was held for the grand jury yesterday afternoon when he pleaded guilty to a burglary charge before Magistrate Peter Fortson.

If, however, Jones says that he is not guilty, he is entitled to a preliminary hearing at which the magistrate will look into the evidence against him and decide whether there are reasonable grounds for holding him for further action. Thus the follow story might report the arraignment:

> The preliminary hearing for a man arrested Tuesday night after a six-block chase by a policeman who saw him crawling out a rear window of the Popular Store was set for 10 a. m. Friday by Magistrate Peter Fortson yesterday afternoon.

Additional information which may be obtained at the arraignment is whether the accused asked for bail, the amount set by the magistrate, and whether the accused was able to make it. This development might be reported:

Bail of $10,000 was set in magistrate court yesterday afternoon for a man accused of burglary after he was arrested Tuesday when seen crawling out a rear window of the Popular Store.

The man, Abner L. Jones, 33, of 200 E. First Street, failed to make the bail and was returned to jail to await a preliminary hearing set for 10 a. m. Friday.

The accused person at his arraignment may waive, or forego, his right to a preliminary hearing after pleading not guilty. In this event, the arraignment might be reported:

Abner L. Jones, 33, of 200 E. First Street, accused of the burglary of the Popular Store, waived a preliminary hearing at his arraignment yesterday afternoon and was bound over to the grand jury.

The preliminary hearing, as has been pointed out, is designed to prevent a person's being brought to trial unless there is presumptive evidence of his guilt. It saves him the trouble and expense of defending himself against further proceedings if the state cannot make out a good case against him. It is similar to a trial in that the magistrate hears evidence against the accused, who can present evidence in his own defense, but it is not actually a trial, since the magistrate court does not have jurisdiction to try prosecutions for felonies. At the preliminary hearing police and other witnesses present evidence to show that a crime was committed and that there are grounds for belief that the defendant did it. The accused is entitled to give evidence to refute the accusation, though he does not have to and often does not.

If the magistrate finds that evidence provides reasonable grounds for holding the accused, he binds him over to the grand jury if an indictment is to be sought, or to the district court if an information is to be filed. In case of such a development, the story of the preliminary hearing might say:

Abner L. Jones was held for grand jury action yesterday after police testified at a preliminary hearing that he had $500 in stolen merchandise in his possession when arrested after being seen crawling out a rear window of the Popular Store.

Jones, 33, of 200 E. First Street, did not give evidence in his defense. He was returned to jail when he failed to make $10,000 bail set by Magistrate Peter Fortson.

On the other hand, if the magistrate does not feel that police have a sufficiently strong case he discharges the accused. This dismissal, however, does not constitute a finding of not guilty and does not preclude rearrest for the crime should police later obtain new evidence. If Jones had been able to refute the police evidence, the preliminary hearing might be reported:

> Abner L. Jones was freed of a burglary charge at a hearing yesterday afternoon when witnesses testified he was in a repair shop on the alley next to the Popular Store when it was burglarized.
>
> Jones, 33, of 200 E. First Street, said he had just left the repair shop when a man called out at him telling him to stop. Fearing it was a hold-up, he fled and was arrested after a six-block chase by a policeman.
>
> The man whom Patrolman John Cassady said he had seen crawling from a rear window of the store apparently escaped in the darkness.

Accusations for Felonies

Some twenty states have constitutional provisions requiring that prosecution for serious crimes be by grand jury indictment. In other states district attorneys have the option of obtaining an indictment or filing an information to bring a person to trial.

The information procedure, however, cannot be followed without the accused person's being given an arraignment and preliminary hearing in an inferior court, and in some states he must waive indictment to be prosecuted by an information. If prosecution is to be by information, the committing magistrate binds the accused over to district or circuit court instead of to the grand jury. The prosecuting attorney then files his information, and the accused is brought into the trial court to be arraigned, that is, to plead to the accusation. Thus, in the Abner Jones case, the magistrate would bind him over to district court rather than to the grand jury if the prosecution was to be by information:

> Abner L. Jones was held for district court yesterday at his preliminary hearing when police testified he had $500 in stolen merchandise in his possession taken from the Popular Store Tuesday night.

When an accused is bound over to a grand jury at an arraignment or preliminary hearing, the prosecuting attorney must go before that body to seek an indictment. A presentment, the second type of accusation emanating from a grand jury, differs from an indictment in that it is based on evidence obtained by a grand jury's own investigations instead of on evidence submitted to it by a prosecuting attorney.

A grand jury is selected by lot from a jury list compiled from tax rolls and voting registration rolls. When the grand jury is convened at the order of a judge, the reporter can get from the district attorney a list of cases to be submitted to it:

> State evidence in one murder case and two manslaughter cases will be presented to the Woods County grand jury to be convened during the week of December 3. The cases will be among 52 to be heard by jurors.
> The defendant in the murder case is Albert Aiken, Middletown merchant, charged with slaying Robert A. Armitage, a business associate, in the latter's Spring Lake cottage October 14. The shooting climaxed an afternoon drinking party at the cottage. . . .

The request for the accusation is in the form of a bill of indictment describing the crime committed or law violated and naming the person believed to be responsible. The district attorney brings in enough witnesses to establish an *ex parte* case, that is, of one side only. If, on the basis of this one-sided evidence, the jurors believe the state has a reasonable case, it votes to return a "true bill," an endorsement placed on the bill of indictment. The terms "true bill" and "indictment" are synonymous in popular usage. If the jurors believe the state's case is insufficient, they endorse the bill "ignoramus" (we ignore it). In popular usage, the grand jury is said to have returned a "no bill," "ignored the bill," or "refused to indict." An example follows:

> All alleged liquor law violations together with bills charging maintenance of gambling devices were ignored by the September grand jury which made its final returns yesterday afternoon.
> The grand jury acted upon 140 bills. Of that number 73 were returned as true bills and 67 as no bills.

The grand jury's findings or report, officially known as a presentment, are given to the judge. All persons named in indictments or true bills must then be brought into court to answer or plead to the accusation at an arraignment. In some instances, a person indicted has not been arrested prior to the grand jury action. The judge orders his arrest by issuing a capias, an arrest order popularly known as a bench warrant.

In addition to the grand jury's function of deciding whether there is probable cause to hold a person for trial on the basis of the prosecuting attorney's evidence, it can conduct investigations of its own of law violations, misconduct of public officials, and the operation of public institutions. A criminal accusation that results from such investigations is sometimes called a presentment. In practice, it usually is a report to the judge asking that the district attorney be instructed to draw up a bill of indictment for the alleged law violation. When the bill has been properly drawn, it is submitted to the grand jury, or another grand jury if the first has been dismissed, for routine approval.

Coverage of Grand Juries

Proceedings of grand juries are secret, and their findings or presentments are not supposed to be made public except by the judge. Reporters frequently, however, are able to speculate on what is happening in the grand jury room through their prior knowledge of cases for which bills of indictment have been prepared, their familiarity with the crimes apparently being investigated, and their information about witnesses summoned to testify. Often, they are able to get witnesses to talk and to obtain information through leaks in the district attorney's office. The following illustrates how reporters sometimes are able to print unofficial and unauthorized information:

> Two witnesses reportedly gave new information Tuesday to the grand jury investigating two slayings by Policeman Michael Moretti.
> Both said they hadn't told their stories to the previous grand jury that failed to indict Moretti by one vote, because they hadn't been asked.
> The two are Frank "Coco" Navarro, 30, of 2943 W. Arthington, part owner of Tito's Hacienda, a saloon at 738 S. Halsted, and Alphonse Toribio, 26.
> Navarro reportedly told the jury he was beaten up by Moretti in the Maxwell Street police station on the night of the shooting early August 24.
> Toribio, who was treated to drinks by Moretti in the saloon that night, was reported as saying Moretti waved his gun and shouted, "We're going to have a real party."—Chicago *Daily News.*

When a grand jury returns its findings, the judge may hold up publication of some of the indictments if the persons accused have not been arrested and it is feared they might go into hiding if informed by a newspaper that they have been charged:

> A series of secret indictments was returned late today by a Woods County grand jury at the conclusion of a week-long investigation of the gambling rackets.
>
> Judge Robert A. Ames directed that the names and the number of those involved not be divulged until they are arrested. Neither may the nature of the charges against them be made public until then.

Grand juries likely to furnish sensational news are those conducting their own investigations of widespread law violation in a community, such as rackets and gambling, or of public officials or institutions. They may have the legal counsel of the district attorney, but frequently a special prosecutor is appointed by the judge to assist the jurors.

Denied access to the jury sessions, reporters must write their stories from their knowledge of the situation that resulted in calling the investigation, the witnesses subpenaed, the length of time they are questioned, hints thrown out by the prosecuting attorney, and statements of witnesses buttonholed after leaving the grand jury room.

The efforts of reporters to interview a witness at a grand jury proceeding are described in the following story:

> Newspaper reporters found Frank J. Sampson, administrative assistant to Mayor Impellitteri and one-time head of Tammany Hall, an elusive person yesterday when they sought to question him after a brief appearance before the grand jury that is looking into several phases of the fire department's activities.
>
> Mr. Sampson, who was before the jury for thirty minutes, left an executed financial questionnaire that had been handed to him on his previous appearance last Thursday, and then slipped out of the building by an unascertained route.
>
> Newspapermen who tried to intercept him before his appointment with the grand jury at 2:30 p. m. discovered that he had arrived a half hour earlier and had gone immediately to the grand jury room on the ninth floor of the Criminal Courts Building at 155 Leonard Street.
>
> The grand jury is reported to be seeking information on two questions concerning purported graft in the fire department. The panel is said to be attempting to learn the identity of the person or persons who "took over" a $500,000-a-year fuel oil shakedown racket last November 15 after James J. Moran, the former first

deputy fire commissioner, had been dropped as the alleged "guiding genius."

The grand jurors also would like to identify, it was said, the recipient of approximately $4,000 from nineteen firemen who admitted they paid fees to insure their promotion to the rank of lieutenant.—New York *Times*.

The grand jury's presentment, in addition to indictments, may contain a newsworthy report on the crime situation or the conduct of public officials, as in the following:

> NEW YORK—Brooklyn's rackets-probing grand jury charged today that a "hierarchy of corrupt officials" in New York City's police department have organized to protect gamblers for graft.
>
> In a sizzling presentment handed up to Kings County Judge Samuel S. Leibowitz, the grand jury called for wholesale house-cleaning in the top echelons of the police department.
>
> The presentment (an official report and not a criminal indictment) said the conspiracy had dated back for ten years.
>
> With few exceptions, the jury charged, it has included every veteran inspector or deputy inspector that commanded a plain-clothes division.
>
> If there are technicalities barring the dismissal of the top brass involved, the jury said, then the officers should be demoted to make it impossible for them "to debase or suborn their fellow officers."

Coroner's Inquests

In cases of sudden death where there is reason to believe that death came about through unlawful means, the coroner and coroner's jury perform inquisitory and accusatory functions. The coroner is authorized to investigate accidental deaths, suspected suicides, deaths from unknown cause, and deaths in which there is suspicion of violence or foul play. The procedure is illustrated in the following story:

> A Middletown man was held for the coroner yesterday after an autopsy disclosed the man's wife died of a head injury and pneumonia.
>
> The autopsy on Mrs. Jacqueline Worth, 44, of 902 Maple, showed she died of an "intercranial hemorrhage, caused by a blow on the head, and pneumonia."
>
> County Detectives David Means and Arthur Sheldon said they are holding James A. Worth, 45, her husband, for action by the coroner.

Means said the investigation began after police discovered the
dead woman's body was covered with marks and bruises which
indicated she had been beaten. . . .

The inquest is conducted in a quasi-judicial manner, with the
coroner presiding and questioning witnesses. When testimony is
completed, the jury returns a verdict. The purpose of an inquest
is to determine the cause of death and to fix responsibility for it.
Possible verdicts are that death was due to accident or to natural
causes, that it was suicide, that it was murder by a person or persons unknown, or that a particular person caused it. In case of an
accusation against a particular person, the coroner, who by virtue
of his office is a committing magistrate, can order the accused
arrested and held for action by a grand jury.

Thomas W. Wales, 33, of 810 Maple, was ordered held for the
grand jury yesterday when a coroner's jury reached a verdict that
he fatally injured his wife in a quarrel last Tuesday.

Since an inquest is required for a suspected suicide, newspapers
usually wait until the coroner's verdict before labeling it as a suicide. Instead of an outright statement such as the following:

Mrs. Arthur A. Waters, 23, of 224 Hamilton Drive, despondent
over the death of her husband in a boating accident in April, committed suicide last night by firing a bullet into her right temple.

the newspaper is more likely to report the death:

Mrs. Arthur A. Waters, 23, whose husband was killed in a boating accident in April, was found dead of a bullet wound in her
right temple last night at her home at 224 Hamilton Drive. A .30
caliber pistol lay on the rug near her right hand.
Police said friends reported Mrs. Waters had been despondent
since the death of her husband. . . .

ASSIGNMENTS

1. Prepare an outline of the court system of your state, explaining the civil and criminal jurisdiction of each and naming the
officers of the courts and their duties.

2. Visit the district or circuit court clerk's office and get from him
an explanation of how dockets and other records are kept. Write a
feature article suitable for newspaper publication that would explain the duties of the clerk to the public.

3. Clip news stories which illustrate the preliminaries in the

prosecution of persons charged with felonies and which indicate the possible disposition of cases at each stage—plea of guilty, plea of not guilty, setting bond, waiving of a preliminary hearing, etc. Discuss the handling of the stories. Are they accurate from a legal point of view? Are they written in such a way that the lay reader can understand the nature and purpose of the proceedings? How much legal detail and explanation do you think should be given in such stories?

4. Write a feature article suitable for newspaper publication explaining the jury system in your state, covering such matters as how juries are selected, the qualifications for jury service, and the functions of juries.

5. Clip news stories that illustrate various problems of covering grand juries.

6. Attend sessions of a justice of the peace or magistrate court and write news stories about the cases handled.

7. Write a follow-up story on the arrest for burglary described in Assignment 4 of Chapter 18. Include as much background information and as much of the new material given below as you think necessary:

> Angus Sinclair and Theodore Patrick are brought into the court of Justice of the Peace Waldo McCormack for arraignment at 2:30 p. m. Each is handcuffed when herded into the court by jailer William Pine, but the handcuffs are removed immediately. Present as witnesses are the four arresting officers, Peter A. Talbott, and Orlando Mayberry, owner of the Oak Park Grocery. Also present are Arthur A. Joiner, an assistant district attorney, and T. L. Carlton, the young men's attorney. In the audience are Sinclair's parents, Mr. and Mrs. Andrew Sinclair, and Patrick's parents, Mr. and Mrs. William A. Patrick.

> McCormack asks the two attorneys if they are ready to go on with the case. Both say "yes." He then reads the warrant obtained after the arrest of Sinclair and Patrick and asks Carlton what his clients intend to do. Carlton says he would like to plead his clients not guilty and to waive the preliminary hearing. Turning to the two defendants, McCormack asks if that is their desire. Both reply "yes."

> Then Carlton continues: "In view of the youth of the two defendants and the fact that neither has been in trouble before, I ask that they be released from jail in the custody of their parents."

> Joiner objects, saying: "I don't think these criminals should be pampered at all. They're not juveniles—one is 19 and the other is 20. They knew they were doing wrong. The crimes they are

charged with were not boyish escapades. They committed two burglaries and attempted another one in the space of three hours. Strict legal procedures should be followed in their case."

Justice McCormack says: "I agree completely with the assistant district attorney. Our juvenile delinquency problem is serious enough without stretching the age limit to young men 19 and 20 years old. I order both defendants committed to the county jail to await action by the grand jury and set bail at $2,000 each."

Carlton explains that neither is prepared at the time to make bail, and McCormack says that the arrangements can be made later. He then calls the next case.

CHAPTER 20

TRIALS AND CIVIL PROCEEDINGS

Arraignments and Special Pleas

AFTER A PERSON is indicted or an information has been filed against him, he is arraigned in the trial court. He is called before the bar, the indictment or information is read to him, and he is asked how he pleads. He has numerous pleas and motions which he can make at this time:

(1) He may plead to the merits of the accusation, that is, either deny or admit guilt.

(2) He may seek to annul or throw out the indictment by a plea in abatement.

(3) He may assert that there are legal barriers which prohibit prosecution by a plea in bar.

(4) He may make several special motions to aid him in preparing his defense and to insure a fair trial.

Pleas to the Merits. Before any trial can proceed, there must be a joinder of issues, that is, the allegation of a fact or facts by the prosecution or plaintiff in a case and a general denial of them by the defendant. In a criminal prosecution, if the defendant pleads guilty—admits the truth of the accusation—no trial ensues, and the judge may pass sentence immediately. If the plea is not guilty, the judge sets the case for trial. In the interim between the arraignment and trial, an accused person may or may not be admitted to bail, at the discretion of the judge; if he has previously obtained bail he may have it continued.

Most convictions are obtained through pleas of guilty. These pleas often result from "bargains" between the prosecutor and the defendant, sometimes concurred in by the judge. The prisoner agrees to plead guilty upon a promise that the district attorney will recommend that a judge impose a light sentence or suspend sentence. Sometimes the guilty plea is obtained through a waiver of the major felony charge and acceptance of a guilty plea for a lesser offense.

Another type of innocence plea is not guilty by reason of insanity. When the accused is obviously of unsound mind at the time of arraignment, the judge may commit him to a mental institution instead of setting the case for trial. The theory of the law, in this instance, is that an insane person cannot plead at an arraignment. However, if the situation is such that the accused was insane at the time of the crime but at the arraignment appears to understand proceedings, the case will be set for trial and the question of insanity left to the jury to determine.

There are situations in which the accused evades a plea to the merits by a special plea of *nolo contendere* (I will not contest it), translated in news stories as a no contest or no defense plea. Its effect is the same as that of a plea of guilty, that is, it permits the judge to pass sentence without a trial. It is used chiefly in prosecutions for violations of business or commerical statutes and in manslaughter cases involving negligent homicide. Since it does not admit the truth of the allegations set forth in the indictment, as in a guilty plea, these allegations would have to be proved in a civil suit arising from the situation that brought on the criminal prosecution.

Pleas in Abatement. These pleas seek to have an indictment annulled on the ground that it is illegal. There are several types: a challenge to the array asserts that the indictment is invalid because of defects in the way it was obtained—that the grand jury was not legally selected or organized, that the members were not legally qualified, and that proceedings were not legally conducted; a motion to quash attacks an indictment because of some defect on the face of it, such as that it fails to state a specific criminal offense; a plea in abatement alleges certain errors in the procedure by which the indictment was obtained, such as that it was not endorsed as a true bill; a plea to the jurisdiction questions the authority of the court to try the case—it may be based on a contention that the offense was not committed within the territorial jurisdiction of the court or that the court has no jurisdiction over the person of the accused. All these pleas are known as dilatory pleas, in that if sus-stained by the judge they merely delay the trial until the errors can be corrected through issuance of a new indictment.

Pleas in Bar. These pleas maintain that prosecution cannot be pursued because of legal barriers: a demurrer is a motion which says that even if the allegations set forth in the accusation are true, they nevertheless do not constitute a crime or cause for action; the plea which takes advantage of the provision in the United States Constitution and most state constitutions that a person cannot twice be placed in jeopardy for the same offense is a plea of former jeopardy or, in some states, a plea of *autrefois acquit* (former acquittal) or *autrefois convict* (former conviction); a plea of limitations is based on the statute which bars prosecution for a number of crimes after a certain period of time has elapsed (statute of limitations); it varies from two to ten years.

Special Motions. Several special motions may be made which are designed to help the accused in conducting his defense and to improve his chances for obtaining justice: if he is not prepared for trial, he may ask for a continuance to obtain a postponement; in an indictment where there is a joinder of offenses or defendants, the accused may make a motion for a serverance, that is, ask a separate trial for each offense alleged or a separate trial from the other persons accused—such a motion is appropriate when the listing of the several counts might be prejudicial to the defendants; when the indictment does not give enough specific details of the offense alleged for the defendant to prepare his defense, he may move for a bill of particulars.

Other special motions cover the following situations: sometimes the admissibility of evidence can be questioned before a case comes to trial—this question is raised by a motion to suppress; when evidence has been obtained illegally, as by wire-tapping or by a search conducted without a warrant, the defense may attempt to make sure it is barred in advance and not introduced at the trial; if the accused feels that he cannot obtain a fair trial in the court because of adverse public opinion which might result in failure to obtain an unprejudiced jury, he may ask for a change of venue, or removal of the trial to another district.

If all these pleas and motions seem confusing to the student, he should not feel he is slow-witted: they are frequently confusing to lawyers, and because they are, many states and the federal courts have consolidated them into a single motion to dismiss—in which is contained a statement of the grounds for the motion. Commenting on the motion to dismiss shortly after its adoption in the federal courts, Homer Cummings, attorney general at the time, said:

> This should result in a reduction of opportunities for dilatory tactics and, at the same time, relieve the defense of embarrassment. Many competent practitioners have been baffled and mystified by the distinctions between pleas in abatement, pleas in bar, demurrers, and motions to quash, and have, at times, found difficulty in determining which of these should be invoked.

Besides the pleas that the defendant can make before trial, the district attorney can halt proceedings by a *nolle prosequi* (I do not wish to prosecute). He may wish to drop charges for several reasons: he may have new evidence showing that the accused is innocent, his case may be so weak he feels he cannot obtain a conviction, key witnesses may have disappeared or changed their testimony, or his staff may so busy it cannot devote the time and effort needed to build a weak case into a strong one.

Coverage of Trials

In order for him to write a news story, it is not necessary that the reporter be in court throughout a trial. On the contrary, most of his trial stories are written from secondhand information received from attorneys and from the minutes of the court. For trials of no great news interest he may want only the jury's verdict and the sentence pronounced by the judge. For more important trials he can obtain summaries of the testimony from one or both of the attorneys in the case, or find out when key witnesses will be called and arrange to be in court during the time of their testimony. If he is unfamiliar with the details of the case, he may plan to be in court for the opening statements of the prosecution and the defense, although he can usually obtain the gist from the district attorney or defense attorney before or afterward. Only for cases of major importance, when his newspaper wants complete coverage, will it be necessary for the reporter to sit through an entire trial.

Special privilege is accorded reporters in coverage of a trial by a press table maintained for them in the courtroom. Because reporters may not want to attend all the court sessions, or because they may have to leave to telephone information to their newspaper, they have frequent occasion to enter or leave the courtroom. These entrances and exits should be made quietly and at times when they are not likely to disturb proceedings.

Ordinarily, a trial is said to begin with the calling of the case and the summoning of a venire from which to select a jury. The trial is conducted according to the following order of procedure:

(1) Members of the jury are chosen and sworn.

(2) The district attorney opens the state's case by describing the crime alleged and outlining how he intends to prove the defendant guilty.

(3) The district attorney presents witnesses to give evidence in support of his case. Cross-examination of each by the defense attorney follows.

(4) The defense attorney opens the case for the defense with an outline of evidence he intends to submit.

(5) The defense attorney presents witnesses to give evidence in support of the defendant. Cross-examination of each by the district attorney follows.

(6) The district attorney may offer rebuttal testimony by calling witnesses.

(7) The attorneys for both sides make their arguments to the jury.

(8) The judge instructs the jury as to its duties and the legal points involved.

(9) The jury retires for its deliberations and verdict.

(10) The judge pronounces sentence if the verdict is guilty or dismisses the defendant if the verdict is not guilty.

A variation in this procedure is for the defense to make its opening statement immediately after the opening statement of the prosecution. Although this is the prescribed order in civil trials, only the State of New York requires the defense to make its opening statement at this time in criminal trials.

Selection of the Jury. The right of trial by jury does not mean just any jury It means a jury free from preconceptions as to the guilt or innocence of the accused, free from any bias that might tend to influence the impartial weighing of facts, and free from any interest in the outcome except that of abstract justice. Both prosecution and defense choose such a jury through challenges of the qualifications of prospective jurors.

The whole venire, or panel, may be subject to a challenge to the array if there is reason to believe there were irregularities in the way it was selected.

A second type of challenge is a challenge to the polls, that is, a challenge as to the qualifications of individual veniremen to sit on the jury. There are two kinds of challenges to the polls:

(1) A challenge for cause, which is based on the grounds that the prospective juror is incompetent to serve because of prejudice, preconceived opinions as to the innocence or guilt of the accused, personal interest in the outcome, or any other reason that might influence his impartiality.

(2) Peremptory challenge, which can be made without the assignment of any reason. The number of peremptory challenges that each side can make is limited by law.

Opening Statement of the Prosecution. The theory of American justice is that the accused is presumed to be innocent. He does not have to prove that he did not commit a crime; it is the task of the prosecution to prove that he did. The burden of proof, therefore, is placed on the prosecution, which must open a trial by setting forth an affirmative accusation. This is done by the district attorney reading the indictment or information. He then gives an outline of what he intends to prove, frequently employing such expressions as "the evidence will show that" or "witnesses will testify that."

In addition to informing the court and jury of what is charged and what must be proved, the opening statement serves as an outline of the facts to be presented in evidence, so that the jury, in particular, can follow the testimony as it is given piecemeal by successive witnesses.

Examination of State Witnesses. After completing his opening statement, the district attorney calls his witnesses to the stand in the order in which he wishes to introduce testimony. When the state is finished with the witness, the defense has the right of cross-examination. The state may re-examine the witness to clear up questions raised or answer points scored in the cross-examination.

The first thing that the state must prove is that a crime was committed. This is known as the *corpus delicti,* or body of the crime. In a murder case, it is likely to be medical evidence to show how the deceased was killed. Subsequent testimony is designed to elicit evidence that the accused committed the crime charged by showing motive, opportunity, and means.

The purpose of the cross-examination is to weaken and to disprove the case of the other party. It is limited to matters touched upon in the examination in chief (the witnesses' testimony under direct examination). Questions in the cross-examination are employed to test the accuracy and credibility of the witness; to contradict, weaken, modify, or explain the evidence given in the examination in chief; to show inconsistent conduct or statements on the part of the witness; to throw light on his character, antecedents, and business; to show his interest, bias, or prejudice toward any of the parties in the case; and to test his power of and opportunity for observation, and the extent or lack of his knowledge.

The re-examination gives the district attorney an opportunity to clarify matters brought out in the cross-examination. Frequently he will seek to reduce the damaging effects of the cross-examination by asking reasons for the statements made in response to the adverse questioning or by seeking to show that his witness misunderstood the questions asked.

Examination of Defense Witnesses. As soon as the prosecution's witnesses are examined, the district attorney announces to the court that "the prosecution rests." At this time the defense may make two types of motions which if sustained serve to end the trial with the acquittal of the defendant. These are a demurrer to the evidence and a motion for a directed verdict.

Both motions say, in effect, that the prosecution has not proved the defendant guilty. They are based on the theory, previously explained, that the state must prove a person guilty and that he does not have to prove himself innocent. A demurrer says that granted the truth of the prosecution's evidence it is not sufficient to warrant a conviction; a motion for a directed verdict merely asks for acquittal on the ground that the prosecution has not proved its case. If the judge upholds either the demurrer or the motion for a directed verdict, the trial ends with the defendant acquitted. The prosecution is not permitted to ask for a directed verdict because of the legal requirement that a conviction must be based upon findings by the jury.

If the judge denies the motions, the defense may then present its case, but, as has been pointed out, it does not have to do so. If the prosecution has presented a weak case, the defense may offer no testimony, in the belief that the jury will not reach a verdict of guilty; sometimes the defense may present no evidence because it may be of so inadequate and inconclusive a nature that it would be of no help.

The procedure in the presentation of defense evidence is the same as that for prosecution evidence: the defense attorney makes his opening statement, calls his witnesses for direct examination, turns them over to the district attorney for cross-examination, and then, if necessary, conducts his re-examination.

A defense may be based on one of several points: one of the best is an alibi, by which the defendant seeks, through the testimony of witnesses, to show that he was somewhere else when the crime was committed. Since by definition many crimes, such as murder, hinge upon intent, the defense may seek to prove the absence of intent. If the act which the state calls a crime is admitted by the defendant, the defense may seek to prove that it was not legally a crime by submitting evidence of justification—self-defense, unprovoked attack, lack of negligence, defense of property, or defense of other persons.

Frequently the defendant offers evidence of his good character and reputation, both of which have been held by the courts to be substantive facts, like any other tending to establish innocence. Character testimony is often effective because, in spite of all evidence to the contrary, it raises a reasonable doubt which would entitle the accused to acquittal. The state is barred from presenting evidence of the defendant's bad character, such as previous convictions for a crime, in determining the probability of his having committed the crime for which he is on trial. If, however, the defendant offers proof of his good character, the state may attack it through cross-examination of witnesses and rebuttal testimony. Naturally, an accused with a previous criminal record will not open up this opportunity to the prosecution.

A high point of a trial is the appearance of the defendant on the witness stand to testify in his own behalf. In any legal proceeding an accused person is not compelled to testify on any matter that might incriminate him, but when he takes the witness stand he waives this immunity. There are, therefore, occasions when he may find it preferable not to take the stand. If he has a previous criminal record, this may be brought before the jury under the guise of impeachment of testimony. Sometimes his counsel advises him not to take the stand if he believes he is likely to be a bad witness for himself or if he is likely to break under cross-examination. Failure of the accused to take the stand ordinarily creates an unfavorable impression, and the tendency of the jury is to believe that he is scared to do so because he is guilty. Statutes provide, however, that failure to take the stand should not be construed as creating any presumption against the defendant, and judges ordinarily instruct jurors not to draw prejudicial inferences from such failure.

The State's Rebuttal. After the defense rests its case, the prosecution is entitled to call witnesses to rebut the evidence given in testimony. Since the defense is presumed to have had ample opportunity to reply to the prosecution's case in its original testimony, it is not entitled to a rebuttal.

The Arguments to the Jury. The prosecution and defense attorneys generally are barred from commenting on the evidence during the examination of witnesses. Their opportunity to explain and interpret the evidence comes when they make their arguments to the jury. The order of presentation is the same as that for the introduction of evidence: the prosecution speaks and then the defense, with the prosecution entitled to a rebuttal. Frequently, however, the prosecution waives the right to make the first address and appears only in rebuttal.

Coming near the end of the trial after a protracted and sometimes monotonous period of questioning of witnesses, the arguments to the jury may be decisive in determining the verdict. The emotional appeals and oratory permitted may outweigh the facts laboriously spread before the jury by the testimony of witnesses. Jury members may be confused by the conflicting evidence, they may have daydreamed through important parts of the examination, they may remember only some rag-tags of insignificant testimony. Thus, they may be quite susceptible to the rhetorical appeals made in the addresses.

The Charge of the Court. In instructing or charging the jury, the judge's principal function is to explain the legal aspects of a case. He informs the jury of the rules of criminal law pertaining to the crime, and explains what evidence is needed to warrant conviction. He explains that the defendant is presumed to be innocent, that the burden of proof is on the prosecution, and that the jury must acquit if it has a reasonable doubt of the defendant's guilt. He also outlines the alternative verdicts possible. Some of his instructions may be merely cautionary in nature, designed to make the jurors appreciate their responsibilities. Thus, the judge may advise them to guard against either sympathy or bias and to weigh the facts impartially.

Verdict of the Jury. After the charge to the jury, the members retire to consider their verdict. No one is permitted to have contact with them during their deliberations. The verdict in a criminal case must be unanimous: when the jury cannot reach such a verdict, it reports back to the court and the members are discharged. Failure of the jury to reach a verdict—known as a "hung jury"—means that a new trial must be held. A valid verdict must be that the accused is guilty or not guilty as charged, though the jury may make recommendations to the judge as to the punishment in the case of a guilty verdict.

Judgment and Sentence. If the jury finds the accused not guilty, the judge discharges him immediately. If the verdict is guilty, the judge may accept this as the judgment of the court and pronounce sentence.

The penalty for crimes is established by statute, but the judge has considerable latitude where statutes provide for indeterminate sentences, such as two to ten years, and where they give a range of fines that can be imposed. When the defendant has been convicted upon a number of counts, the judge can decide if the sentences shall be served consecutively or concurrently. For example, a man sentenced to three years on each of two counts would serve six years if the sentences were to be served consecutively, but only three years if the sentences were to be served concurrently. Where there are mitigating circumstances, such as the extreme youth of the convicted person or bad family or social and economic background, the judge may suspend sentence or place the prisoner on probation.

After the jury reaches its verdict, the defense attorney may seek to obtain freedom for his client through a motion in arrest of judgment. The motion is based on grounds similar to those made before the trial in a demurrer or a motion to quash. If denied, the court goes on to pronounce judgment and to sentence the convicted person.

Soon after the pronouncement of judgment and sentence, the defense may make a motion for a new trial based upon errors committed in the course of the trial or upon newly discovered evidence. If this motion is denied, the only recourse is an appeal to a higher court.

Rules of Evidence

As has been pointed out, a trial can proceed only when there is a joinder of issues, that is, the allegation of one set of facts and the denial of them by an opposing party. In criminal cases, the facts in issue are two—that a crime was committed and that the defendant committed it. These are set forth in the indictment or information. The issues are joined when the defendant pleads not guilty.

In the presentation of evidence by one side or the other, the opposing counsel may object to testimony as being irrelevant, immaterial, or incompetent.

To be admissible, evidence must be relevant, that is, it must relate to facts in issue. For example, it has been held relevant to describe the habits of a deceased person to show that the accused had an opportunity to administer poison. The fact that a murdered man had been pressing the accused for payment of a debt has been held relevant to show motive.

Evidence that is of no importance or consequence or that is lacking in definiteness is held to be immaterial and inadmissible on the grounds that it consumes time, distracts attention from the real issues, and is unfair to the adverse party, who is not prepared to meet it. For example, in a trial for murder by arsenic poisoning a witness testified that some ten years earlier he had seen the deceased taking arsenic for her health. This testimony was halted on the ground that the evidence was too remote, that is, immaterial.

To be competent, evidence must be fitting, suitable, or sufficient for the purpose according to the nature of the thing to be proved. Hearsay evidence—what someone else told the witness—is excluded as incompetent, for its value does not depend solely on the veracity of the witness, but rests also on the veracity and competency of some other person. In contrast, eyewitness testimony is considered to be competent. Opinions or conclusions by laymen may be barred as incompetent. A medical examiner would be allowed to state that a blow on the head caused death; a layman would not be permitted to make this statement.

Civil Actions and Trials

Despite the fact that most matters handled in the courts deal with civil litigation, newspapers devote comparatively little space to it.

The reason is fairly obvious: much of it is of concern only to the litigants. Civil litigation becomes of general interest when it affects the public welfare, when the persons involved are prominent, or when the cases are unusual or have human-interest appeal.

While civil law is much more complicated than criminal law, from the reporter's standpoint civil cases are easier to report. He covers criminal cases from beginning to end—from arrest to conviction—and therefore must concern himself with all stages of procedure. But the reporter usually does not give continuous coverage to the civil cases he considers newsworthy: he will report chiefly on their inception and conclusion—the bringing of a cause for action and the trial and judgment of the court.

There are two broad fields of private or civil law: (1) actions at law and (2) suits in equity. In most states the procedures by which the individual obtains his rights in both fields are similar and both types of cases are handled in the same courts. Law actions deal largely with the recovery of property and the collection of damages. Equity actions largely consist of those resulting in a court order to perform specific actions or to stop specific actions. If an industrial plant produces fumes or waste products that ruin the crops of a nearby farmer, the farmer could sue for damages for his losses. This would be an action at law. If he wanted to prevent further destruction, he could bring a suit in equity seeking an injunction directing the plant to stop the practices that caused the damage.

Because of the large number of civil suits and because many of them, no matter how well reported, would be of little interest to the public, the coverage of civil litigation is confined mostly to a few types of actions. Perhaps the most common cases with news interest of any kind are damage suits. Other actions of public interest are those in which a division of government is a party; those involving organizations whose activities are sometimes of public concern, such as labor unions and utility firms; and divorce suits involving prominent people. Probate matters, especially if a large estate is involved or if the maker of the will was a prominent person, also are usually reported.

A person initiates a civil suit by filing, through his attorney, a complaint in a court. The complaint is known variously as a declaration, bill, or petition, depending upon the type of action and the civil procedures of the state in which the action is brought. The complaint consists principally of a set of allegations which set forth the cause of action, and a conclusion asking the court for whatever relief is sought.

All complaints are listed in a civil appearance docket in the court clerk's office and are given a serial number. The information recorded includes the names of the plaintiff and the defendant and the nature of the action. The reporter covering the clerk's office checks the docket regularly for new cases: if he comes across one that seems to be newsworthy he looks up the petition. The petition usually gives him most of the details needed for a story.

Since the petition gives only one side of a case, it may be unfair at times to write a news story from it without consulting the defendant to get his side of the story. A petition, at this stage of a suit, is not considered privileged nor is it a public record. Hence, if it contains libelous material, the newspaper prints the information at its own risk. A petition becomes privileged only when it is brought to the attention of a judge, as when he rules on a motion or demurrer, and it thereby becomes part of a judicial proceeding.

We have seen that in a criminal prosecution a number of preliminaries must be completed before a case comes to trial. The same is true of a civil suit, but here the preliminaries take the form of pleadings. After the court clerk receives a petition, he serves notice of the suit to the defendant, who is given a period of time in which to file an answer. As was pointed out in the discussion of criminal procedures, a trial cannot take place until there is a joinder of issues—a set of allegations on one side and a general denial of them on the other. The defendant's denial of the allegations in a civil suit is contained in his answer.

But the court may be asked to rule on a number of motions before the issues are joined. All these motions in the case are known as pleadings. The defendant may enter a demurrer, that is, declare that even if the allegations are true they nevertheless do not constitute a cause for an action. He may also move for a bill of particulars to make the allegations more specific, enter a motion to strike, or eliminate, certain parts as being superfluous or immaterial, and make other motions similar to some of the special pleas in a criminal case. These are heard by the judge on a motion and demurrer day in court. One reason why the reporter seldom covers pleadings is that they involve legalistic questions that, except for cases with widespread public interest, can have little appeal to most newspaper readers.

Though the reporter may not find the pleadings worth reporting, he nevertheless should check the civil appearance docket at intervals for developments in important suits. Quite often they are settled out of court before trial, and he may not hear of the settlement unless the attorneys in a case inform him of this outcome, or unless he finds it in the court records.

The stages in a civil trial are the same as for a criminal trial except that the counsel for the defense must make his opening address immediately after that of the counsel for the plaintiff. Another difference is that much of the evidence is presented by deposition. Witnesses are interrogated before the trial by the attorneys for both sides and their testimony in written form is submitted at the trial. Many civil trials, also, are conducted without a jury, the attorneys and their clients choosing to have the judge decide the facts as well as rule on points of law.

ASSIGNMENTS

1. Make a collection of news stories that illustrate as many as you can find of the special pleas and motions mentioned in this chapter. Do you think the stories make the points of law involved sufficiently clear for the average reader's understanding?

2. Clip daily the newspaper reports of an important trial given full and detailed coverage. Write a report analyzing the series of stories, paying particular attention to legal principles involved. Note, also, interpretations given by the news writer to make the courtroom events clearer to readers.

3. Attend sessions of your local district or circuit court in which criminal cases are being tried. Take notes on the proceedings and try your hand at writing a news story covering the period of your attendance. Compare your story with the published report in the local newspaper.

4. During a period of one week clip from a metropolitan newspaper all news stories dealing with civil actions. Look up in a legal dictionary all legal terms mentioned in the stories. What are the elements of news interest in the stories that made the cases worth reporting?

5. Write a news story based upon the petition given below which was filed in a civil action.

IN THE COURT OF COMMON PLEAS OF CENTRE
COUNTY, PENNSYLVANIA

SCHOOL DISTRICT OF SPRING
TOWNSHIP, IN COUNTY OF
CENTRE AND STATE OF PENNSYL-
VANIA,

Plaintiff,

vs.

ANNIE ZELESNICK,
Defendant.

IN EQUITY

PLAINTIFF'S BILL

To the HONORABLE M. WARD FLEMING,
President Judge of the said Court.

The School District of Spring Township, the above named plaintiff,
brings this bill against Annie Zelesnick, the above named defendant.

The plaintiff complains and says:

1. The plaintiff is a municipal corporation created and existing under
the laws of the Commonwealth of Pennsylvania.

2. The defendant is a resident of Spring Township, in the County of
Centre and State of Pennsylvania.

3. The plaintiff condemned and acquired title in fee simple for school
purposes to land previously belonging to the said defendant, as such title
was finally adjudged by your Honorable Court in a certain suit in equity
in your Honorable Court to No. 3 September Term, 19____, in equity,
wherein the said Annie Zelesnick was plaintiff and the said School District
of Spring Township and Merrill Weaver, Freeman S. Hile, John H. Barn-
hart, Lloyd A. Stover and Clayton Walters, the then School Directors of
said School District, were defendants, and wherein the said Annie Zelesnick endeavored to have declared invalid such condemnation and acquisition, but wherein, as above indicated, the said Court entered a Final
Decree dated March 23, 19____, adjudging and decreeing thereby that the
said condemnation and acquisition of said real estate by the said School
District was valid and that the land so acquired is vested in fee simple
in the School District of Spring Township, the plaintiff in the above
entitled case, subject to the rights of the said Annie Zelesnick, the defendant in the above entitled case, to the appointment of viewers and
assessment of damages with right of appeal from said assessment of damages, as provided by the School Code, and in which prior suit to No. 3
September Term, 19____, in equity, the injunction theretofore granted
therein was dissolved and the said plaintiff's bill therein dismissed at the
cost of the plaintiff but subject to a conditional provision for payment of
costs by the defendant therein, as more fully appears in a copy of said

decree dated March 23, 19___, marked Exhibit A, hereto attached and made part hereof.

4. The said Annie Zelesnick never took any further proceedings in said suit in equity to No. 3 September Term, 19___, and after the expiration of the time for an appeal from said decree, without any appeal having been taken, the said School District of Spring Township in accordance with said decree, paid the record costs therein to the Prothonotary of Centre County in full of said costs.

5. In said suit in equity No. 3 September Term, 19___, the land thus condemned and acquired was described, as follows:

"ALL that certain messuage, tenement and tract of land situate in Spring Township, Centre County, Pennsylvania, bounded and described as follows: Beginning at an iron pin, corner of D. R. Rimmey, Annie Zelesick and present school site South 20 degrees and 20 minutes West 252 feet to an iron pipe; thence along lands of Annie Zelesnick North 69 degrees 34 minutes West 466.96 feet to an iron pipe in stone; thence North 61 degrees 44 minutes West 457.62 feet along lands of George Showers and C. H. Rimmey to a tack in stake, being corner of C. H. Rimmey and old school plot; thence South 41 degrees 36 minutes East along old school lot 173.30 feet to an iron pin the place of beginning. Containing 2.228 acres."

The land thus acquired, as thus appears, is bounded to the southeastward and to the southward thereof by other land of the said Annie Zelesnick, and to the northwestward thereof by land of George Showers and C. H. Rimmey, and to the northeastward thereof by the old school ground.

6. The said Annie Zelesnick has not heretofore instituted any proceeding for the appointment of viewers and assessment of damages by reason of said condemnation and acquisition in fee simple of said real estate by the said School District.

7. The said School District, the above named plaintiff, is ready and willing to pay and will pay such damages as may finally be ascertained and adjudged as payable by said School District by reason of said condemnation and acquisition of said real estate when thus ascertained and adjudged in any proper proceeding that may hereafter be instituted by the said Annie Zelesnick for the appointment of viewers to assess said damages, or as may be otherwise thus finally ascertained and determined by such proceeding.

8. Since such acquisition in fee simple by the said School District of title to said real estate, the said Annie Zelesnick by herself, or by her agents, representatives and employes, has persistently disregarded the said ownership by the said School District of said real estate, and has repeatedly planted and cultivated and reaped crops thereon for her own benefit, including potatoes heretofore planted thereon during this present year, and has interfered with and obstructed the possession and enjoyment of, said real estate by the said School District by removing a pole or poles and other appliances erected by the said School District upon the said real estate for recreational uses by the pupils of the school, erected on the said adjoining old school ground, and has otherwise treated the said real estate as if it were her property and not the property of the said School District.

9. A stone wall constitutes a division monument between the land herein involved and the above mentioned land of George Showers and C. H. Rimmey; and at the time of said condemnation there was an old fence, constituting a division fence between the land herein involved and the said old school ground, which said old school ground is otherwise owned by the plaintiff; but there has not yet been erected any division fence between the land herein involved and other land of the said Annie Zelesnick along the first two lines mentioned in the description of the said land contained in paragraph numbered 5 of the Plaintiff's Bill.

10. Subsequent to said condemnation and acquisition, the said plaintiff removed the said old fence between the land herein involved and the said old school ground, as no longer needed as a division fence; but, after such removal, the said Annie Zelesnick replaced or caused to be replaced the said fence, thus manifestly for the purpose of maintaining said fence as a division fence; and such fence still remains as thus replaced.

11. In order to define the two lines constituting division lines run between said property and other property of the said Annie Zelesnick (that is to say, on the two above mentioned lines running respectively South twenty degrees twenty minutes West two hundred and fifty-two feet as to the first of said lines, and thence North sixty-nine degrees thirty-four minutes West four hundred and sixty-six and ninety six-onehundredths feet as to the second of said lines), the said School District has endeavored to erect a fence on said two lines as a division fence in accordance with the Acts of Assembly relative to such division lines, to be adjusted by fence viewers in accordance with said Acts of Assembly, or otherwise, to be erected, and for this purpose had an accurate survey made, among other things, locating said two division lines; but the said Annie Zelesnick by herself or through her agents, representatives or employes, caused stakes placed by the surveyor on these two lines to be removed, and has otherwise obstructed and interfered with the erection of such division fence, so that the same is not yet erected.

12. The said Annie Zelesnick by these and other unwarranted acts has continuously obstructed and interfered with the possession by the said School District of the said real estate for school purposes.

13. The plaintiff has no adequate remedy at law and is entitled to equitable relief to restrain the unwarranted and unlawful acts of the defendant committed in disregard and violation of the rights of the plaintiff.

WHEREFORE, the plaintiff prays your Honorable Court as follows, to wit:

(a) Upon hearing relative to application for injunction and the taking of testimony at such hearing, with notice of such hearing to the defendant, to enter a decree granting an injunction preliminary after such hearing and to continue in force until final hearing in this suit, and to become perpetual upon such final hearing, restraining and enjoining Annie Zelesnick, the defendant, her agents, representatives and employes, from exercising any possession or control of the land described and designated and defined in paragraph numbered 5 of the Plaintiff's Bill, filed in this suit, and from planting, cultivating or reaping crops thereon other than potatoes heretofore planted thereon during this present year, and from removing any pole or poles and other appliances and structures that may be erected upon the said land, and from removing any stakes, fence posts, rails or wire constituting a fence, or any fence that may be erected upon any of the boundary lines of said land as a division fence that may be erected between the said land and other land of the said Annie Zelesnick, whether erected as a division fence in accordance with the Acts of Assembly relative to such division lines, or otherwise erected, and from in any way interfering with or obstructing the entire possession and enjoyment of said land by the said School District of Spring Township under its exclusive management and control.

(b) To grant the plaintiff such other and further relief as to your Honorable Court may seem meet and proper.

SCHOOL DISTRICT OF SPRING TOWNSHIP,
the above named Plaintiff,

Merrill Weaver,
President

Blanchard & Blanchard
Attorneys for Plaintiff

CHAPTER 21

NEWS OF GOVERNMENT

The Fourth Estate

"THE GALLERY in which the reporters sit has become a fourth estate of the realm," Thomas Babington Macaulay wrote early in the nineteenth century. British journalists adopted this designation to show the importance of their function in the operations of government, and it has been found applicable in the United States because of the threefold separation of governmental powers into legislative, judicial, and executive.

But recognition of the importance of the press in government goes back much earlier than Macaulay's often quoted statement. The First Amendment to the Constitution, for instance, guarantees freedom of speech and press, and the founding fathers considered the press as "the palladium of liberty." "The basis of our government being the opinion of the people," wrote Jefferson, "the very first object should be to keep that right; and were it left to me to decide whether we should have a government without newspapers or newspapers without a government, I should not hesitate to prefer the latter."

Other recognition of the essential function of the press in the conduct of government exists in the development of such privileges as those which provide for reporting legislative and judicial proceedings and for access to public records. The theory behind second class mailing privileges for newspapers and magazines is that low postage rates for them is desirable in order to promote the dissemination of information. Because a well-informed citizenry is so important in a democracy, the press has a real responsibility to cover government fully and accurately and to rise above partisanship in politics.

On the state and national level, government on the whole is well reported. Competing newspapers and press associations insure complete and impartial coverage. Little occurs in state capitols and on Capitol Hill in Washington that does not come to the attention of reporters. But the same cannot always be said of local government—the city hall and county courthouse—whose activities touch more intimately the lives of the people than do activities in the statehouse or in Washington.

One critic, Oxie Reichler of the Yonkers *Herald Statesman,* describes the city hall as "the great untold story of America," and another, James W. Bloomer of the Columbus (Georgia) *Ledger,* said in a speech to the Georgia Press Association: "We spend much time and effort finding fault with our national news gathering agencies, but it seems to me that they are doing a much better job on the national and international level than we are doing on our local level. The average American today is better informed on national and international questions than he is on those of his own community."

The reason for the poor coverage of local government may occasionally be a publisher who hesitates to expose maladministration and inefficiency because officials may be his friends or because he is fearful of making influential enemies; but more often the reason may lie in the indifference of reporters. Explaining tax procedures and presenting the facts of a municipal budget may not be so dramatic as a five-alarm fire or a cops-and-robbers chase, but such information can be made interesting by the reporter who masters the details of local government and who attempts to make the story meaningful to his readers.

One of the major problems of local government is the apathy of citizens toward public affairs, even in the matter of voting. The newspaper can help develop a continuing concern in what goes on in the city hall and the county building not only by full coverage and interpretation, but also by stories designed specifically to arouse interest. In any community controversy, for example, informal polls and the collection of opinions on issues stimulate the people's interest and often lead to their participation in government.

Covering City Hall

Basically, the American system of government is one of the oldest systems of government in the world. Yet, in one respect, it faces a crisis today—the failure of the system to meet the problems of local government created by the increasing urbanization of the nation. When the nation was founded, 95 percent of the people were rural dwellers; today about 65 percent of the people live in municipalities and 46 percent live in cities of more than 100,000 population.

Since there was no orderly plan for the development of a system to cope with the needs created by urbanization, local government today is not unlike a jungle—a chaos of units with overlapping and sometimes conflicting powers and functions. The statistics are revealing: in 1952 there were 3,049 counties, 16,778 municipalities, 17,202 townships, 67,346 school districts, and 12,319 special districts or authorities for such services as water, sewage disposal, and housing. In the New York metropolitan area there were 1,071 governments; figures for other metropolitan areas were: Chicago, 960; Philadelphia, 702; Pittsburgh, 616; St. Louis, 420; Oakland, 372; and Detroit, 355.

To take the leadership in pointing out the problems of local government through adequate news coverage and in suggesting solutions through interpretive reporting is one of the major challenges of newspapers today. Because the system lacks uniformity, differing not only from state to state but from city to city within a state, the reporter planning to equip himself for coverage of his local governmental units must make a special study of his own community.

In general municipalities—cities, boroughs, towns, and villages—derive their powers and functions from the state. They are corporations, chartered by the state, either under general laws that apply to cities of several classes according to size, or under home-rule laws that permit them to frame and amend their own charters. The reporter's first step in preparing himself to cover the city hall is to study the charter or laws under which his municipality operates.

There are three principal forms of city government: the mayor-council, the council-manager, and the commission. In the New England states there is a fourth type—the town meeting plan, which provides for all residents to attend meetings and vote on questions. Only 92 towns operate under this plan, however, and they comprise only 3.6 percent of the places with more than 5,000 population.

The most popular form of city government is the mayor-council plan. Of cities with more than 5,000 population, 1,315, or 52 percent, have adopted this form. The mayor-council plan, however, is a generality, for there is little uniformity under this system. The powers of the mayor vary, according to whether the weak mayor plan or the strong mayor plan is in effect. Although the unicameral council is most prevalent, a few cities have a bicameral system. The number of councilmen varies, ranging from 2 to 50 with 7 the average. In 59 percent of cities councilmen are elected at large; in 24 percent they are elected by wards; and in 16 percent some are elected at large and some by wards. In about 40 percent of cities they are elected by partisan ballot and in about 60 percent by nonpartisan ballot. Their terms vary, with two-year and four-year terms the most frequent.

In the mayor-council plan the council performs legislative functions—adopting ordinances to protect the health, safety, and welfare of citizens; approving measures to raise money through taxation and special assessments; and passing upon expenditures and budgets of city departments. Under the strong mayor plan, the mayor is the chief executive with power to hire and fire employees and to veto measures passed by the council. Under the weak mayor plan, he shares responsibilities with the council.

The council-manager plan is a variation of the mayor-council plan. The council, elected by the people, has two main functions: to pass ordinances for the city and to select and supervise the city manager. The city manager, an expert in municipal affairs, is the actual and responsible head of the administration. In most council-manager cities the office of mayor has been retained, but the mayor's duty is principally to serve as the ceremonial head of the government. The council-manager plan is followed in about 30 percent of the nation's cities.

Under the commission plan commissioners are elected to direct the several administrative departments of city government—accounts and finance, public safety, public affairs and health, streets and improvements, and parks and public property. The commission form has been adopted by about 30 percent of American cities.

The mayor, city manager, and members of the council or the city commissioners are the most important sources of news concerning municipal affairs, but complete coverage involves the reporter's seeing scores of other officials, either appointive or elective, and the members of the numerous boards, commissions, and authorities established for specific functions.

The problems of covering council meetings are about the same as those for any meeting—the reporter must write advances on what business will be taken up at a meeting and must attend sessions to find out what happened. Council meetings are open to the press and the public, and delegations of citizens often appear before the council when measures affecting them personally are brought up—changes in zoning regulations, special assessments for paving streets or installing sewer lines, or increasing the tax levy. As both advocates and opponents of measures may be present, the conflicts of interest can result in tumultuous sessions which are as interesting as any event the reporter may be called upon to cover.

As with other legislative units, much of the work of the city council is carried on through committees. A proposed ordinance or a municipal problem, for example, is turned over to a committee for study. The reporter should check with committee members and other council members for their attitudes toward such matters, and should cover committee meetings at which they are considered. The committee, when it reaches a decision, reports back to the council with its recommendations.

The principal function of city government is to do the things that the people cannot do for themselves. With the concentration of large numbers of people in limited geographical areas, the problems of everyday living are such that they can be solved only through community cooperation. The main services of the municipality are in the areas of public safety, public works, public health, public welfare, public parks and recreation, public utilities, planning and zoning, and education.

The machinery for carrying out these services varies widely. In some cities they are performed by departments with appointive heads; in others general supervision and policy making are in the hands of a board or commission; and, increasingly in recent years, new functions are performed by specially created authorities outside the regular municipal administration.

The varieties of services performed by the city in these areas include the following:

Public Safety. The main areas in which the city is concerned with public safety are police and fire protection, both discussed in other sections of this book.

Public Works. Activities assigned to the public works department, or engineering department, include construction and maintenance of streets, sidewalks, alleys, sewers, street lighting, public buildings, and other facilities.

Public Health. The city health department has powers to enforce standards of sanitation for private, public, and commercial water supplies; foods, especially milk and meat; restaurants and cafes; and swimming pools. It may also have the power to act to halt practices by industrial and manufacturing firms that endanger the public health or comfort. It enforces rulings to prevent the spread of communicable diseases through quarantine, and it sets up safety measures when there is danger of an epidemic. Among its other functions are public health education programs, public nursing services, and public school health examinations.

Public Welfare. In recent years the national and state governments through the social security program have either undertaken many of the public welfare programs of the cities or have obviated the need for some of them. Nevertheless, cities still provide public assistance in the form of general home relief, aid to the aged and the handicapped, medical services, and assistance to widows and children.

Public Parks and Recreation. A park department or park board is charged with the construction and maintenance of these facilities for making urban living more pleasant. Especially important are the summer playground programs of supervised recreation to keep children off the streets and out of mischief.

Public Utilities. Public utilities consist of indispensable services often operated as monopolies. Several, in America, are recognized as the province of private enterprise—railroads and telephones. Others are generally accepted as being legitimate functions of the city—streets, sidewalks, bridges, parks, sewerage systems. Others—water, light and power, natural and artificial gas, and transportation such as street cars and buses—in some cities are provided by the municipality and in others by private corporations. Privately owned utilities, however, are subject to city regulation, with a corporation given the right to operate through a franchise.

Planning and Zoning. Because of the rapid growth of urban areas in recent years, planning for future growth and the zoning of areas for residential, business, or industrial purposes have become increasingly important. Most of the planning and zoning programs are worked out by an appointed board or commission, which makes recommendations to the city council for action.

Education. Except for a municipally owned university, the public school system of a city is operated separately from the city administration by an elected board of education. School revenue comes from the school district's share in the general property tax and from special school taxes.

All divisions of the government today are faced with acute problems in raising the revenue needed for supporting the services asked by the people, but the financial difficulties of municipalities are probably the greatest. Part of the problem is due to the fact that the bulk of a city's income comes from the general property tax, which it shares with the county, townships, and school districts. The general property tax, primarily a tax on real estate, has proved inadequate for the increased services which local government units are expected to provide, and it has placed an undue burden on property owners.

In recent years reliance on the property tax as the chief source of revenue has had adverse results for cities because of the growing trend for people to live in suburban developments outside the city limits. Thousands of people earn their livings in a city and make heavy demands upon a city's services without contributing to its support because they cannot be reached for taxation purposes. To make up for this loss of revenue many cities have adopted income or wage taxes and sales taxes.

In addition to the general property tax, cities receive income from a variety of other sources: occupation taxes, business taxes, special assessments for improvements such as paving and sewer lines, license and permit fees, parking meters, police court fines, and charges for such services as garbage and trash removal. Where cities operate public utilities, such as water and electric plants, the tendency is to make these enterprises revenue producers. Cities also share in some of the revenue derived from certain statewide taxes.

The monthly or annual reports on the income received from these various revenue sources provide news stories. Information can be obtained from the departments collecting the fees, from the city treasurer or comptroller, and from the tax collector.

The biggest financial story of the year is the budget, prepared for a fiscal year beginning either January 1 or July 1. The procedure begins several months before the start of the fiscal year when department heads are asked to make out estimates of needs. These estimates go to the city's chief fiscal officer or to the mayor or city manager, who draws up a tentative budget based on expected revenue. The final action on the budget is its adoption by the city council. All steps of the procedure provide news for the reporter.

Of especial news importance are the decisions of officials to increase service fees, to adopt new fees, and to make such special assessments as those for paving streets, extending sewer lines, or constructing new sidewalks. The city council or its appropriate committee holds public hearings on these proposals, and many citizens take advantage of the opportunity to attend and have their say either for or against.

The County Building

Each of the forty-eight states is divided into areas which are usually called counties. As subdivisions of the state government, counties enforce state laws, administer justice in the courts, conduct elections, maintain roads and highways, and carry on other functions. They are also local units of government, performing for rural areas many of the services performed for urban residents by the municipality.

Sometimes called the "dark continent" of American government, county government is little understood by most city dwellers. The average newspaper reader hears about it chiefly through the reports of trials in the district court. The property owner has contact with county officials perhaps only once a year when his real estate is assessed for tax purposes and when he pays his taxes to the treasurer. If a person buys or sells property, or borrows money on it, he may have contact with the county clerk or recorder whose job it is to record such transactions. Otherwise, activities which go on in county government remain largely unknown to the majority of citizens.

To the reporter, perhaps the most important news sources in the county building are the officials charged with law enforcement and the administration of justice. The importance of these functions is indicated in the name usually given the county building: the courthouse.

The sheriff's office is the reporter's source for information about crimes and investigations taking place outside incorporated municipalities. The sheriff's staff includes deputies and special investigators, and he also has charge of the county jail. Coverage of his office is like coverage of a police station, since he keeps similar records of complaints and investigations. Suspects arrested by city police to be prosecuted on felony charges are transferred to the county jail, and federal prisoners may be temporarily lodged there also.

Since the county or district attorney conducts the prosecution in all felony cases, he is an important news source. He frequently takes an active part in criminal investigations, working both with city police and the sheriff. The attorney is also the legal counsel for all other county officials.

The county judiciary consists of the district judge and judges of special courts such as county court and probate court. Coverage of the courts and the court clerk's office has been discussed in the chapters on civil and criminal legal procedures.

Certain administrative functions of county government are prescribed by the state in the creation of certain elective offices. The offices vary from state to state, but they generally include the following: board of county commissioners or supervisors; clerk, recorder, or registrar of deeds; school superintendent; treasurer; and assessor.

County Commissioners. The board of county commissioners exercises powers comparable to those of a city council except that it has few legislative functions. It has charge of construction and maintenance of county buildings; it builds and maintains roads that are not a part of the state highway system; it has charge of the distribution of poor relief and maintains county homes and farms for the aged and indigent; generally, it can levy taxes for county purposes; it approves the budgets of county offices; and it authorizes the expenditure of county funds.

The commissioners in some states are elected at large and in some states by districts. The number may range from three to seven. The county clerk keeps the minutes of board meetings and the records of board transactions. Official business of the board is transacted at meetings open to the press.

County Clerk. While the county clerk performs essential duties, he seldom is a source of highly important or interesting news. The clerk records real estate transactions—deeds, mortgages, leases, transfers of title, and so forth. Some newspapers, especially in rural areas, print these, but in metropolitan areas they are too numerous for publication. Other functions of the clerk may include issuing licenses, keeping county records and official documents, and receiving applications for corporation charters.

School Superintendent. In many states a county superintendent of schools is an elective official having general supervision of dependent school districts coming under the state department of education. His main duties are to provide leadership in planning courses of study, improving standards of instruction, giving teachers' examinations, and seeing to it that buildings and other facilities are adequate.

County Treasurer. The chief financial official of the county is known variously as treasurer, auditor, or tax collector. He is the custodian of county money, makes out the warrants for paying county bills, collects taxes, and may have other duties that vary from state to state.

County Assessor. As has been pointed out, the most important source of revenue for local government is the general property tax. More than 90 percent of the money for carrying on city, township, county, and school district functions comes from this tax. The tax is placed on real property (land, buildings, and improvements) and on personal property. Personal property includes tangible property (household furnishings, jewels, livestock, and crops in storage) and intangible property (stocks, bonds, and savings accounts).

A tax is levied against the value of the property in terms of mills, a mill being one-tenth of a cent. Thus, if the tax rate is 10 mills on each dollar, the owner of a piece of property valued at $10,000 would pay $100 in taxes.

The determination of the value of property is the task of the assessor. In some states, each unit of local government that derives income from the general property tax has an assessor and determines the tax rate according to its needs, but the most widespread plan is for the assessment to be done by an assessor who is an elected county official.

The assessor maintains an assessment roll, or list of taxable property. Since keeping the roll is a vastly complicated undertaking, it is easy to see that only the most prominent property—land and buildings—may be perceived by the assessor. Actually, about 80 percent of the revenue derived from the general property tax comes from real property. The assessor cannot make an accurate check of tangible personal property and usually has no way at all of checking on intangible personal property.

Property is seldom assessed at its true value—a home that would sell for $25,000 is perhaps listed on the assessment roll as being worth only $15,000—and there are numerous gross inequalities because of the loose method of assessment. When the assessor does not have time to make a firsthand examination of property, he usually lists the value as being that of the previous assessment. Property owners frequently report their own valuation of the property, which the assessor accepts without personal inspection of it. When a property owner believes that the valuation of his property is too high, he may ask the assessor to lower it. If the assessor refuses, the property owner may appeal the decision to a county equalization board.

Property of corporations and utilities, such as railroads, natural gas lines, telephone lines, and power lines, is usually assessed by the state, with the county assessor notified of the valuation within his county.

In covering the work of the assessor, the reporter writes stories announcing that the work of assessment has begun and reporting when the assessor will be in certain places in the county to assess property. The completion of the assessment rolls, when the total worth of the county is determined, is the occasion for a major news story. In addition, the rolls will supply a host of features for the reporter who digs into the material.

After the assessed worth of a county is determined, officials can then determine the tax rate. In some states this is done by a county equalization or excise board, which allocates the levy among the county, cities, school districts, and other units sharing in the general property tax. In other states the several units use the county's valuation as a basis for fixing their individual rates. The rates, limited in most states to prescribed maximums, unless a special election is held to exceed the maximums, is determined according to the budgetary needs of the governmental units. The fixing of the tax rate, of course, is an important news story since it affects all property owners.

Besides the county functions discussed, a county election board, usually of three members, has charge of all elections, working under the supervision of a state election board. It attends to the registration of voters, selects polling places, names election officials, distributes ballots, and counts the votes when the election is over.

The county building is also a principal source of farm news, since it generally houses the offices of the agricultural agent and home demonstration agent, who are paid in part from county funds and in part from federal funds. Some of the other federal programs for aiding farmers also have local representatives who occupy quarters in the courthouse.

Township Government

Townships, outside the New England states, are subordinate governmental units. Their functions and place in the governmental system vary greatly. Formerly, they were chiefly important in rural areas, but today, with the urbanization of the countryside in developments outside incorporated cities, they have become the basis for carrying out such services and functions as police and fire protection, education, streets, and water supply performed by municipalities.

Where townships are organized for governmental functions, the officials are a committee or board of supervisors. The board has about the same role as a city council or board of county commissioners.

ASSIGNMENTS

1. Analysis of surveys by the Continuing Study of Newspaper Reading shows that local government news has only nominal readership, scoring between 16 and 20 percent (See Chapter 1). During a week's period clip from the local newspaper all stories dealing with local government and monitor radio and television programs, noting the time devoted to information in this category. Approximately what percentage of space and time is given to informing the people about their local government? What departments of the government receive the most attention? What departments seem to be neglected? Do you think local government is adequately reported by the news media in your city? Do you have any suggestions for improving coverage and treatment of the news of government to increase the public's interest in it?

2. Study the charter or laws under which your city operates and write a report on its organization. List the city officials, indicating how they are selected, their terms of office, their salaries, and their duties. Do the same for special departments, boards, commissions, and authorities. Illustrate the type of news emanating from each office with story clippings from the newspaper.

3. Attend a session of your city council and write a news story about it.

4. Consulting the compiled statutes of your state, write a report on the organization of your county government. List the officials, indicating how they are selected, their terms of office, their salaries, and their duties. Find news stories to illustrate the kind of public information each office produces.

5. Write a news story based on the following action taken by the city council at its weekly meeting in the city hall:

> Roll call: Councilmen Hansford Billings, Richard Croce, Henry Peterson, T. R. Gander, Jerome Whitcome, Leslie Throgmorton, and Paul Fitzpatrick and Mayor Toby Michael, all answering present.
>
> Billings, as chairman of the public health committee, reports on the rough draft of a proposed anti-smog ordinance; other committee members are Peterson and Whitcome. The report proposes that an air pollution control board be established by ordinance to work in close cooperation with the city building inspector.
>
> The board would include a registered professional engineer trained in chemical engineering, a doctor, and at least two private citizens whose occupations are wholly independent of all phases of the manufacturing or transportation industry.
>
> The ordinance would make it unlawful to contaminate the air with dust, fumes, gas, mist, odors, smoke, vapor, or any combination of these in such a way as to pollute the air. It also would make it unlawful to burn garbage, trash, junked vehicles, or any other material in an open fire except at such places and times and under such safeguards as may be prescribed by the air pollution control board.
>
> Penalties would include fines and sentences ranging upward to 90 days in jail.
>
> Discussion of the report indicated approval and it was directed that it be turned over to City Attorney Charles A. Canfield to be drafted into proper legal form. It will be submitted for a first reading at next week's council meeting.
>
> George Grainger appeared before the council to ask reconsideration of a request that an area in the south part of the city be rezoned from a Residence 1 to Residence 3 area. The council last month turned down a similar request by a vote of 5 to 2. Grainger, major developer of the area, known as Floral Gardens, explained that he wanted to build an apartment house of several multiple units. He exhibited plans and architect's drawings of the building, explaining that it would not detract from the area as a residence area.
>
> Councilman Croce, in whose district the Floral Gardens area

is included, said he voted against the change because he had understood residents were opposed, fearing the type of development that might result if the district were rezoned. He said subsequent investigation had shown there was actually no real opposition to rezoning. The council voted 6 to 1 to put the area in the Residence 3 class, with Throgmorton casting the negative vote.

City Manager Joseph Wadsworth submitted his resignation, to take effect as soon as a successor could be employed. Wadsworth said he was resigning to become general manager and chief engineer for the Wentworth Manufacturing Co. He explained that his new job meant a considerable increase in salary. His job as city manager pays $15,000 a year. Wadsworth was named city manager ten years ago. After his graduation from the college of engineering at the state university, he worked five years as an engineer for the state highway commission. He then served three years as city engineer in Belleville.

PART IV

Special Writing Problems

CHAPTER 22

WRITING FOR RADIO AND TELEVISION

Differences in Media

A NEW ERA in journalism was opened in 1920 when a small, experimental "radiophone" station, 8MK, operated by the Detroit *News* broadcast the Michigan primary elections. A little later that year KDKA, operated by the Westinghouse Electric and Manufacturing Co. in Pittsburgh, broadcast the Harding-Cox presidential election.

These broadcasts marked the beginning of regular news reports disseminated not by the traditional medium of print but by sound waves. They created a new field of journalistic endeavor involving new reportorial and writing problems.

The journalistic situation was radically changed again when regular television broadcasts were inaugurated, adding a new dimension—the visual—to the reporting of current events by air. Again newsmen were faced with new problems of reporting and writing.

Though radio and television involve different techniques from those of the newspaper, all three have such a sufficiently common basis that the person trained and experienced in one medium can without great difficulty shift to another. Radio in its early days recruited its newsmen from newspapers and press associations, and television followed the precedent by recruiting its newsmen from radio. Many reporters working for press associations and for news-papers with radio-TV affiliations write for more than one medium.

The factor common to all three media, of course, is news. While they treat news differently, fundamentally what is news for one medium is news for the other two. But there are differences which give each medium certain advantages over the others and which require special abilities.

Between radio and newspaper, one of the most obvious differences is the time interval between the occurrence of an event and the reception of it by the public. The radio newscast can be given within minutes after an event happens and new developments can be reported as quickly. This immediacy is not possible for the newspaper, since the story about an event must be set in type, along with scores of other stories, and the paper must be printed and delivered. Moreover, radio can go right to the scene for an on-the-spot report.

Television shares with radio certain advantages of immediacy, since its cameras can give a visual and aural report of an event as it happens. These on-the-scene reports, however, are limited to major and usually scheduled happenings, such as a political convention, a speech by the President, or a press conference by a high public official. The time lag between the newspaper report and the event exists also for regular television newscasts, since a well planned television newscast involves the writing of a script and the processing of photographs and films for telling the visual part of the story.

But though the newspaper may be slower than the other two media, this delay has certain advantages. The newspaper has time to correct errors made in the first reports of happenings. Also, it is not so likely as the other two media to give disproportionate emphasis to any particular event. Once radio and television are set up to report a happening on the spot, they must continue their coverage even though nothing of interest or importance happens, or more newsworthy events are taking place elsewhere.

In comparison with the newspaper, both radio and television suffer because they lack completeness and comprehensiveness in their coverage. Both tend to skim the surface of the news. The typical radio and television news program gives only the highlights of an event, frequently only a half-minute or minute of time being devoted to the report. People who want fuller details, and there are many of them, have to go to a newspaper.

Moreover, there are many areas of news not covered at all either by radio or television. Both the latter media concentrate on the top news of the day. The scores of little happenings in a community—club meetings, minor accidents and crimes, deaths of unimportant people—are reported in newspapers, but not by radio and television. The news appeal of radio and television is primarily to the mass;

newspapers, because they carry a great volume and variety of news, have an appeal not only to the mass but to special groups as well. Since the advent of television, however, this advantage of newspapers has been lowered to some extent by the increasing practice of radio, in meeting the competition of its new rival, to broaden its coverage and to carry programs of specialized appeal.

On the other hand, radio and television have an advantage over the newspaper in that people can absorb the news with little effort. To get the news from a newspaper requires some mental concentration; to get it from radio or television requires very little. In addition, radio and television have resources by which they can more easily capture interest than can the newspaper. The personality of the newscaster and his voice and appearance, if pleasing, can add to the interest of a news report. It is possible, also, on radio and television to create close rapport between the listener-viewer by bringing newsmakers before the microphone or camera, either by means of live or recorded and filmed appearances.

But to offset these advantages, the newspaper can be read anywhere and anytime. A radio or television newscast, once given, is gone forever. The permanent form of the newspaper is of value, too, because readers can check back over stories to make sure they have the facts in mind correctly and can clip items which they might like to have for future reference.

Writing for the Ear

The essentials of all journalistic writing are simplicity, directness, and clarity, but in radio and television writing, which is designed to be spoken and heard, more effort must be put forth to achieve these qualities than in writing for print. It has been said that the journalist must write not just so that he can be understood, but so that he cannot be misunderstood. The opportunities for being misunderstood are more numerous for radio and television than they are for the newspaper. The chief factor that leads to misunderstanding in spoken journalism is that the listener has only one chance to grasp the meaning. In reading the newspaper a person can go back over material and figure out the meaning of a word or sentence if it is not clear at first, but in listening to a broadcast a second chance is denied him.

Besides being simple, direct, and clear, radio-television writing is marked by a degree of informality not present in other writing. It should convey the impression that it is talk or conversation; the listener should not be aware that the announcer is reading aloud from a prepared script. As a result, colloquialisms, partial sentences, and vernacular expressions not permitted in other types of writing are acceptable, and even desirable, in radio and television. This informality, however, does not extend to the toleration of bad grammar and vulgarisms.

The problem of writing for radio and television involves two fundamental factors: (1) in choosing words the writer must use those common to the everyday language—those that an ordinary person would be likely to use in his own speech, and (2) he must use short, uncomplicated sentences.

In writing for the eye, even when the prose is simple, an occasional word not in everyday use may be acceptable: the reader can guess the meaning from the context. But in writing for the ear, puzzlers should be avoided, since the listener who is forced to ponder over it misses what follows. Only instantly recognizable words should be used. When an unfamiliar word must be used because no other word conveys the same meaning, the writer should define or explain it rather than leave it up to the listener to figure out the meaning.

Thus, in radio and television the short, common word is preferable to a less familiar word even at the sacrifice of shades of meaning: home or house instead of residence or domicile, read instead of peruse, ask instead of inquire, try instead of attempt or endeavor, cost instead of expense, start or begin instead of inaugurate, poor instead of indigent.

Another reason for preferring the everyday word to the literary word is that the news script must not be stilted. It must, as has been pointed out, capture the flavor of actual speech. Few people, for example, say that they "arose betimes" or "retired at a late hour." They get up early or go to bed late.

Besides choosing everyday words to give the impression of a person talking informally, the writer can employ certain colloquialisms. One of the marks of the spoken language is frequent use of contractions: he'll instead of he will, won't instead of will not, it's instead of it is. Slang, too, is acceptable in radio and television writing if it has become a part of everyday speech and if the matter being discussed does not require a dignified treatment. It would be inappropriate, of course, to say that the President of the United States "hit the sack" when he retired for the night, but this expression would be all right in a story about soldiers at an army base.

Direct address is another device for obtaining naturalness of speech in writing for radio and television. This is avoided in most newspaper writing, but it is entirely suitable for the radio or television newscaster. He is a person talking to people, and nothing could be more natural than for him to address his listeners as "you." Exactly as if he were in his own living room among friends and members of his family, he may, in broadcasting, properly speak as follows:

> If you have been worrying about making out your income tax report, you'll be interested in what the Internal Revenue Service has been doing to make your job easier. It has . . .
>
> You may recall the news story yesterday about the call for blood donors for the little girl with a rare disease. Well, we have a cheerful report for you today about her condition.

Another area in which writing for the ear differs from writing for the eye is in the handling of numbers and statistics. Generally, radio and television practice is to use round numbers rather than exact figures. Some examples follow:

For the Newspaper	For Radio-Television
The Borough Council today approved a budget of $515,260 for next year, an increase of $25,220 over that of last year.	The Borough Council has approved a new budget for next year. It is for slightly more than $500,000—an increase of about $25,000 over that of last year.
Final returns gave Senator Alfred Andrews 151,211 votes to the 124,801 of his opponent, James D. Hanson.	Final returns gave Senator Alfred Andrews slightly more than 150,000 votes. His opponent, James D. Hanson, had almost 125,000 votes.

In the early days of radio, writers were warned against sibilants—words beginning with or containing the letter "s." Engineering has corrected the tendency of sibilants to hiss or whistle when passing through the microphone, but nevertheless they should be avoided when several appear in one word or in sequence at the start of several words. The foregoing sentence, for instance, because of the prevalence of "s" sounds, is unsuitable for broadcasting. Alliteration, as in such tongue-twisters as "the practical possibilities presented by the plan," must also be avoided. Announcers are likely to stumble over them and commit a verbal fluff or bloop.

In addition to using simple words to obtain clarity and listenability in radio-television scripts, <u>the writer must for the most part relate the news in simple, declarative sentences</u>. It is not a matter, however, of cutting sentences down to an arbitrary length of ten or fifteen words. A newscast written entirely in sentences of this length would be choppy and monotonous. The writer can, and should, use complex sentences, but he must use them very discriminately.

In writing complex sentences—those containing a main clause and one or more dependent clauses—several rules should be followed:

1. Long, involved dependent clauses should be avoided.

2. Preferably, not more than one dependent clause should appear in a single sentence.

3. A long, dependent clause should not intervene between the subject and verb of the main clause.

4. Dependent clauses are better at the start of a sentence than at the end.

In writing for print, the long, modifying "who" clause in the following sentence would be acceptable:

> When members of the audience caught sight of the president, who entered the auditorium at the rear, smiling and waving his hand in greeting as he strode down the center aisle to the stage, they broke out in spontaneous cheers and applause.

But such a sentence should be broken up for radio-television:

> When members of the audience caught sight of the president, they broke out in spontaneous cheers and applause. The president entered the auditorium from the rear. As he strode down the center aisle to the stage, he smiled and waved his hand in greeting.

Piling clause upon clause, as in the sentence below, makes for difficulty in understanding:

> At the hospital, after an examination showed that Senator Smith's injuries were not serious and that he would be in good shape, his secretary announced that he would continue his campaign tour tomorrow, speaking in Middleburg in the afternoon.

In writing for listenability, some of the subordinate clauses should be placed in separate sentences:

At the hospital, an examination showed that Senator Smith's injuries were not serious. Attendants said he would be in good shape after a night's rest. His secretary announced that the senator would continue his campaign tour tomorrow. He is scheduled to speak at Middleburg in the afternoon.

Clauses or phrases interposed between a subject and a verb are especially dangerous, since listeners may hear only the latter part of the sentence and thereby grossly misapprehend what was said. In newspaper writing identifications and explanatory phrases conventionally come after the name, but this placement should be avoided in radio-television writing. For instance:

John A. Parker, secretary to Governor Alvin Jones, was killed early tonight when his car overturned near Middleburg.

Listening with only a part of his attention given to the newscast, the hearer is likely to miss the name of the secretary and to become alert only when he hears the familiar name of the governor. The chances are that he will mistakenly believe it was the governor who was killed. For radio-television writing, therefore, it is best to avoid the newspaper method of giving the name followed by the identification. Instead, the radio-television writer leads up to the name:

A member of Governor Alvin Jones' official family was killed in an automobile accident early tonight. The victim is John A. Parker, the governor's secretary. Parker was killed when his car overturned near Middleburg.

Another radio-television departure from newspaper writing is the avoidance of dangling attributions at the end of sentences. In newspaper writing the place for emphasizing important facts is at the first of a sentence; in writing for oral delivery it is at the end. A newspaper story might report the news:

Automobile accidents in the city during May numbered 153, an increase of 22 over the previous month, a police department report showed today.

For radio-television the preferable way to tell the story is:

A police department report shows that automobile accidents in the city during May numbered 153. This is an increase of 22 over the month of April.

Or better:

> There were more automobile accidents in the city during the month of May than during the month of April. A police department report lists 153 accidents in May. The number is 22 accidents above the number reported for April.

Examination of the newspaper sentences recast for radio-television in the foregoing discussion will disclose another characteristic of writing for the ear: individual sentences are not overloaded with meaning. Generally, radio-television writing follows the rule of one idea, one sentence. It will be noted also that frequently more words are needed to tell a story for radio-television than for the newspaper. There is a loss in conciseness but a gain in clarity.

In the discussion of diction appropriate in writing for the ear, it was pointed out that naturalness of speech can be obtained through the use of colloquialisms. Another way to obtain this effect is through use of broken and incomplete sentences. These are marks of ordinary talk, and radio-television writers make greater use of them than writers for other media.

Direct quotations pose a difficulty in maintaining naturalism when writing for the ear. The newspaper reader can see the quotation marks; the radio-television listener has to have them spoken for him. Generally, direct quotations appear less in radio-television copy than in newspaper copy, since indirect statements and loose paraphrase suffice for most utterances. But when it is essential that the exact words of a speaker be used, then the artificiality of saying "quote" and "end quote" or some other expression must be resorted to.

Frequently, only the initial expression indicating a direct quotation is needed, the fact that the quotation is ended being obvious from the context:

> Discussing the council's action, the mayor said—quote—"The vote of the council was a scandal. I will do everything possible to get the resolution rescinded." The mayor then went on to explain . . .

Some variations for the "quote" and "end quote" labels are:

> The mayor said—and we quote—"The vote of the council . . ."
> The mayor sharply attacked the council's action. His exact words were: "The vote of the council . . ."

The mayor was bitter in his criticism of the council. To quote him: "The vote of the council . . ."

As the mayor expressed it: "The vote of the council . . ."

In the words of the mayor: "The vote of the council . . ."

As the mayor said: "The vote of the council . . ."

The mayor's statement said in part: "The vote of the council . . ."

You have just heard the mayor's statement about the council's action.

That was the way the mayor described the council's action.

Those were the words of the mayor in summing up his opinion of the council's action.

With these words of criticism, the mayor then went on to . . .

Radio News Programs

A radio station, in its daily operation, is likely to present a rather wide variety of news programs, either of local or network origin. The backbone of the station's news programming, however, is the straight news summary or roundup. These are of four types according to length: the one-minute spot summary, the five-minute summary of top news, the ten-minute summary, and the fifteen-minute summary. Similar to these are the specialized news reports: sports, women's interests, science, agriculture, religion, education. For interpretation and opinion, the station may have its own commentator or analyst, or carry the network programs of nationally known figures. Other types of news programs or semi-news programs are on-the-spot coverage of special events, interviews and press conferences, roundtables, and documentaries and dramatizations.

The beginner needs to be instructed only in planning and writing summary or roundup programs dealing with general and specialized news, since they constitute the bulk of radio newscasts. Most reporting of special events consists of extemporaneous explanation and description by the newscaster, while interviews, roundtables, and press conferences are usually conducted without scripts. Documentaries and dramatizations call for special and advanced writing ability. Commentators and analysts write their own scripts.

Preparing a news roundup program consists primarily of assembling and editing separate items received from the wire service and those written by the radio station's own staff reporters. In selecting items, the script editor must consider what kind of listening audience his program has. Early morning shows, noontime shows, and evening shows usually must be designed to appeal to all types of listeners. The in-between listening audience consists principally of women, but this does not mean that all newscasts should be directed toward them: many men have irregular hours of work and may be at home during the day, and there are thousands of men on the highways listening to their automobile radios.

Because the one-minute and five-minute summaries must be so brief, the organization of items offers no particular problem. For the ten-minute and fifteen-minute programs, however, some degree of unity and planning is desirable. The most natural method is to organize the news according to its geographical origin: foreign, national, state, and local. This arrangement avoids the splintering effect of presenting a series of unrelated items, and helps the listener get the news in focus.

Generally, the summary should begin with the most important item in one of the four categories, with secondary items following. The same plan should be used with items in the other categories. The advantage of this arrangement is that it creates several high points of interest during the program, thereby holding the listener's attention throughout.

Another popular arrangement is to start the broadcast with a series of capsule summaries similar to newspaper headlines. These are of one sentence, as in the following from a press service radio wire:

> Governor Thomas Stanley has handed the Virginia General Assembly his plan for keeping the races segregated in schools in the state.
>
> Egypt's official reply to the Western demand for talks on the Suez crisis will be made tomorrow.
>
> There is speculation in London that Cypriot Archbishop Makarios may be brought to trial as a leader in terrorist activities on the Mediterranean island.
>
> Adlai Stevenson and Estes Kefauver have started their 34-state grass roots trip to confer with local Democratic leaders.

These headlines are designed to whet the listener's interest: a forecast of what will come up during the program alerts him to the items which he will find of especial interest. The details of each event, with news items of minor interest intervening, are given in the body of the broadcast.

Unlike the newspaper story, in which information is given in dwindling order of interest and importance, the radio newscast should end on a strong note. An often-used ending is a short humorous or entertaining feature, designed to give the listener a lift after he has heard the serious news of the day. Another good ending is a bulletin or news report received after the newscaster went on the air.

Unless a single event so dominates the news that it would be ridiculous to give only a few details, the summary consists ordinarily of ten or twelve items, with the longest of not more than one minute or one and one-half minutes in length. As has been pointed out, radio skims the surface of the news. The newspaper reader can select the stories that he wants to read, but the radio listener must hear what the script editor chooses to give him. Hence, only events of transcendent interest are reported in detail on the radio.

In the ten-minute and fifteen-minute roundup, it is desirable to tie together related news and to shift to new topics by means of transitional phrases and clauses. These transitions must be inserted in the copy by the script editor. Some examples are:

Time transitions

At the same time	Coincident with
Meanwhile	On the heels of
Later today	Afterward

Place transitions

Now for news from abroad	In our own state
Across the Atlantic	From our state capital
In the Far East	Here at home
In the nation's capital	Now for news from our home
Elsewhere in the nation	city
On the home front	On the local scene
	Locally

Topic transitions

On the political scene	Now for news of
Other news of labor	Some other headliners in the
Other happenings today	news today
	Turning now to

The general principles of writing for listenability are discussed in the previous section, but a few additional principles must be considered in writing the radio news story. In writing for radio, the newsman accustomed to the newspaper inverted-pyramid pattern will have to reverse his thinking about how to present the news. Instead of stressing the most important or most interesting facts at the start of his sentence and summarizing the whole event in the lead, the radio writer builds up to his main points slowly. It is like the windup before a ball is pitched. The opening sentence of his lead oftentimes is a general statement indicating the nature of the news, not what it is. The reason for this method is that the listener needs some forewarning to prepare himself for reception of the essential information.

The radio lead may start with introductory sentences like the following:

> The number of automobile accidents caused by the icy streets continues to mount. Three persons were seriously injured early this evening . . .
> There is important news tonight from the foreign ministers' conference in London.
> Officials in Washington are watching closely new developments in the Middle East situation.

In newspaper stories, reporters subordinate factors such as the when and where and the source of information. These are often placed first in radio news stories:

> Shortly after noon today, the mayor announced that . . .
> A spokesman for the State Department has revealed that . . .
> News from Moscow tonight is that . . .

The differences between newspaper and radio leads can best be shown by comparison of stories written for the two media. The newspaper story tells the news like this:

> John A. Parker, 65, president of the First National Bank, was killed this morning when his automobile collided with another automobile at E. First Street and Maple Avenue.

For radio the event would be reported like this:

> One of the city's financial leaders was killed in an automobile accident this morning. The president of the First National Bank, John A. Parker, died of injuries suffered when his automobile collided with another automobile at E. First Street and Maple Avenue.

The mechanics of preparing radio copy are especially important, since material must be presented in a form that the newscaster can read without stumbling over words and in such a way that it can easily be timed. As to the time element, a fifteen-minute newscast, for example, does not take up fifteen full minutes of air time. Usually, the actual news time runs only eleven or twelve minutes, with the remainder of the period devoted to the opening and closing by the studio announcer and the commercials.

If the following method is used, each page of copy will approximate one minute of air time: using standard 8½ by 11 inch paper, leave one-inch margins at the right and left and type fifteen lines to the page. This will be between 150 and 175 words, the average words-per-minute speed of delivery of most newscasters.

In writing the copy, the rules below should be followed to help the newscaster read easily and without error:

(1) Double or triple space, according to the practice of the station. To make local copy conform to wire copy, many stations prefer that stories be typed in capital letters.

(2) In case of typographical error, do not strike over the incorrect letter or correct with conventional copyreading marks, but x-out the whole word and rewrite it.

(3) Give the phonetic spelling of an unusual or difficult word in parentheses after the word: "Doctors in Galveston, Texas, report no significant change in the condition of the famed woman athlete— Babe Didrikson Zaharias (Zah-hair'-ee-us)."

(4) Do not divide words at the end of a line of copy.

(5) Preferably, try to end each page with a completed paragraph, but in any case do not continue a sentence from the bottom of one page to the top of another.

(6) Do not abbreviate words except for some of the most commonly used titles before a name: Gov. Smith, Sen. Adams, Gen. Roberts.

(7) In writing numbers and figures, follow the rules below:

    a. Spell out all single digit numbers: one, two, three.

    b. Use Arabic numerals for two or three digit numbers: 50, 90, 500.

    c. Spell out or write large numbers in combination with Arabic numerals: one thousand, 12 hundred, five million, 25 million, 2.5 million.

    d. Spell out fractions: one-half, one and three-fourths.

    e. Spell out dollars and cents after a number: 25 cents, two dollars, 500 million dollars.

Television News Scripts

The types of television news shows are similar to those of radio. Television roundup type programs, however, run longer—fifteen or thirty minutes—and contain fewer news items, because more time is required for the visual devices of presentation. The other types of shows include on-the-spot coverage, interviews and press conferences, roundtables, and documentaries.

To obtain interesting variety and to make use of all the visual aids available, producers of the roundup type program generally plan a melange that includes the following presentation devices:

(1) Part of the program consists of a live telecast showing the announcer or narrator in the studio. The views vary, and include close-ups and medium shots of him reading his script or moving about to point to props, such as maps and charts, which illustrate the news.

(2) Still pictures may be flashed on the screen to synchronize with the news item being read by the announcer. Still pictures include regular photographs, with a dull rather than a glossy finish to prevent light reflections, and projections of single scenes from film strips. Two methods are used to show photographs, charts, graphs, maps, lettered headlines, and drawings: they may be mounted on "flipcards" and placed on an easel in sequence ready for projection by a studio worker on cue from the program director; or they can be projected by a device which may be either a balopticon or telopticon. The shortened expression "flip" is used to indicate projection by the first method and the expressions "balop" or "telop" to indicate projection by the second. Stills are flashed on the screen, and are in view for only ten or fifteen seconds. The sources of stills include pictures taken by staff photographers, the station's photograph and film files, and pictures transmitted by wire or facsimile by the Associated Press, International News Service, and United Press.

(3) Persons figuring in the news may be brought to the studio for a brief live telecast of an interview.

(4) A tape recording of the voice of a person figuring in the news may be used, although this device does not seem to be popular with many television news directors.

(5) Newsreels, by far the most effective way of visual reporting

other than the live telecast of an event, may be used. The newsreel film may be one produced locally by the station's own staff or, for national news, one obtained from one of the special television news services—INS-Telenews of the International News Service, or Movietone of the United Press and 20th Century-Fox. The special services for television stations deliver a complete package of films and mimeographed scripts.

(6) Studio props may be used to assist in the visual presentation of news. They include the maps familiar in weather programs and objects that can be exhibited—perhaps a gun or knife used in the commission of a crime, the pumpkin or ear of corn that won the blue ribbon in the county fair, the actual report made by the city planning commission.

Planning a roundup telenews program is a major operation which must be started early in the day, hours before the show is timed for telecasting. The first step in the procedure is to draw up a schedule of events likely to need coverage. The television news director, like the city editor of a newspaper, keeps a future book for upcoming happenings. The schedule, of course, will have to be revised during the day to take care of unexpected occurrences, but on the whole it should serve as a reliable guide to the content of the newscast.

After the tentative schedule is made up, the next task is to decide what type of coverage is needed and what visual devices should be used in telling the story—still pictures, films, or other visual representations. Staff members must then be assigned to their particular jobs in the overall coverage. Although still pictures may sometimes be obtained from the photograph and film files, many events require coverage by a photographer. Because of the time and expense, the filmed portion of the newscast must be devoted to an event of major news interest and one that especially lends itself to pictorial treatment.

Writing the script, allocating the time for reporting each event, and choosing the background music which will set the mood for stories are jobs that can be done as the program shapes up. Parts of the script may be prepared some time in advance of the telecast, but the final form of the script will have to be written as close to the program hour as possible in order to include latest developments. Several copies of the script are needed—one for the newscaster, one for the program director, and one each for members of the technical crew staging the show.

Radio and television news scripts have almost equal requirements in respect to simplicity, clarity, and informality. But preparing a television script involves several special problems, most of them concerned with relating the commentary to the visual representations.

One problem is a matter of timing—coordinating picture and copy so that both coincide with what the viewer sees. No difficulty confronts the script writer when the camera leaves the commentator to focus on a still picture flashed on the screen for a few seconds. The problem does arise when film is used. Generally, for a commentary accompanying a film, it is better for the audio portion to run shorter than the visual portion. Since the viewer's attention is held by what he sees on the screen, periods of silence are not discouraged so much in television as they are in radio.

Perhaps a danger for the beginning television script writer is a tendency to say too much—to fail to let the picture tell the story. The narration should not be cluttered with verbal descriptions of events and scenes that the viewer can see for himself.

As in the radio script, the television script should provide transitions to guide the listener-viewer in changes of place, time, and situation, not only for shifts from one story to another but sometimes within a single story. For example, if the film shows the governor at his press conference in the morning, but the script relates something that happened later in the day, the viewer must be informed that what he is hearing about occurred afterward.

After the opening by the studio announcer and the showing of the commercial, no long introductory matter is required in the news script. The narrator can begin immediately with the news after a brief salutation such as, "Good evening." The radio technique of headlining the news—giving viewers an outline of what the major items will be—is used in many television newscasts. For example, the following from a news script of KSD-TV in St. Louis:

> Good evening everyone. The important news tonight comes from Chicago, where the speculation over which Democrat Harry Truman will support for the nomination goes on . . . from Egypt, where there's been a challenge of Britain's right to call an international conference on the Suez crisis . . . from New York, where six big railroads have asked for a 45 percent increase in first class passenger fares . . . and from East St. Louis, where an associate of Buster Wortman was scolded by a federal judge.

The copy for a news script, in most stations, is written on a sheet ruled for two columns, the one at the left headed "Video" and the one at the right, about twice as wide, headed "Audio." The video column gives the cues needed by crew members in staging the show and the type of visual representation of the audio commentary. Information in the video column includes the following: focus of the camera on the narrator; the type and source of visual representation—film (with the footage and amount of time required for showing), a flip card or easel picture, or a balopticon or telopticon projection; the type of shot—close-up, middle shot, high shot, or long shot; and the subject of the picture. The audio column gives the written script to be read by the narrator.

A sample telecast that illustrates the mechanics of preparing a script is the following, consisting of portions of a news program of KCMO-TV of Kansas City, Missouri:

VIDEO	AUDIO
CAMERA ON MAC *("Mac" is the name* *of the narrator.)* FILM 1:03	Almost two years of waiting came to an end today with the dedication and opening of the New Broadway Bridge across the Missouri river. *(Scene)* The ceremonies began with a motorcade at City Hall at 12th and Oak . . . With Mayor Bartle, Lieutenant Governor James Blair and bridge queen Miss Patricia Wilkinson, 14-year-old daughter of Willard Wilkinson, head of Local 663 of the construction laborers union. The motor car parade followed a rather circuitous route to the bridge approach . . . a tradition for parades. *(Scene)* And when the cars arrived a large crowd of spectators was on hand at the south toll gate for the round of speeches and formal dedication. Taking part were Blair, Bartle, R. N. Bergendoff, Rabbi Samuel Mayerberg, city councilmen and *(Scene)* the dedicatory address was given by Robert L. Mehorney Junior of Kansas City who pointed to the bridge as further proof of the Kansas City spirit and said it filled a need for the future growth of Kansas City. *(Scene)* Symbolic dedication was performed by Miss Wilkinson who broke a bottle filled with Missouri river water on a concrete abutment.
CAMERA ON MAC	Following the ceremonies the motorcade crossed the bridge to the north to the parking area and

VIDEO	AUDIO
	returned. Friday tolls go into effect. Tomorrow it is free.

VIDEO	AUDIO
CAMERA ON MAC	President Eisenhower touched on various items at his weekly news conference in Washington today. On the problems of school integration
FLIP: IKE	in Tennessee, Texas and Kentucky, the president said he didn't believe the federal government should enter the picture except where local authorities are unable to cope with the problem and so far the president says they have moved swiftly to meet each situation. As for
FLIP: IKE-HAGERTY	the president's campaign plans, he interrupted his conference briefly for a huddle with news secretary James Hagerty. The upshot is this . . . There will be a number of speeches this month following the kickoff at his Gettysburg farm September the 12th. He will speak twice on farm matters. On the 21st at Neweton, Iowa, and over radio and television less than one week later. And there is another TV-radio speech set for September the 19th.
CAMERA ON MAC	Incidentally, his opponent Adlai Stevenson will speak at the Newton, Iowa national plowing contest, one day after the president speaks.

ASSIGNMENTS

1. Write a comparison of the news presentation of the newspaper, radio, and television covering the following questions: From the standpoint of meeting the essential needs of the people for information, which in your opinion does the best job? How in your opinion do the three media compare in the reliability of their news? Which medium would you say is the weakest from the standpoint of stressing the entertainment value of news over its informational value? Which medium do you think shows the least bias in its news? Do you think the general public would agree in your personal attitudes toward the three media?

2. Clip five stories from a newspaper and rewrite them for delivery over radio or television.

3. Using clippings of stories from a daily newspaper, write a fifteen-minute radio newscast, following suggestions given in the

chapter for the organization or arrangement of items and the rules set forth for preparing copy.

4. From information obtained from newspapers and other sources, write a fifteen-minute radio script of news commentary and analysis.

5. Write a fifteen-minute radio news script for a specialized program—sports, science, religion, education, or other subject in which you are interested. Obtain your information from newspapers and other sources.

6. Prepare a working schedule for a 10 p. m. television news show based on the news situation as revealed in the morning and afternoon editions of newspapers. Indicate the time that will be devoted to each item of news and the type of visual representation that will be used for each.

CHAPTER 23

INTERPRETIVE ARTICLES AND FEATURES

The Debate over Interpretation

IN A SPEECH at the University of Missouri, Newbold Noyes, Jr., of the Washington *Evening Star* mentioned a meeting of managing editors of Associated Press papers at which interpretive reporting was discussed. The report presenting the consensus of the discussion, however, referred to the need for giving "the meaning of the news as well as the fact of it"; the expression "interpretive reporting" was avoided. Noyes quoted one editor as explaining: "You can't say those words these days without immediately finding yourself in the middle of a hell of an argument."

The argument revolves around the belief of many editors that interpretive reporting violates, or tends to violate, the canon of objective reporting. "Stick to the facts," the opponents of interpretive reporting urge, "and cite your sources. Let the readers decide the meaning of the facts."

The theory of objectivity—in the sense of impartial and unbiased presentation of the news—has been held to be one of the glories of American journalism. But increasingly in recent years it has been subjected to scrutiny, and some of the deficiencies of the press in informing the people have been attributed to it.

Objectivity has been blamed for the superficiality of much news reporting. Walter Lippmann, in his book, *Public Opinion,* said of news that it was not "a mirror of social conditions, but the report of an aspect that has obtruded itself." Concerned chiefly with surface manifestations, newsmen have given only a one-dimensional picture of the world.

The need for reporting in depth has been cited both by journalists and persons outside the profession. As early as 1934, J. Charles Poe of the Chattanooga *News* said in a talk before the American Society of Newspaper Editors:

> Is not the time ripe for a shift away from the diet of dull routine, inconsequential crime and cheap flippant entertainment in our news columns to a more intelligent and withal more nourishing news menu? . . . [The people] want a chance to know about those social questions which heretofore have been chiefly the concern of scholars. They would like, perhaps, to try to relate themselves constructively to the pattern of their times.

The controversial report, *A Free and Responsible Press*, issued by the Commission on Freedom of the Press, said the first requirement for the media of mass communication in adequately performing their function was to give "a truthful, comprehensive, and intelligent account of the day's events in a context which gives them meaning." At a panel arranged by the magazine *Editor & Publisher* to discuss the report, Kurt Riezler, a philosopher, criticized the concept of news as the reporting of events that have obtruded themselves, saying:

> I think in our world the most important things happen without conspicuous events or without providing the stuff of news in that sense, a news story. There are slow developments about which we don't hear anything but which are important, and that is a question of the standards of reporting that the news should not be published without some background.

Another criticism of the cult of objectivity is that it makes the press a vehicle for spreading dubious information, if not outright misinformation. Many utterances by speakers and other persons considered newsworthy are carried in the press, despite the fact that reporters have no way of telling whether they are true. Objectivity seems to be a matter of getting the utterances down correctly, whatever their truth or falsity. Roland E. Wolseley, a journalism professor at Syracuse University, cites, for instance, the experience of a Chilean journalist visiting this country. He heard a great many lecturers who spoke on South America and was appalled at the amount of dubious information they spread. "And newspapers, alas, are quite willing to spread all this imperfect knowledge," Wolseley commented.

They are also willing to print untruths that are known to be untruths. Irving Dilliard of the St. Louis *Post-Dispatch* cites an incident involving Oliver K. Bovard, that newspaper's managing editor for thirty years. Bovard pointed to a story in the paper, saying:

> Here is a lie. I know it is a lie, but I must print it because it its spoken by a prominent public official. The public official's name and position make the lie news. Were the source some unknown person, I could and would gladly throw it in the wastebasket. I have done what I can to show that I know that the statement is untrue by putting it under a small headline and printing only enough of it to make an entry in the record of the day's news. Printing these lies, even in this way, is one of the hardest things I have to do.

But in calling for more interpretive reporting, the advocates of this type of news presentation state that interpretation is not incompatible with objectivity. They are careful, in theory at least, to demarcate between opinion and interpretation based on facts. Lester Markel of the New York *Times,* for example, sought to explain the distinction at a meeting of the International Press Institute:

> There is a tremendous difference between interpretation and opinion; the first is objective, or as objective as human beings can make it; the second is subjective. Let me illustrate:
> To report that the Kremlin is launching a peace offensive is news;
> To explain why the Kremlin is setting the doves cooing at this time is interpretation;
> To state that any Kremlin peace offer should be rejected out of hand is opinion.
> Interpretation is an essential part of the news columns; opinion should be confined, almost religiously, to the editorial columns. This is a prime point and it cannot have too much emphasis.

Another newspaperman who has attempted to define the difference between interpretation and opinion is John M. Hightower of the Associated Press. He said in *The AP World*:

> One point about interpretive writing ought to be stressed at the outset. As practiced in the Associated Press, it should represent an extension of fundamental principles of accuracy, reliability and fairness—not a withdrawal from them.
> Essentially this means to me that a reporter must be as diligent in distinguishing between his own opinions and his objective facts in writing an interpretive story as in writing a straight news account.

The argument that the interpreters of news are, or can be, as objective as the reporters who confine themselves to gathering facts has not convinced some newsmen. They feel that it opens the door to editorializing in the news columns. Describing interpretive writing as "a stunning reversal of American journalism," Richard F. Pourade of the San Diego *Union* at a meeting of managing editors of Associated Press papers said that

> it may shake the confidence of the reader of American newspapers. After you have raised him in the American tradition of objective reporting and then suddenly tell him you are now giving him interpretive writing, he will begin to read with a question in his mind, as already have so many of our top figures of today.

Pourade cited as an example of dubious interpretation an Associated Press story by Hightower, the lead of which said: "U. S. prestige and popularity have been on the skids all over the globe for about a year and a half. Today the trend appears to have leveled off." With Pourade, one is inclined to ask where Hightower got his information that U. S. prestige had been on the skids and what evidence he had that the trend had been reversed "today" (why not yesterday or the day before?).

Robert Lasch of the St. Louis *Post-Dispatch* from time to time punches holes in the claims of objectivity in his department, "I See by the Papers," in *The Progressive*. He cites for example a foreign ministers conference in Geneva at which Russia refused to accept Western terms for reunification of Germany.

When the conference ended, Lasch wrote, "the wire service correspondents had themselves an orgy of pessimism and recrimination." The big powers had broken up "in confessed failure." The West "bitterly accused Molotov of bad faith." In twenty-one days the conference "scored a series of massive failures." It "contributed nothing to the relaxation of international tensions and the consolidation of confidence between states." It had, instead, "created new distrust." Commenting on the reporting of the conference, Lasch wrote:

> All of these judgments may have been correct, but I kept wondering whether it really is the function of a news agency to preoccupy itself so much with an editorial opinion about an event as to neglect information about it. Should the A. P. be so interested in establishing the fact of the conference's failure that it is not interested at all in facts that might explain the failure? Why did we get such a starvation diet of actual news about the conference—news of the positions taken by each side, reasons given

for those positions and their historical background—and such a
plethora of blame, indignation, and disappointment?

Whatever opinions one may have on the values and defects of
interpretive writing, there can be no doubt it is here to stay. Editors
of papers served by the press services have repeatedly asked for more
interpretation. Voices like those of Pourade and Lasch are drowned
out in the crescendo of demands for news stories that tell the reader
or listener *why* as well as *what*.

Interpretation in News Stories

Though there is an increasing demand for interpretation in news
stories, it is quite clear that some events do not require interpretation. A tornado that devastates a Kansas or Oklahoma town, an
explosion and fire caused by a gas leak, a suit to obtain damages
for injuries suffered in an accident—dozens of events like these can
be reported purely factually. Naturally they *could* be interpreted,
but to try to give the significance of every one of such happenings
would be a pointless if not impossible task.

To report a single automobile accident, all the newsman has to
do is to find out who was involved, where and when it happened,
and what caused it. It does not require interpretation. But automobile accidents in general could be considered a subject for an
interpretive article explaining the causes of accidents and how they
might be prevented by better highway engineering or adoption of
more stringent tests for drivers or better enforcement of traffic
regulations.

In one respect, interpretive reporting seems to be needed for
accounts of general conditions which the press has taken cognizance
of only in isolated instances. From a sociological point of view,
many news reports might be looked upon as individual case histories. Correlating these case histories in a general statement of
conditions would be the task of interpretive reporting. This would
fulfill the need mentioned by J. Charles Poe that people "want a
chance to know about those social questions which heretofore have
been chiefly the concern of scholars."

The field for this type of interpretation is almost as broad as the
news reported every day, and it can be enlarged if we include in
our definition of news those important undercurrents which Kurt

Riezler pointed out as happening without "conspicuous events." For example, the denizens of Skid Row in many of our cities have not been considered newsworthy individually even when brought into police court. But taken collectively they have provided the material for interpretive articles attempting to explain this sore on our urban society.

Besides the explanation of general conditions, the field of interpretation includes some reports of events that have obtruded themselves, in the Lippmann definition of news. These are events which cannot be understood without an understanding of what went on before they assumed a "certain definable shape." The function of interpretation here is to provide background, which is conceived of by Lester Markel of the New York *Times* as being "the deeper sense of the news." "It places a particular event in the larger flow of events," he explains. "It is the color, the atmosphere, the human elements that give meaning to a fact. In short, it is setting and sequence and, above all, significance."

For instance, residents of a South American capital may break out in a demonstration against the United States and storm the American embassy. The report of the event may be a masterpiece of vivid writing and a superb example of reporting in which all the details have been gathered, but it is meaningless to readers if it does not indicate what led to the demonstration. In fact, the background may be more important—more newsworthy—than the event itself; it is not the event that is significant, but what caused it.

Because of the impossibility of anybody's keeping informed of developments all over the world, international news requires more interpretation than any other class of news. But interpretation, in the sense of providing background, may at times be needed even on the local level. Suppose the mayor makes a sweeping reorganization in the police department, removing the chief and demoting some bureau heads and replacing them with other men. This certainly calls for explanation—and it is a job for background reporting.

Background may consist of a number of things. It may be merely milieu—the color and setting for an event, as in a descriptive story about people and place; it may be a biographical account of a person in the news; it may provide geographical, historical, social, or economic information; or it may be an analysis of motives and causes. Whatever form it assumes, it gives depth to the report of an event and contributes to the reader's understanding of it.

The significance of some events, however, cannot be made clear solely through background. Events themselves may be causes as well as results, and the interpretive reporter's task may be that of explaining what the outcome will be. In some areas of information this task may not be difficult. If the state legislature passes a new tax program, any reasonably skillful reporter can find out from tax experts and economists what the effect will be, or is likely to be, on the public and on business, or he himself can estimate fairly accurately whether it will bring in the revenue needed. But in other areas there may not be sufficient information available to predict what will happen, or the event may be of a sort not susceptible to forecast. For example, when Stalin died, every foreign correspondent, columnist, editorial writer, and radio commentator had his say on what the event would mean to Russia and the world. In a single issue of a newspaper a reader could find a half dozen conflicting versions. In this instance, interpretation, instead of clarifying the situation, merely added to its obscurity.

The reporter needs a certain degree of clairvoyance to perceive events in the making and to write of them before they become manifest so that the public will be somewhat prepared. But unhappily, in explaining the shape of things to come, many reporters try to become fortune-tellers, apparently willing to predict anything, from the horse that will come in first in the third race at Bowie to whether there will be war next year. Unhappily, too, these reporters are read—no matter how often they have gone wrong in the past—because of the urgent desire of people to know what is to be. While it is important to prepare the people for possible eventualities, the preferable—and safer—task of the interpretive reporter is to explain what has happened, not to predict what will happen. In this respect, hindsight is better than foresight.

If the press is to assume, as it seems to have done, the task of explaining the meaning of events, it is obvious that a very superior type of reporter will have to be developed. The ideal reporter in the past was the all-round man who could cover anything—a city tax muddle, a brutal axe murder, a complicated Supreme Court decision, and a golden wedding anniversary—perhaps all in the same day. A reporter could do this so long as his job was merely to find out information and to write it quickly and simply into a news story. But if he is to explain the significance of the information as well, he must become a specialist. This means that he must have the broad as well as specific knowledge of a subject which can come only from years of study. Thus, there is increasing demand today for the specialist—in science, in labor, in municipal government, in education, and so forth.

But specialization has its difficulties and dangers. No newspaper can afford a specialist in every field, and in news work often the person who knows the most about a subject is not the best person to explain it to those who know very little. As Louis M. Lyons, curator of the Nieman Foundation at Harvard University, said in a speech to California editors:

> The reader needs a reporter closer to the reader's own layman's approach to the specialty. It is hard for the specialist to realize all that has to be explained—to appreciate where the reader begins. The newspaperman turned specialist must work to keep himself in the middle position between expert and lay reader, so that he can interpret the expert. Experts always need interpreting—not merely to get out of their own jargon into the common tongue, but to know where to begin and how to tie on the special information to the pattern of what the reader knows and can take for granted.

It would be impossible for any reporter to become so omniscient as to be able to interpret soundly anything or everything that comes along, but he can make interpretation itself a job of reporting. In his own area or areas of specialization, he can interpret from his own background knowledge. In other areas he can, as a reporter, go to the sources of the news for explanation and can interview experts for their diagnosis or prognosis of a situation. Both methods have been used in the past for special stories and articles that claimed to be nothing more than a report of what the source or the expert had to say on the subject. The methods can be used by today's interpretive writer to obtain background which can be fitted into his own analysis and presented as his own thinking on a subject.

In addition to going to news sources and to experts, the reporter can obtain help from reference books and other published material. This means that the newspaper's morgue or library should be a keystone in any system for interpreting the news. In fact, it has been proposed that qualified researchers be added to newspaper staffs to supply reporters and writers quickly with needed background information. In the book, *Your Newspaper,* Nieman Fellows at Harvard University suggested the plan of employing a group of editorial assistants like those on *Time* and *Newsweek.* "Their job," the book says, "would be to provide reporters and writers with brief digests of long reports, look up facts in books and encyclopedias, get information by telephone and interviews and verify facts of which the reporter is not sure. Such researchers can save writers' and editors' time and thus make possible more effective use of the paper's high-priced talents."

Interpretation in Special Articles

In most discussions of interpretive writing the point is made that the reader should be able to tell whether he is reading a straight news report or an interpretive report. Without being labeled as such, by-line articles, columns, and editorials are usually recognized as interpretive writing. All three forms of interpretation provide the writer with considerable freedom to present his facts and his thoughts about them in a cogent article.

Perhaps as good a way as any to illustrate the problems and methods of interpretation is to show how writers went about interpreting one event: the Maine election of September, 1956. Maine, of course, is famous for the slogan, "As Maine goes so goes the nation," which has become a cause for jocular comment ever since 1936, when only Vermont followed Maine in the Republican column in that year's election. But the slogan is well known and it is always recalled when Maine people cast their votes in the state elections in a presidential election year. It is the first election of the season and, before public opinion polling became popular, was eyed for national trends.

In the 1956 Maine election Edmund S. Muskie, a Democrat, won re-election as governor by a resounding margin. This was a phenomenon in Maine, traditionally rock-ribbed Republican in politics, but even more sensational was the fact that the Democrats won a seat in the United States House of Representatives for the first time since 1934, and were only narrowly defeated in two other congressional races.

The Associated Press story for the morning papers on the day after the election was a model of objective reporting, in which the results were given and quotes were obtained from leading politicians as to the election's national significance. The story began:

> PORTLAND, Me. (AP)—Maine Democrats scored a smashing victory in usually Republican Maine's first-in-the-nation election Monday, retaining the governorship and winning their first United States House seat in 22 years.
>
> Republican leaders predicted today, however, that the Democratic success would not hurt President Eisenhower's November chances of re-election. But the Democratic national chairman saw the results pointing toward a Democratic victory in November.
>
> President Eisenhower said in Washington he saw no national trend in the Maine Democratic triumph.
>
> After Governor Edmund S. Muskie's record-vote, second-term win, the New York stock market got the jitters, but the break was short-lived and losses were trimmed gradually. Brokers explained the Democratic gains caused much selling because Maine has been an "Eisenhower market."

This lead, in several respects, is admirable. The first paragraph summarizes what happened and implies the significance of the election by pointing out that it was the first in the nation and that it occurred in a state that usually went Republican. The next three paragraphs summarize opinions on the significance of the election expressed in political and financial circles. The story itself continues with details about the vote totals in the several races and with quotations from party and congressional leaders as to what the vote portended, if anything, for the November presidential election.

This news report, appearing on the morning after the election, is unsatisfactory, however, as interpretation, despite its inclusion of quoted statements on the significance of the event. Any reader would know that the comments of politicians on such a thing would mean very little; naturally, the Democrats would hail it as a great victory, as they did, and the Republicans would minimize its importance, as they did. This story illustrates the inadequacy of going to news sources for explanations of the significance of an event in which they are involved: they are all too likely to be biased.

The significance of the Maine election called for interpretation beyond the resources of the straight news reporter. The nation's political analysts, columnists, and editorial writers rose to the occasion, and most of the advantages of interpretation and most of its liabilities can be found in their comment.

The purpose of interpretation, ostensibly, is to elucidate—to make events clear to people. Fortunately for the reader, his sampling of the interpretations put forth is limited; otherwise he sometimes would be more confused than if he had not had the benefits of any expert explanations. For example, in the Maine election an initial question was whether the outcome was a surprise. The Kansas City *Times* said it was, describing Governor Muskie's re-election as an "upset." So did W. H. Lawrence of the New York *Times,* who labeled the Democratic victory a "surprise." The Washington *Post and Times-Herald,* on the other hand, said in an editorial that Governor Muskie's re-election was "almost a foregone conclusion," and the New York *Herald Tribune* stated that it was "pretty much expected." The Pittsburgh *Post-Gazette* interpreter could not make up his mind: in a single editorial he said that "no one could foresee the outcome" and a few paragraphs later that the governor's "victory was not a surprise."

In all the comment about the Maine election considerable importance was attached to the fact that the Democrats scored a victory in a state that usually went Republican. Nearly every columnist, analyst, and editorial writer devoted a part of his comment to exclaiming over this, stressing that the outcome was a warning to the Republicans they would have to fight to win in November and their candidates could not ride to victory on the coattails of President Eisenhower. The New York *Times* said "the complacency with which some Republicans have been viewing the presidential campaign this fall ought to be severely shaken"; the New York *Herald Tribune* commented that it "will jolt every candidate and party worker out of anything resembling complacency"; and the Atlanta *Constitution* editorialized that it gave the GOP "a case of jitters." Undeniably, all these interpretations of the significance of the election are true. But the person who is skeptical about the value of interpretation may be inclined to ask: Were they necessary? Were they not conclusions that any person who had read the news stories was likely to reach? In other words, much of the interpretation seemed to be devoted to expounding of the obvious.

Another topic which received extended treatment was that the Democratic victory in Maine could not be taken as a guide to what would happen in the November election. A number of reasons were cited: local issues and personalities were involved; the name of President Eisenhower did not appear on the ballot, as it would in the November election; the Eisenhower popularity did not rub off on other Republicans; the campaign was fought on state and not national issues (despite the fact the GOP slogan in Maine was that a Democratic vote was "a vote against Ike"); the Democrats presented a united front while the Republicans were split into factions; and the saying, "As Maine goes so goes the nation," had been exploded years ago and never had any validity anyway. As with the interpretations devoted to the jolt the election gave the Republicans, it would appear that the expert analysts were belaboring the fairly obvious, if not the completely obvious.

In the examples of interpretation cited, it is clear that the crucial question about the Maine election has not been touched upon: Just why did a majority of voters in Maine vote Democratic? Readers seeking for an answer could not find one.

A few commentators wrote that Governor Muskie had been a popular governor and that his first administration had been a good one. Certainly this was one explanation—though not the complete story—but, lacking any convincing detail, it was ordinarily buried in the article.

Perhaps the three or four writers who considered the registration figures as well as the election figures were on the most rewarding trail of an explanation, but none really pursued it to the end. Doris Fleeson, for example, included in her column the statement; "Reliable sources say that a very heavy independent registration, including many new voters, is responsible for this break with Maine's past." But she did not give any supporting detail, nor did she attempt to explain why the independents and the new voters chose to back the Democrats. A fuller consideration of this factor was given by syndicated columnist David Lawrence, who wrote:

> The Maine election can be analyzed by the partisans to suit themselves, but the big unanswered question is this:
> Why did the Republican candidate for governor poll only about 11,000 more votes than he did two years ago, and why did the Democratic candidate poll 45,000 more votes than in 1954—and where did these extra 45,000 votes come from?
> Certainly, Governor Muskie, the re-elected Democrat, didn't subtract any votes from the Republican nominee, who actually increased his vote over 1954. Then are not the 45,000 new votes for the Democratic party a recruitment from the stay-at-home vote of the two major parties and the "independents"?
> There have been unofficial estimates that in Maine the Republicans registered this year about 270,000 and the Democrats 100,000,

and that the balance of the registered vote of 130,000 is "independent."

Thus out of the reservoir of 270,000 Republican votes, the Republican nominee for governor polled this time less than half; the Democratic nominee, on the other hand, must have received not only the 100,000 Democratic votes, but 81,000 out of the "independent" column or from the stay-at-home voters of other years for him to get a total of 181,000 votes—the highest ever polled in Maine by any candidate of either party for governor.

While Lawrence's column poses a question rather than answers one, his analysis is set apart from that of most of the other interpreters in that it is an analysis. The fact that he went beyond the news stories to discover information on his own brings out in somewhat bold relief the failure of interpretation in the Maine election. The job of interpretation calls for more than a mere rehash of front-page news stories mixed with a few generalizations—usually ones that readers could make for themselves—by the columnist, the editorial writer, and the by-line reporter. It calls for the interpreter to find out additional information to supplement the surface and current facts reported about an event. This is what most of the interpreters of the Maine election failed to do.

But the Maine election did produce at least one example of reporting and writing which can serve as a guide to methods that should be followed by practitioners of the science of interpretation. It was an article by W. H. Lawrence on the front page of the New York *Times*. Most of the interpreters apparently rushed to their typewriters as soon as the results were in, composing their pieces from scraps of information vaguely remembered about Maine and its politics, the principal memory seeming to be the famous but discredited adage. Lawrence, as should all good reporters, interpretive or otherwise, did some legwork and library research before presuming to explain things to the less well informed.

He emphasized in his opening sentence a point not underscored by other writers—that the meaning of the Maine election was not so much its bearing on the presidential race but on "the battle to retain control of the Congress." Later he amplified upon this:

> From the national standpoint, the big news from Maine was that the Democrats captured a House seat in a state that had not sent a Democrat to Congress since 1934. The vote on another seat was so close that the issue was still in doubt.

The last time Maine elected a Democrat to the House the country as a whole chose 322 Democrats and 103 Republicans in the mid-term election of President Franklin D. Roosevelt's first term. There were seven Progressives and three members of the Farmer-Labor party in the House at that time.

As did other commentators, Lawrence brought out that Governor Muskie's re-election was not so surprising as his "whopping margin" of victory. In filling in details on the significance of the election in the congressional races, Lawrence went to the *Congressional Quarterly* and *Editorial Research Reports*. He made use of some of the data discovered as follows:

In advance of Tuesday's balloting, Congressional Quarterly put together the statistics on how Maine's Republican congressmen had fared in percentages in recent elections. It also reported what the nation as a whole had done in giving Democrats or Republicans control of the House.

Congressional Quarterly pointed out, for example, that in 1952 the three Maine Republican House candidates, taken together, had polled 67 percent of the vote in September. After the November elections, in which President Eisenhower swept to a popular and electoral vote landslide, the make-up of the House was 221 Republicans to 213 Democrats, plus one Independent.

Two years ago, midway through President Eisenhower's term, Maine re-elected its three Republican representatives, giving them about 55 percent of the total vote. After the November elections, the Democrats controlled the House 232 to 203.

Congressional Quarterly drew this conclusion before Maine voters went to the polls:

"In sum, it would appear that if this year's Republican candidates for the House together receive less than 60 percent of Maine's vote, the G.O.P. will be unlikely to win control of the House in November."

Editorial Research Reports, as long ago as September, 1948, when most experts expected former Gov. Thomas E. Dewey to replace President Truman in the White House, said "the old adage should be revised to read: 'If Maine goes Republican by more than 65 percent, the Democrats lose in the nation.' "

Lawrence also pointed out that the Democratic victory in Maine was not an isolated phenomenon:

For the Democrats, the Maine results continue a trend of local, state and national victories that have gone on almost without interruption since their defeat in 1952 by President Eisenhower.

They showed gains in 1953, in 1954, and again in 1955 when the president himself was not on the ticket.

Several commentators, including Doris Fleeson and David Lawrence, cited Democratic gains in voter registration in Maine, but only the *Times* reporter attempted to explain why:

> There has been a gradual change in Maine's economic make-up as a result of industrialization. Cities and their working class districts have grown as the economy shifted.

This, out of all the thousands of words spent in interpreting the Maine election, would seem to be the most rewarding approach in explaining why the vote went the way it did. But it was tacked on as a last paragraph to the *Times* article, and the St. Louis *Post-Dispatch,* which also carried the article, omitted it entirely.

This analysis of the explanations of the Maine election underscores the difficulties of interpretation: it is not a form of journalism that just anyone can master; it requires reporting and research to uncover the facts; time is needed to study the information to decide what is important; and conclusions must be the product of logical thinking. The public, no doubt, needs interpretation, but it must be *informed* interpretation.

ASSIGNMENTS

1. Find three examples of interpretive news articles and analyze them, considering the following questions: Do they contain information not given in the straight news stories about the events? What were the sources of this new information? Do the articles contain expressions of opinion? Are the conclusions reached justified by the facts given? Do you think the articles contributed to reader understanding of the events?

2. Clip straight news stories of events that you think require interpretation and state what additional information is needed to place the events "in a context that gives them meaning."

3. Choose one of the events about which background material can be found in the library and write an article interpreting it.

4. As was done in the discussion of the Maine election, clip news stories, by-line articles, columns, and editorials about an event and critically analyze the interpretation of it.

5. Choose a situation or condition in your community—juvenile

delinquency, city revenue, automobile accidents, educational needs—about which an interpretive article could be written. Interview persons who know about the situation, conduct other research for information, and write such an article.

APPENDIX A: PREPARATION OF COPY

1. Typewrite all copy double or triple space on standard 8½-inch by 11-inch paper. The space between lines is needed by copyreaders for writing in corrections and changes in copy.

2. In the upper left-hand corner of the sheet about one-half inch from the top write your name and a "guideline" or "slug" to indicate the nature of the story. This designation, usually chosen by the city editor, consists of a single word. Some typical slugs are "weather" for a weather story; "council" for a city council meeting; "drowning" for a story about a death by drowning. The guideline is the story's "name," used for purposes of identification and record-keeping.

3. Start your story about three or four inches from the top of the page and leave one-inch margins at the left and right sides. The wide margin at the top leaves room for instructions to typesetters and for a headline. The one-inch margins at the sides make it easy to estimate the length of a story, four typewritten lines equaling about one inch of type matter one column wide.

4. Indent five or ten spaces at the start of each paragraph.

5. End each page with a paragraph; do not have a paragraph run over from one page to the next. The reason for this rule is that separate pages of your stories may go to different compositors for setting in type.

6. If your story takes up more than one page, write the word "more" at the bottom and continue the story on a second sheet. Do not write on the back of the page.

7. Instead of numbering the second page as page two, label it "first add" or "add one" followed by the slug. Any of the following versions may be used: *first add council, 1st add council, add one council,* or *add 1 council.*

8. Indicate the end of your story by the double cross mark (#) or the number *30.* Use of the number *30* as an end mark is traditional in journalism; the origin of this practice is not definitely known.

9. After completing your story, copyread it carefully with a soft-leaded pencil to correct errors and to improve the writing. Use the copyreading marks shown in Appendix B. If your handwriting is illegible, print.

10. Get into the habit of turning in "clean copy." If your copy is hard to read because of numerous strikeovers and penciled corrections and changes, retype if time permits. Dirty copy is hard to edit, slows up typesetters, and may result in errors getting into print.

APPENDIX B: EDITING MARKS

⌐Three men were seriously hurt.	Indent for paragraph.
to City Hospital. ⌐Attendants	Start new paragraph.
charged with reckless driving.⌐ ⌐Police said the accident was	Run in; no paragraph.
The condtion of one∕is serious. *(of the men)*	Insert matter.
A public⎮hearing will be held.	Separate words.
He re͡ceived 124, 000 votes.	Close up.
The two ~~shifty-eyed~~ prisĩoners	Delete.
He ~~perused~~ the report quickly. *read*	Delete, insert word.
He ⟨refused ⎸quickly,⟩ to accept it.	Transpose words.
He will be arraigned Thru͡sday.	Transpose letters.
The judge ~~sustained~~ the motion. *(stet)*	Do not make correction.
The democratic candidate won.	Capitalize word.
The ⱡecretary of ⱡtate spoke.	Do not capitalize.
He was charged on ③ counts.	Spell out number.
He lived there ⟨twenty⟩ years.	Use Arabic numeral.
⟨Governor⟩ Smith will not attend.	Abbreviate word.
The address was 200 E. Elm ⟨Ave.⟩	Spell out abbreviation.
Her name was Hazelle Jones. *⟨Folo Copy⟩*	This is correct; follow copy.

327

APPENDIX C: STYLESHEET

A stylesheet or stylebook is designed to obtain consistency and uniformity in certain usages not subject to universal rule or practice. The rules adopted for this stylesheet are a composite of those used by major newspapers and press associations. They represent, insofar as a single stylesheet can, practices prevailing throughout the country.

1. Abbreviations

1.1 Abbreviate names of months (except March, April, May, June and July) when they precede a number to form a specific date: *He was born Jan. 14, 1935, in Brazil*. But: *January 1957* (without commas before or after the year). (See 3.5 and 4.7)

1.2 Do not abbreviate names of days of the week.

1.3 Spell out academic and other degrees and do not capitalize: *He has a master of arts degree*. Degrees may be abbreviated after a name: *Arthur A. Adams, M. A.*

1.4 Abbreviate the words *company, corporation, brothers, incorporated* and *limited* when they are the last word of a firm name: *J. W. Smith and Co*. Do not use the ampersand (&) unless the firm itself uses it; when in doubt spell out.

1.5 Abbreviate names of states (except Idaho, Iowa, Ohio, Maine and Utah) as follows:

(a) When they follow the name of a city; *Springfield, Mo.*

(b) When they are interpolated parenthetically between the name of a city and an organization or publication: *Portland (Ore.) Chamber of Commerce*.

(c) When they are needed in giving the party affiliation of a member of Congress or state legislature: *Sen. A. B. Morehead (R.-Ind.)*. (See 4.22)

1.6 Do not abbreviate United States territories and possessions (except when they follow the name of a city), nations and countries. *U. S.* is acceptable when used as an adjective: *U. S. people*. The Union of Socialist Soviet Republics should be written: *USSR*.

1.7 Do not abbreviate names of cities or counties.

1.8 Do not abbreviate Christian names.

1.9 Abbreviate and capitalize commonly used professional, civilian, ecclesiastical and military titles when they precede a name. (See 2.1)

1.10 Abbreviate street, boulevard, avenue, drive, etc., and the direction in addresses: *200 N. W. First St., 450 N. Elm Ave.*

1.11 Terms for weights, measurements, distances and quantities (pounds, inches, miles, gallons) may be abbreviated when used with figures in tabular matter and listings.

1.12   Governmental agencies and commissions, clubs, societies, unions and other organizations frequently designated by their initial letters should be spelled out in full on first mention in an article unless they are well known. On subsequent mention the initial letter designations may be used in capitals and without periods for those with three or more letters: *ICC* (Interstate Commerce Commission), *TVA* (Tennessee Valley Authority), *FCC* (Federal Communications Commission). The no-period rule applies also to certain phrases or expressions: *AWOL, RSVP*. Use periods for two-letter designations: *U. N.* (United Nations), *U. S.* (United States).

1.13   Use periods for abbreviations in small letters: *c.o.d., a.m., p.m.*

2. Capitalization

2.1   Capitalize titles or offices when they precede a name: *Sen. James A. Smith, Prof. Arthur B. Morris, Secretary of Agriculture Louis A. Perkins.* Do not capitalize and do not abbreviate when they follow a name: *Louis A. Perkins, secretary of agriculture.* Do not capitalize when standing alone without a name: *He was secretary of agriculture in the previous administration.* (See 1.9)

2.2   Do not consider as titles nouns preceding a name that have an adjectival force or that are in close apposition with the name: *halfback John Biggers, grocer Matthew Smith, author William Farnsworth.*

2.3   Capitalize names of national and state legislative bodies when referring to specific ones: *the U. S. Senate, the state Legislature.* Do not capitalize the adjectives *congressional* and *senatorial.*

2.4   Capitalize the full names of committees of legislative bodies: *the Senate Foreign Relations Committee.*

2.5   Do not capitalize the names or titles of legislative bills or acts: *the pure food and drug act.*

2.6   Capitalize official names of federal, state, county and city departments, boards, commissions, bureaus, agencies, etc.: *the Federal Trade Commission, the Planning and Resources Board, the Department of Health.* Do not capitalize the general terms *department, board, commission, bureau, agency,* etc., when used without the designating part of the name: *He has been head of the department five years.*

2.7   Capitalize the names of specific courts: *the U. S. Circuit Court of Appeals, the District Court.* Do not capitalize when referring to courts in a general sense: *In most states the supreme court is the court of final appeal.*

2.8   Capitalize the full names of educational institutions and subdivisions: *Harvard University, University of Kansas, College of Engineering, School of Law, Department of Economics.*

2.9   Do not capitalize school or college classes: *the freshman class.*

2.10   Capitalize the names of military branches, services, commands and units: *the U. S. Navy, the Coast Guard, the 45th Division, Company A.*

2.11   Capitalize common nouns or generic terms as well as identifying words in the names of organizations and institutions, natural features like rivers and lakes, and buildings and other structures: *Kiwanis Club, Applied Arts Institute, Red River, Grand Lake, First National Bank Building, Triborough Bridge.* Do not capitalize the common noun when used alone: *The bridge was built in 1910.*

2.12   Capitalize descriptive terms for specific geographical regions: *the South, the Middle East, Western Germany, the Northside.*

2.13   Capitalize names of specific holidays, celebrations, special weeks and expositions: *Thanksgiving, Pioneer Celebration, Homecoming Week, the Minnesota State Fair.* Do not capitalize meetings, conventions or conferences: *the fifth annual meeting, the Pennsylvania press conference.*

2.14   Capitalize important historical events, notable documents and treaties, and geological and historical eras: *the Revolutionary War, the Declaration of Independence, the Treaty of Versailles, the Devonian Age, the Era of Good Feeling.*

2.15   Capitalize fanciful appellations and personifications: *the Empire State, the Dodgers, the Union* (when referring to the United States), *Old Sol, Mother Nature, Old Glory.*

2.16   In referring to breeds or strains of animals, fowls and plants that have been given special names capitalize the identifying part of the names but not the common nouns indicating classes or groups: *Hereford, Black Angus, Irish setter, Radiance rose, Elberta peach.*

2.17   Capitalize names of races and nationalities: *Negro, Caucasian, Oriental, Filipino.*

2.18   Capitalize the names of religious faiths or doctrines, denominations and churches, and adherents to a faith: *Buddhism, Christianity, the Methodist church, a Baptist, a Buddhist, a Christian.*

2.19   Capitalize the names of sacred writings and adjectives derived from them: *the Bible, the Talmud, the Koran, the Scriptures, the Old Testament, Biblical, Talmudic.*

2.20   Capitalize all words denoting the deity: *God, the Holy Father, the Heavenly One.*

2.21   Capitalize the names of decorations: *Congressional Medal of Honor, Silver Star, Navy Cross, Croix de Guerre.*

2.22   Use quotation marks and capitalize the principal words (all words except prepositions, conjunctions and articles unless they come first or last) in titles of books, songs, pictures, speeches and sermons: *"War and Peace," "My Wild Irish Rose," "The Angelus," "The Art of Living."* (See 4.37)

2.23   Capitalize, but do not quote, the names of newspapers, magazines and other periodicals: *the Baltimore Sun, the Saturday Review, the Congressional Record.*

2.24   Capitalize derivatives of proper names except those which through long usage have acquired independent common meanings: *pasteurize, india rubber, dutch oven, plaster of paris.*

2.25   Capitalize nouns and adjectives designating political parties and members of parties: *the Democratic party, a Republican candidate, a Communist.*

2.26   Capitalize nouns preceding Arabic or Roman numerals: *Room 2, Ward 3, Section VI.*

3. Numerals

3.1   Spell out cardinal and ordinal numbers below 10 and use Arabic figures for those above, with the exceptions noted in the rules below: *one, first, 10th, 20th.*

3.2   Use figures for a related series of more than two numbers: *The room contained 6 chairs, 2 tables, 1 sofa and 4 pictures.*

3.3   Spell out numbers used to start a sentence: *Two hundred persons attended the meeting.*

3.4   Use figures for exact measurements, weights, quantities, etc., as indicated below:

Measuremens: *3 inches, 5-foot rope.*
Distances: *3 miles, 100-yard dash.*
Weights: *1 pound, 3-ounce bottle.*
Quantities: *5 bushels, 2-quart kettle.*
Calibers: *.22 rifle.*
Degrees of temperature: *9 degrees.*
Percentages: *6 percent.*
Betting odds: *odds of 5 to 1.*
Ages: *age 9, 4 years old, 5-year-old boy.*
Latitude and longitude: *latitude 2 degrees 8 minutes north.*

3.5   Use figures for dates, omitting *st, nd, rd* and *th*: *April 1, Dec. 4.* (See 1.1)

3.6   Use figures for the time of day, omitting the zeros after even hours: *8 a. m., 1 o'clock, 12 noon.*

3.7   Use figures for all sums of money; spell out the word *cent* but use the dollar mark; omit zeros after sums in even dollars: *1 cent, $5.50, $10.* (See 3.9)

3.8   Use commas with any number containing five or more digits except serial numbers and telephone numbers: *5000, 500,000, series E20-000, telephone Chronicle 7-2711.*

3.9   For numbers and sums of money in the millions and billions write as follows: *2 million, 3½ billion, $1 million.*

3.10   Spell out fractions except when they are combined with whole numbers: *three-fourths, five-eighths* but *1½.* (See 4.30)

3.11   Hyphenate compounds formed by a number and a noun used as an adjective: *three-act play, 6-inch board, 2-year-old boy, 4-quart bottle.* (See 4.31)

3.12   Do not use the apostrophe in forming plurals of numbers: *three 6s.*

3.13   Use an apostrophe when the century designation is omitted in a date: *the class of '57.* Spell out expressions like *in the fifties* in referring to decades in a century.

4. Punctuation

Period:

4.1   Use a period after declarative and imperative sentences, after abbreviations except for certain initial letter designations (See 1.12 and 1.13), between dollars and cents and as a decimal point.

4.2   Use three periods to indicate omissions in quoted matter within sentence. At end use required punctuation plus three period's. *"The principal problem . . . is reaching an agreement on the tax rate," he said.*

4.3   Use periods instead of dashes after numbers or letters for items in a series when they are on separate lines:

He listed the following as the main planks in his platform:

1. Construction of a municipal auditorium.
2. Reorganization of the police department.
3. Reduction of expenses through more efficient methods in conducting the city's business.

Comma:

4.4   Use commas to set off identifications after a name: *Arthur A. Taylor, professor of history, presided.*

4.5   Use commas to set off nouns in loose apposition but not in close apposition: *Mary, his 3-year-old daughter, was not hurt.* But: *His daughter Mary was not hurt.*

4.6   Omit commas before and after prepositional phrases formed with *of* and *by* in indicating position, place of residence or authorship: *John Smith of the Department of English, Taylor P. Barnes of Chicago, "Bleak House" by Charles Dickens.*

4.7   Use commas before and after the year in dates in which the day of the month is given: *He was born Feb. 20, 1910, in Paris.* Omit commas when only the month and year are given: *May 1957.*

4.8   Set off the name of a state by commas when used after a city: *He moved to Columbus, Ga., in 1950.*

4.9   Omit the comma before *and* and *or* in a series: *Bacon, eggs and toast.*

4.10   Use commas in a series of adjectives modifying a single noun if each separately modifies the noun: *a belligerent, objectionable attitude.* Do not use when one adjective modifies the whole expression following it: *carefree college days.*

4.11   Use a comma in compound sentences between two long coordinate clauses that are not closely related in thought: *He challenged the reliability of the figures, but the committee overruled his objections.* The comma is not needed between short, closely related clauses: *He started early but he failed to arrive on time.*

4.12   Use a comma to set off a long subordinate clause or phrase preceding a main clause: *When committee members had collected all the information available about the extent of juvenile delinquency in the city, they drafted a report to send to the mayor.* The comma is not needed after a short clause or phrase: *When they pay the fee they will be given membership cards.*

4.13   Set off loose or nonrestrictive modifying clauses or phrases by commas: *The audience, which showed no impatience during the long wait, applauded when the governor finally appeared.* Do not use commas for close or restrictive modifying clauses or phrases: *People who violate rules may expect to be punished.*

Semicolon:

4.14   Use a semicolon between the main clauses of a compound sentence when the conjunction is omitted: *The building was erected in 1910; the wing was added in 1920.*

4.15   Use a semicolon in enumerations to separate items that contain commas: *New officers are Paul Johnston, president; Martha Perkins, vice president; and Thomas Dain, secretary-treasurer.*

Colon:

4.16   Use a colon after expressions that introduce or point to something that is to follow: *The president named the following committees: entertainment, Thomas Paine and Alice Roberts; registration, John Adams and Roland White; and housing, Curtis Talbot and Richard Parker.* Do not use a colon to introduce a short listing: *Members of the committee are John Payne, Lyle Duggan and Martha Danforth.*

4.17   Use a colon after a speech tag or attribution introducing a long quotation: *The governor's report stated: "The study of the state's penal institutions shows a drastic need for reorganization and for more funds to employ competent personnel. Trouble is bound to arise when conditions are such as they are now."*

4.18   Use a colon in expressing clock time: *1:30 p. m.* and in Biblical citations: *Luke 4:2.*

Parenthesis:

4.19   Use parentheses around material inserted in a sentence unrelated to the rest of the sentence in construction: *The new magazine (the first issue will appear in May) is designed to inform employees of company policies.*

4.20   Use parentheses around explanations interpolated in quoted material: *"They (the members of the council) were not fully acquainted with the facts," he said.*

4.21   Use parentheses to set off figures or letters in a series within a sentence: *He said the principal issues are (1) high taxes, (2) foreign policy and (3) the high cost of living.* (See 4.3)

4.22   Use parentheses around political party designations after a name: *Thomas O. Trotter (D.-Pa.).* (See 1.5)

Dash:

4.23   Use a dash to mark a sharp change in thought or sentence construction: *"I think I shall go—no, it probably wouldn't be the thing to do,"* he said.

4.24   Use a dash when a word or phrase summarizes or repeats in other words what has just been said: *Intelligence, initiative, industry—all are needed to attain success.*

4.25   The dash may be used for parenthetical matter or asides rather than commas or parentheses: *It was her last—and her finest—performance.*

Hyphen:

4.26   Use a hyphen between a prefix ending with a vowel and a word beginning with the same vowel: *pre-eminent.*

4.27   Use a hyphen between a prefix and a proper name: *un-American.*

4.28   Use a hyphen to distinguish between words of the same or similar spelling but different meaning: *re-cover* (to cover again) and *recover* (to get again).

4.29   Use a hyphen between two nouns indicating twofold occupation or office: *secretary-treasurer, soldier-statesman.*

4.30   Use a hyphen between compound numerals that are spelled out: *twenty-one, fifty-eighth.*

4.31   Use a hyphen in a compound of a number and a noun or adjective used as a modifier: *3-foot board, three-act play.* (See 3.11)

4.32   Use a hyphen for clarity with a pair of modifiers: *a light-green scarf* (a scarf pale green in color), *a light, green scarf* (a green scarf made of light material).

Apostrophe:

4.33   Use an apostrophe in contractions: *haven't, don't.*

4.34   Use the apostrophe and *s* ('s) to indicate a singular possessive and the *s* and the apostrophe (s') to indicate a plural possessive: *the boy's bicycle, the students' teacher.* For words ending in *s* use only the apostrophe to form the possessive: *Burns' poems.*

4.35   Follow the official form as to the use of the apostrophe in the names of organizations, companies, institutions and geographical places: *Harper's Magazine, Johns Hopkins University, the Associated Press Managing Editors Association, Harpers Ferry.*

Quotation Marks:

4.36   Use quotation marks at the beginning and end of all direct quotations. In a quotation extending over several paragraphs, use marks at the beginning of each paragraph and at the end of the last paragraph of the quotation. Use a single quote mark (') for a quotation within a quotation.

4.37   Use quotation marks for titles of books, plays, short stories, poems, musical compositions, sermons and speeches. (See 2.22)

4.38   Do not enclose in quotations names of periodicals, ships, trains, airplanes, animals or characters in literature or drama. (See 2.23)

4.39   Use quotation marks for nicknames inserted between the first and last name of a person: *John "Butch" Malone.*

4.40   The comma and period are placed inside the quotation marks. Other punctuation marks go inside the quotation marks only if they are part of the quoted matter. *His novel, "Bushwhack's Folly," appeared last year. The speakers and their subjects are A. B. Riley, "Power Politics"; T. R. Warner, "Party Finances"; and D. B. Donald, "Public Opinion Polls." He asked, "What will the governor's attitude be?"*

INDEX

② length

① number of
   stories

③ placement

④ pix

(1) each cand's activities (F-U-N)
(2) addit election coverage (F-to whom - N)

(1) each cand's activities
(2) omissions

(1) where
(2) head size
        (a)